The Black Ghetto
Promised Land or Colony ?

Edited and with an introduction by
Richard J. Meister

THE PROBLEMS IN AMERICAN CIVILIZATION SERIES
(Arranged in approximate chronological order)

(continued inside back cover)

The Black Ghetto: Promised Land or Colony?

PROBLEMS IN AMERICAN CIVILIZATION

Under the editorial direction of
Edwin C. Rozwenc

The Black Ghetto: Promised Land or Colony?

Edited and with an Introduction by

Richard J. Meister
University of Michigan—Flint

D. C. HEATH AND COMPANY
Lexington, Massachusetts   Toronto   London

23144

CONTENTS

IV THE IMPACT OF THE GHETTO

V GHETTO REVOLT

INTRODUCTION: THE BLACK AMERICAN AND THE CITY

The urban experience has not been the same for the black American as it has been for the white. For whites, the city has offered opportunity and mobility. The city has not offered blacks these same avenues of progress. The purpose of this collection is to explore how black Americans have viewed the city and to examine how they have responded to it. As early as the seventeenth century American towns held recognizable black populations. But because one's skin was black, whether he was enslaved or free, meant that his position in society differed from that of the white urban dweller. His mobility was limited by written and unwritten laws. Even when northern states abolished slavery after the American Revolution, the newly freed blacks still faced white racism. Blacks withdrew into their own neighborhoods and established their own institutions. Whether black separatism was caused by white hostility or motivated, at least partially, by group consciousness is debatable. By the mid-nineteenth century certain political, economic, and social patterns regulated the role of blacks in the pre-industrial cities. Blacks, even those with property, were disfranchised in most of the northern states. Only occupations which whites did not desire were opened to blacks. And when such an occupation became desirable blacks were forced out. Although their neighborhoods were scattered throughout the city, blacks had little contact with whites. Blacks had their own churches, benevolent societies, and social clubs. Following the Civil War there were a few signs of progress in race relations. But these were short lived.

In the late nineteenth century the place of the black man in the city was in a state of transition because of a changing urban environment. The industrial revolution caused cities literally to explode. Cities expanded their boundaries as new methods of transportation were introduced. Advances in intra-urban transportation changed the spatial make-up of the city. Land use became specialized, sorting out people and businesses according to income and function. The population of the cities grew rapidly with much of the increase caused by the influx of southern and eastern Europeans. These newcomers attempted to isolate themselves by establishing their own neighborhoods. Also contributing to the ever-increasing urban population were southern black migrants. The movement of blacks from the rural South to the urban North had begun.

To understand the forces at work within the black urban community today one must have some understanding of how these forces came into being. The first four selections help to explain why isolated black neighborhoods of the late nineteenth century became the black ghettos of the twentieth century. In the opening selection, W. E. B. DuBois discusses the Black North. Writing a series of five articles for *The New York Times* in 1901, he examines the cities of New York, Boston and Philadelphia. Two years before, DuBois's *The Philadelphia Negro,* a classic in American sociology, had appeared. In the articles for the *Times,* DuBois summarized his research on Philadelphia and added studies of the other two large eastern cities. In addition to his statistical examination he provides a historical sketch showing that blacks faced white hostility from the very beginning. These problems multiplied and became more complex in the late nineteenth century with the accelerated migration of blacks from the South to the North, especially the migration of the young. Although DuBois's examination of these three cities is brief, he does point out the major characteristics of the black population in the North. These characteristics and DuBois's comments on them should be kept in mind when reading the later selections in this collection.

These articles, as St. Clair Drake has recently written, "indict a social system that bred poverty and bore down with extra weight upon Negroes due to the racism institutionalized within it." DuBois blamed not only the social system, but also the "social failures" among the blacks, who were responsible for supporting the race stereotypes that whites had of blacks. In the tradition of his time, DuBois called for blacks to pull themselves up by their bootstraps.

A major problem faced by the blacks in the northern cities was the imbalanced population. The young unmarried men and women, between the ages of 18 and 30, dominated the population, with women outnumbering men. The lure of the city encouraged the migration of thousands of young blacks. And it was for the young that the freedom of the city offered the greatest dangers. The second selection is taken from Paul Laurence Dunbar's novel, *The Sport of the Gods,* which appeared in serial form in *Lippincott's Monthly Magazine* in the same year as DuBois's articles. Although it is not a great novel, it does provide us with a look at the city through the eyes of the first major black writer. Dunbar wrote this naturalistic novel partly for the purpose of encouraging blacks to remain in the South. The novel presents the city as a danger to be avoided by rural blacks. The South, despite its racial practices, is portrayed as home for black people. At the end of the novel, Berry and Fannie Hamilton no longer have a family. Their daughter Kit is a singer in a road show and their son Joe is in jail for murder. The old folks leave New York and turn "their faces southward, back to the only place they could call home."

The third and fourth selections are taken from recently published secondary works. Osofsky and Spear in their studies of the black communities of New York and Chicago deal with the making of the ghetto during the crucial years between 1890 and 1920. Osofsky discusses the role of the subway, the importance of land speculation, the entrepreneurial activity of Philip A. Payton, Jr., and the influence of black institutions in the making of the black ghetto. Spear examines the creation of the physical ghetto in Chicago. This ghetto, Spear argues, was created by white hostility. In reaction to white racism, blacks in Chicago responded by institutionalizing the ghetto. They had hopes of creating a city within a city.

The creation of the ghetto gave some blacks confidence in the possibilities of race cohesion. The black middle class, whether they viewed the ghetto as an end in itself or a stage of transition, were optimistic about the future of Black America. The rapid growth in size and in population of the ghettos, no matter how small an income the newcomer had, meant more opportunity for the enterprising black entrepreneur. The middle class continued the earlier process of institutionalizing the ghetto. They believed that their institutions, though mirroring the institutions of white society, could be made independent of white institutions and had a dynamism in their own right. Whether one was a spokesman for integration or separatism, the rapidly expanding ghetto offered political, economic, and social advantages to the middle class. It also offered to those able to take advantage of it a limited amount of social mobility. Even the Universal Negro Improvement Association depended upon the urban experience for its ideas of race pride and self-confidence. Unlike the black bourgeoisie, the Garveyites rejected the American way of life. For the followers of Marcus Garvey, the ghetto was no "promised land." But it provided fertile soil for organizing the most successful mass movement in the history of Black America.

In Part II, "The Ghetto as Promised Land," four selections support the view that the ghetto offered opportunity for the black newcomer. The first selection is taken from the Chicago Commission Report of the Riot of 1919. Although the Chicago riot blemished the image of the "promised land," the Commission Report is important for it shows how the image was reinforced between 1917 and 1919 by the articles that appeared in the Chicago *Defender.* Also this selection details the reasons for the Great Migration, not only to Chicago, but also to the industrial North. St. Clair Drake and Horace Cayton discuss the "Fat Years" in Chicago. To the middle class of the Black Metropolis the period after World War I, despite the violent racial conflict of 1919, generated a feeling of optimism. Though the middle class might question the ultimate success of institutionalizing the ghetto in private, they never did so in public.

Black intellectuals supported the optimism of the middle class. The achievements of the New Negro Movement provided the educated black man with another reason for his confidence in race cohesion. The black experience, through literature, poetry, theater, music, and art, became meaningful. The selection taken from Robert Bone's *The Negro Novel in America* discusses the coming of the Harlem Renaissance and relates it to the optimism of the twenties. Complementing Bone's selections is James Weldon Johnson's "Harlem: The Culture Capital." This selection portrays Harlem as "not merely a Negro colony or community, [but as] a city within a city, the greatest Negro city in the world" (p. 301). Johnson, the general secretary for the NAACP during the twenties, was an active participant in the Harlem Renaissance. His essay appeared in *The New Negro, An Interpretation* (1925), edited by Alain Locke. Locke argued that "With this renewed self-respect and self-dependence, the life of the Negro community is bound to enter a new dynamic phase. . . . The migrant masses, shifting from countryside to city, hurdle several generations of experience at a leap, but more important, the same thing happens spiritually in the life-attitudes and self expression of the Young Negro, in his poetry, his art, his education and his new outlook" (p. 5).

The four selections in Part III show that the city was not the "promised land" that many blacks thought it to be. Elliott Rudwick's study of the East St. Louis race riot in 1917 points out that this and other race riots were not isolated phenomena, but represented growing white hostility to the influx of blacks into northern urban centers. Rudwick in the selection included here discusses the causes of racial conflict by comparing the East St. Louis riot with the Chicago riot of 1919 and the Detroit riot of 1943.

Middle-class blacks in Washington, D.C., did not have the same view of the ghetto as the middle class in Chicago. These doubts and the reasons for them are found in Constance McLaughlin Green's study of race relations in Washington. While reading the selection one might first ask why the middle class of Chicago was optimistic and why this was not true in Washington. One might also ask why it was that many of the black middle class of Chicago overlooked the signs of stagnation that were evident to the middle class of Washington?

The Depression destroyed the confidence that blacks had in themselves. Middle-class businessmen closed their stores. Blacks were forced to leave the ministry, medicine, and law. The lower-class black found himself not only oppressed, but also out of a job. In the early thirties a number of black ghettos lost population as blacks returned to the South. Alain Locke wrote of the destruction of the New Negro Movement, "The rosy enthusiasm and hopes of 1925 were cruelly deceptive mirages." The ghetto the social worker knew in the twenties became the ghetto that black writers finally saw in the thirties. Even the Garveyite movement virtually disappeared, partly because of the economic crisis of the early thirties. The Depression thus eroded confidence in a movement that had rejected the American Dream. Even the ideology of black separatism depended on the prosperity of white America. An account of the impact of the Depression on the black urban population is found in the selection by E. Franklin Frazier, written in 1938. Much of what Frazier wrote as an observer in the thirties has stood the test of time.

The Depression showed urban blacks just how dependent they were on whites. One response to this dependency was the Harlem riot of 1935. This riot was the requiem for the myth world of the previous decade. When the riot was over, three blacks were dead, two hundred stores raided, and two million dollars worth of damage was done. The final selection in Part III is taken from the last chapter of Ralph Ellison's novel, *Invisible Man.* Ellison provides the reader with a frightening portrayal of a Harlem riot. This selection, written in the late forties, is also a prophecy for the violent outbreaks of the sixties—Watts, 1965, Cleveland, 1966, Newark, 1967, Detroit, 1967, and Washington, 1968.

The three selections in Part IV deal with ghetto culture. When discussing the culture of the ghetto a number of areas of disagreement emerge. Many blacks reject the thesis that the ghetto produces a pathology. They are reacting especially to the excessive number of studies which portray the ghetto only as a problem. James Farmer wrote in 1965, "we are sick unto death of being analyzed, mesmerized, bought, sold, and slobbered over while the same evils that are the ingredients of our oppression go unattended." Some blacks even reject the use of the term *ghetto,* for it is pregnant with pathological implications. They see black urban communities producing strong and positive antidotes to white racism. There is a culture, they argue—one which functions positively. A difficulty with viewing a positive culture within the ghetto is that those who see the ghetto in pathological terms also see a separate culture within the ghetto, but a culture that acts as a negative rather than a positive force.

Part of the problem found in attempting to evaluate the impact of a cultural influence in the ghetto is seen in the controversy over the Moynihan Report. The Moynihan Report, or more accurately entitled, *The Negro Family: a Case for National Action,* issued by the Labor Department in 1965, questions whether economic assistance alone could break the cycle of poverty in the ghetto. The report, in suggesting that there existed a subculture in the ghetto, brought an immediate reaction from black civil rights spokesmen. James Farmer replied bitterly, "By laying the primary blame for present-day inequalities on the pathological condition of the Negro family and community, Moynihan has provided a massive academic cop-out for the white conscience and clearly implied that Negroes in this nation will never secure a substantial measure of freedom until we learn to behave ourselves and stop buying Cadillacs instead of bread." Elizabeth Herzog in Part IV responds to the Moynihan Report, questioning both its use of statistics and the conclusions.

Many critics of the Moynihan Report attack the report's negative view of the black family in the ghetto. The report sees the matriarchal structure as a fault and gives little credit to black women for holding the family together. Less is said in the report of the black male. There is no indication that the black man who fails to assume responsibility as head of the household is making a contribution to society, either his own or the larger one in America. A year after the publication of the report, Charles Keil, a white anthropologist, published his book *Urban Blues.* In this book Keil uses the blues singer and his audience to show the distinctive traits of the black American culture. The bluesman becomes a cultural model of maleness for the blacks of the ghetto, a model that is quite independent of white culture. Keil disagrees with the Moynihan Report, arguing that there is within the black community positive responses to life around it. There is within the ghetto a culture that is independent of white society. Another view of black male models was developed in Elliot Liebow's *Tally's Corner* (1967). Liebow's conclusions differ with those of Keil. While both Keil and

Liebow studied the unattached, highly mobile black male, Liebow views ghetto life in terms of a problem rather than a culture. His emphasis is placed not on cultural determinism, but on economic determinism. Street corner society is formed by socioeconomic pressures of white society.

The concluding essay in Part IV is by Ulf Hannerz, a Swedish anthropologist, who made a study of the Washington ghetto. Hannerz's results were published in 1969 under the title *Soulside.* In this book he holds that there is a black culture, "largely evolved in America as a response to black American conditions." He sees that culture provides a means of adapting to a given situation rather than being a "completely autonomous determinant of behavior." In this essay, published in 1969 in an anthology edited by Lee Rainwater, Hannerz takes another look at the black culture of the ghetto. He argues that Liebow's ecological economic interpretation of the role of the ghetto male is not necessarily dichotomous to Keil's cultural interpretation.

The activity of black leaders since 1965 may be seen as an attempt to restore the self-confidence that blacks had in themselves in the twenties. Today, black nationalism, whether seen in cultural, economic, or separatist manifestations, is an attempt by black Americans to direct their own destinies. Once again the question arises whether black responses to white America are any more independent of white America today than they were in the twenties.

In Part IV much of the discussion revolved around the culture of the ghetto. Those who see the ghetto in a positive fashion judge that there is a dynamic force at work within the ghetto, a force that is responding positively to white racism. In Part V, Ghetto Revolt, we examine this dynamic force, which is generally called Black Power. Black Power means many things to many people. Stokely Carmichael and Charles V. Hamilton defined it as "a call for black people in this country to unite, to recognize their heritage, to build a sense of community. It is a call for black people to begin to define their own goals, to lead their own organizations and to support those organizations. It is a call to reject the racist institutions and values of this society."

A basic premise found within the Black Power movement is that the ghetto is a colony. Kenneth B. Clark in *Dark Ghetto* sees that "the dark ghetto's invisible walls have been erected by the white society, by those who have power, both to confine those who have no power and to perpetuate their powerlessness. The dark ghettos are social, political, educational, and above all—economic colonies" (p. 11). This view of the black American in a colonial situation is developed more fully by Stokely Carmichael and Charles V. Hamilton in the first chapter of their book, *Black Power: The Politics of Liberation in America.* Many white authors cannot accept the black militant view that the black man forms a colony within white America. Theodore Draper, writing in *Commentary* in September, 1969, rejects the premise that "black people in this country form a colony." He charges those who hold this view with a confusion of terms. He argues that "A colony requires something more than political, economic, and social discrimination or oppression, especially of a minority. It requires precisely what Carmichael and Hamilton deny—a historic relationship of a people to a land" (p. 41). In Part V Christopher Lasch, a white spokesman for the New Left, challenges Carmichael and Hamilton in the excerpt taken from his book, *The Agony of the Left.* Lasch feels that there is too much ambiguity in their presentation. He questions whether black people can be considered a "nation" and a revolutionary class at the same time. Some of Lasch's criticisms are answered in the third selection. Robert Blauner in "Internal Colonialism and Ghetto Revolt" defines colonialism more precisely. He distinguishes between colonization as a process and colonialism as a social, economic, and political system. In America blacks experience colonialism as a process. Urban riots, cultural nationalism, and the movement for ghetto control, Blauner argues, are collective responses to colonized status.

The last selection, taken from Harold Cruse's book *The Crisis of the Negro Intellectual,* comments on the Black Power movement. Cruse attempts to get at the heart of the black nationalism that is presently such a dynamic force within the black community. In reading this selection one might ask the following questions. Does he see the present black militancy as new? What weaknesses does Cruse find in the Black Power movement? What alternatives does Cruse offer?

In examining the black experience in the cities, were ghettos created only by white hostility? Or did blacks, like the European immigrant groups, establish their own ghettos as a means of strengthening their group consciousness and of protecting their cultural inheritance? Is there a positive, dynamic black culture in New York, Chicago, and Washington? Is this culture determined by external or internal forces? Is this culture an ethnic or a class culture? DuBois and Moynihan both discuss the destructive forces at work within the ghetto. Are DuBois's conclusions similar to Moynihan's? What are the implications of their findings? Do their conclusions agree with those of Hannerz and Cruse? Is colonialism applicable to the black American experience? Why? What is the relationship between colonialism and cultural nationalism?

I THE MAKING OF THE GHETTO

W. E. Burghardt DuBois

THE BLACK NORTH: A SOCIAL STUDY

W. E. B. DuBois (1868–1963) is the major black intellectual of the twentieth century. During his life DuBois challenged the leadership of Booker T. Washington, helped to organize the NAACP, edited The Crisis, *supported Pan-Africanism, espoused first socialism and then communism, and in 1963, the year of his death, he renounced his American citizenship, becoming a citizen of Ghana. He was a teacher, historian, novelist, sociologist, social critic, and journalist. His major sociological work,* The Philadelphia Negro, *was published in 1899. He later studied New York and Boston. The results of his work appeared in a series of articles for the* New York Times Magazine Supplement *in 1901. Excerpts from these articles are included below. Among DuBois's major works are* Suppression of African Slave Trade to the United States of America *(1896),* The Souls of Black Folk *(1903),* The Quest of the Golden Fleece *(1911),* Black Reconstruction *(1935), and* Dusk of Dawn *(1940).*

New York City

Let us now examine any peculiarities in the colored population of Greater New York. The first noticeable fact is the excess of women. In Philadelphia the women exceed the men six to five. In New York the excess is still larger—five to four—and this means that here even more than in Philadelphia the demand for Negro housemaids is unbalanced by a corresponding demand for Negro men.

This disproportion acts disastrously today on the women and the men. The excess of young people from eighteen to thirty years of age points again to large and rapid immigration. The Wilmington riot alone sent North thousands of emigrants, and as the black masses of the South awaken or as they are disturbed by the violence this migration will continue and perhaps increase.

The North, therefore, and especially great cities like New York, has much more than an academic interest in the Southern Negro problem. Unless the race conflict there is so adjusted as to leave the Negroes a contented, industrious people, they are going to

From W. E. Burghardt DuBois, "The Black North: A Social Study," *New York Times Magazine Supplement*, November 17, 1901–December 15, 1901; "New York City," November 17, p. 10 and November 24, 1901, p. 11; "Philadelphia," December 1, 1901, p. 11; "Boston," December 8, 1901, p. 20; "Some Conclusions," December 15, 1901, p. 20.

migrate here and there. And into the large cities will pour in increasing numbers the competent and the incompetent, the industrious and the lazy, the law abiding and the criminal.

Moreover, the conditions under which these new immigrants are now received are of such a nature that very frequently the good are made bad and the bad made professional criminals. One has but to read Dunbar's *Sport of the Gods* to get an idea of the temptations that surround the young immigrant. In the most thickly settled Negro portion of the Nineteenth Assembly District, where 5000 Negroes live, the parents of half of the heads of families were country bred. Among these families the strain of city life is immediately seen when we find that 24 per cent of the mothers are widows—a percentage only exceeded by the Irish, and far above the Americans, (16.3.)

In these figures lie untold tales of struggle, self-denial, despair, and crime. In the country districts of the South, as in all rural regions, early marriage and large families are the rule. These young immigrants to New York cannot afford to marry early. Two-thirds of the young men twenty to twenty-four years of age are unmarried, and five-eighths of the young women.

When they do marry it is a hard struggle to earn a living. As a race the Negroes are not lazy. The canvass of the Federation of Churches in typical New York tenement districts has shown that while nearly 99 per cent of the black men were wage earners, only 92 per cent of the Americans and 90 per cent of the Germans were at work.

At the same time the work of the Negroes was least remunerative, they receiving a third less per week than the other nationalities. Nor can the disabilities of the Negroes be laid altogether at the door of ignorance. Probably they are even less acquainted with city life and organized industry than most of the foreign laborers. In illiteracy, however, Negroes and foreigners are about equal—five-sixths being able to read and write. . . .

Ten per cent of the colored people are skilled laborers—cigar-makers, barbers, tailors and dressmakers, builders, stationary engineers, etc. Five and one-half per cent are in business enterprises of various sorts. The Negroes have something over a million and a half dollars invested in small business enterprises, chiefly real estate, the catering business, undertaking, drug stores, hotels and restaurants, express teaming, etc. . . .

These are the most promising enterprises in which New York Negroes have embarked. Serious obstacles are encountered. Great ingenuity is often required in finding gaps in business service where the man of small capital may use his skill or experience.

One Negro has organized the cleaning of houses to a remarkable extent and has an establishment representing at least $20,000 of invested capital, some ten or twelve employes, and a large circle of clients.

Again, it is very difficult for Negroes to get experience and training in modern business methods. Young colored men can seldom get positions above menial grade, and the training of the older men unfits them for competitive business. Then always the uncertain but ever present factor of racial prejudice is present to hinder or at least make more difficult the advance of the colored merchant or business man, in new or unaccustomed lines.

In clerical and professional work there are about ten Negro lawyers in New York, twenty physicians, and at least ninety in the civil service as clerks, mail carriers, public school teachers, and the like. The competitive civil service has proved a great boon to young aspiring Negroes, and they are being attracted to it in increasing numbers. Already in the public schools there are one Principal, two special teachers, and about thirty-five classroom teachers of Negro blood. So far no complaint of the work and very little objection to their presence has been heard.

In some such way as this black New York seeks to earn its daily bread, and it remains for us to ask of the homes and the public institutions just what kind of success these efforts are having.

*   *   *

Taking all available data into consideration we may conclude that of the 60,000 Negroes in New York about 15,000 are supported by workers who earn a good living in vocations above domestic service and common labor. Some thirty thousand are kept above actual want by the wages of servants and day laborers. This leaves a great struggling, unsuccessful substratum of 15,000, including "God's poor, the devil's poor, and the poor devils," and, also, the vicious and criminal classes. These are not all paupers or scamps, but they form that mass of men who through their own fault or through the fault of conditions about them have not yet succeeded in successfully standing the competition of a great city.

Such figures are of course largely conjectural, but they appear near the truth. So large a substratum of unsuccessful persons in a community is abnormal and dangerous. And yet it is certain that nothing could be more disgraceful than for New York to condemn 45,000 hard working and successful people, who have struggled up in spite of slavery, riot, and discrimination, on account of 15,000 who have not yet succeeded and whom New Yorkers have helped to fail.

In no better way can one see the effects of color prejudice on the mass of the Negroes than by studying their homes. The work of the Federation of Churches in the Eleventh and Thirteenth Assembly Districts, where over 6,000 Negroes live, found 19 per cent living in one and two room tenements, 37 per cent in three rooms, and 44 per cent in four or more rooms. Had the rooms been of good size and the rents fair this would be a good showing; but 400 of the rooms had no access to the outer air and 655 had but one window. Moreover, for these accommodations the Negroes pay from $1 to $2 a month more than the whites for similar tenements—an excess rent charge which must amount to a quarter of a million dollars annually throughout the city. One fourth of these people paid under $10 a month rent; two-thirds paid from $10 to $20.

We may say, then, that in the Tenderloin district, where the newer Negro immigrants must needs go for a home, the average family occupies three small rooms, for which it pays $10 to $15 a month. If the family desires a home further from the vice and dirt of New York's most dangerous slum, it must go either to Brooklyn or, far from work, up town, or be prepared to pay exorbitant rents in the vicinity of Fifty-third Street.

More than likely the newcomer knows nothing of the peculiar dangers of this district, but takes it as part of the new and strange city life to which he has migrated. Finding work scarce and rent high, he turns for relief to narrow quarters and the lodging system. In the more crowded colored districts 40 per cent of the families take lodgers and in only 50 per cent of the cases are the lodgers in any way related to the families. Unknown strangers are thus admitted to the very heart of homes in order that the rent may be paid. And these homes are already weak from the hereditary influence of slavery and its attendant ills. . . .

The most sinister index of social degradation and struggle is crime. Unfortunately, it is extremely difficult today to measure Negro crime. If we seek to measure it in the South we are confronted by the fact that different and peculiar standards of justice exist for black and white. If we take a city like New York we find that continual migration and concentration of Negro population here make it unfair to attribute to the city or to the permanent Negro population the crime of the newcomers. Then, again, it has been less than a generation since, even in this city, Negroes stood on a different footing before the courts from whites, and received severer treatment. In interpreting figures from the past, therefore, we must allow something at least for this. . . .

No very exact data of Negro crime are available until about seventy-five years ago. In 1827, 25 per cent of the convicts in New York State were Negroes, although the Negroes formed but 1 per cent of the population. Twenty years later the Negroes, forming the same proportion of the population, furnished 257 of the 1,637 convicts, or more than 15 per cent. In 1870 the proportion had fallen to 6 per cent.

Since then we may use the arrests in New York City as a crude indication of Negro crime. These indicate that from 1870 to 1885 the Negroes formed about 2 per cent of the arrests, the best record they have had in the city. From 1885 to 1895 the proportion rose to 2½ per cent, and since then it has risen to 3½ per cent. A part of this rise is accounted for by the increase in the proportion of Negro to white population, which was 1⅓ per cent in 1870 and 1¾ per cent in 1900. The larger proportion of the increase in arrests is undoubtedly due to migration—the sudden contact of newcomers with unknown city life. From the mere record of arrests one can get no very good idea of crime, and yet it is safe to conclude from the fact that in the State in 1890 every 10,000 Negroes furnished 100 prisoners that there is much serious crime among Negroes. And, indeed, what else should we expect?

What else is this but the logical result of bad homes, poor health, restricted opportunities for work, and general social oppression? That the present situation is abnormal all admit. That the Negro under normal conditions is law-abiding and good-natured cannot be disputed. We have but to change conditions, then, to reduce Negro crime.

We have so far a picture of the Negro from without—his numbers, his dwelling place, his work, his health, and crime. Let us now, if possible, place ourselves within the Negro group and by studying that inner life look with him out upon the surrounding world. . . .

To see what this means in practice, let us follow the life of an average New York Negro. He is first born to a colored father and mother. . . . The child's neighbors, as he grows up, are colored, for he lives in a colored district. In the public school he comes into intimate touch with white children, but as they grow up public opinion forces them to discard their colored acquaintances, and they soon forget even the nod of recognition. The young man's friends and associates are therefore all Negroes. When he goes to work he works alongside colored men in most cases; his social circle, his clubs and organizations throughout the city are all confined to his own race, and his contact with the whites is practically confined to economic relationships, the streets, and street cars, with occasionally some intercourse at public amusements.

The center of Negro life in New York is still the church, although its all-inclusive influence here is less than in a Southern city. There are thirty or forty churches, large and small, but seven or eight chief ones. . . .

Next to the churches come the secret and beneficial societies. The Colored Masons date from 1826; the Odd Fellows own a four-story hall on Twenty-ninth Street, where ninety-six separate societies meet and pay an annual rental of $5,000. Then there are old societies like the African dating back to 1808, and new ones like the Southern Beneficial with very large memberships. There is a successful building association, a hospital, an orphan asylum, and a home for the aged, all entirely conducted by Negroes, and mainly supported by them. Public entertainments are continually provided by the various churches and by associations such as the Railway Porters' Union, the West Indian Benevolent Association, the Lincoln Literary, etc.

Here, then, is a world of itself, closed in from the outer world and almost unknown to it, with churches, clubs, hotels, saloons, and charities; with its own social distinctions, amusements, and ambitions. Its members are rarely rich, according to the standards of today. Probably less than ten Negroes in New York own over $50,000 worth of property each, and the total property held may be roughly estimated as between three and four millions. Many homes have been bought in Brooklyn and the suburbs in the last ten years, so that there is a comfortable class of laborers.

The morality and education of this black world is naturally below that of the white world. That is the core of the Negro problem. Nevertheless, it would be wrong to suppose here a mass of ungraded ignorance and lewdness. The social gradations toward the top are sharp and distinct, and the intelligence and good conduct of the better classes would pass muster in a New England village. As we descend the social distinctions are less rigid, and toward the bottom the great difficulty is to distinguish between the bad and the careless, the idle and the criminal, the unfortunate and the imposters.

Philadelphia

From early times there was a steady northward flow of free Negroes and fugitive slaves, and these immigrants invariably sought the cities. Thus we find the Negro population concentrating and growing in the City of Philadelphia. At the time of the first census there were 2,500 Negroes there, and a century later there were 40,000. Today there are 62,613 Negroes in Philadelphia—a population larger than that of the whole city when it was the capital of the Nation. . . .

In other words, of the 63,000 Negroes in Philadelphia, 37,500 actually work in gainful occupations. Of these at least 26,500 are servants and ordinary laborers, while 4,500 others are laborers of a little higher grade. Another 4,500 are clerks and artisans, while 2,000 are business and professional men. . . .

The servants and laborers are composed mainly of the recent Southern born immigrants to the city. They find little else open to them, and only a few are fitted for other work. Some of them are artisans and they find some work in the building trades, and in a few large establishments, notably the Midvale Steel Works. For the most part, however, they are entirely shut out from mechanical labor by the trades unions, which in nearly all cases frankly or covertly debar the Negro. The cigar-makers' union is almost the only exception.

The descendants of the free Negroes and other Northern trained colored people, together with some of the best of the Southerners, have gone into business and professional lines. The openings in the large business firms for colored boys are very few. The business ventures by Negroes are mostly small shops. The physicians are the most successful professional men. . . .

Among the Negroes of Philadelphia and of most large cities there is a marked excess of females and a preponderance of young people between the ages of twenty and thirty years. Sixty years ago the Negro women of Philadelphia outnumbered the men more than three to two. Today the proportion is a little less than six to five.

This is the result of open chances for young women to work as servants and restricted chances for young men. The age distribution shows that the young people of the South are hurrying Northward in search of large opportunities. Such a migration, however, has its dangers, for all experience shows that the ages of twenty and thirty are peculiarly a period of temptation to excess and crime.

Moreover, the Negro home life is, on account of slavery, already weak, sending forth children poorly equipped to meet the allurements of a great city. The excess of young women further complicates the situation, so that under this peculiar moral and economic stress it is well to ask just how this population is standing the strain.

There is without doubt a great deal of crime among Negroes. When any race passes through a vast and sudden change like that of emancipation from slavery the result is always that numbers unable to adjust themselves to the new circumstances easily sink into debauchery and crime. . . .

The North has a direct interest in the race problem in the South, and cannot expect permanent improvement in the criminal rate of its Negro population as long as Southern conditions breed crime and send it North. At the same time the city itself is partially responsible.

Receiving, as it does, a population easily tempted to crime, it ought not to make yielding to temptation easier than honest labor.

And yet, by political protection to criminals and indiscriminate charity, it encourages the worthless and at the same time, by shutting Negroes out of most avenues of honest employment, the city discourages labor and thrift.

The fight for a livelihood and the temptation to crime are both a severe strain to physical health. It was a generation ago confidently asserted that Northern cities would never have a large Negro population because of the cold climate and the stress of competition. The continued growth of this population afterward was laid solely to migration. This is only partially true.

The death rate of Negroes in Philadelphia is higher than that of whites for obvious reasons. The majority live in the most unsanitary sections of the city, and in the worst houses in those sections; high rents lead to crowding, and ignorance of city life to unhealthful habits. As a consequence, the death rate of the Negroes exceeds that of the whites just as the death rate of an unsanitary region exceeds that of a clean, orderly city. . . .

Looking now at the social conditions of this mass of 60,000 souls, we are first struck by the fact that a rapid differentiation into social classes is going on. The common measure of this would be that of accumulated property. . . .

Only one Negro is reputed to be worth over $100,000. Four have estates worth from $50,000 to $100,000; eleven, $25,000 to $50,000, and thirty-seven from $10,000 to $25,000. One obstacle to saving is the high rent which Negroes are compelled to pay for houses. Over $1,250,000 are annually spent for rent by this race, and the rents paid are from 10 to 30 per cent higher than whites pay.

The average monthly rent per family is $10.50. Twenty-two per cent of the families pay less than $5 a month; the mass, or 57 per cent, pay between $10 and $20. The result of high rents is crowding, so that through a system of subletting fully a third of the families in one of the most populous wards live in one-room apartments.

If in addition to economic differences we bring in considerations of education and morals we may divide the colored people of Philadelphia, roughly, into four classes. The lowest class are the slum elements—criminals, gamblers, and loafers who form the "submerged Tenth." They live in the alleys of the older ward, center about "clubs" and near saloons, and form, perhaps, 6 per cent or more of the city Negro population. They are a dangerous class both to their own people and to the whites, are responsible for much serious crime, and tempt the hardworking immigrants from the South into excess and immorality.

Above these come the poor and unfortunate. They are the class of Negroes who for various reasons have not succeeded in the sharp competition of city life. They include unfortunates who want work and cannot find it, good-natured but unreliable workmen who cannot keep work, hard workers who spend regularly more than they earn, and in general people poor but not criminal nor grossly immoral. Thirty per cent of the Negroes would probably fall in this class.

Above these would be the bulk of the laborers—hard-working, good-natured people, not as pushing and resourceful as some, but honest and faithful, of fair and rapidly improving morals, and with some education. Fifty-two per cent of the Negroes fall into this class. Their chief difficulty is in finding paying employment outside of menial service.

Finally about 12 per cent of the Negroes form an aristocracy of wealth and education. They correspond to the better middle-class population of modern cities, and have, usually, good common-school training, with here and there a high school or college man. They occupy comfortable homes, are educating their children, and own property.

They, too, have difficulty in finding careers for their children, and they are socially in an anomalous position. The world classes them with the mass of their race, and even in a city like Philadelphia makes but little allowance for their culture or means. On the other hand, not being to any considerable extent themselves employers of colored labor, or bound to them by ties of industrial interest, they cannot easily assume leadership over their own people. Indeed, a natural instinct of self-defense and self-preservation drives them away from the lower masses of their people.

They feel that they can only maintain their position and advance further by drawing social lines against the incompetent and criminal of their own race. Thus they face a peculiar paradox, and stand between black and white, the representatives of all that is best in the one and at the same time suffering vicariously at the hands of the other for all that is worst among their own people.

Boston

Slavery in Massachusetts began with the undoing of the Pequods in 1638 and the sailing of the slaver *Desire* about the same time. At the beginning of the eighteenth century there were 400 Negroes in Boston. A century later there were 1,200.

At the beginning of the twentieth century there were 12,000 Negroes in Boston. The growth of this population was slow and steady until 1850, when it increased more quickly. Since 1880 it has grown rapidly. . . .

The 12,000 Negroes of Boston today are largely immigrants since the war, as the excess of adults shows. Nevertheless, this urban Negro population is peculiar in being the only one among the larger Northern cities to have a normal distribution of the sexes—5,904 males and 5,687 females in 1900.

This immediately leads us to expect better family life and social conditions than we have yet studied. Thanks to Massachusetts schools, the illiteracy of this group is about that of England and France (13½ per cent).

The oldest colored settlement was on the north side of Beacon Hill, in the West End. For a century and more this has been the historic center of the blacks. Here was the African meeting house, where the anti-slavery movement was launched, here was the first Negro school, and here still are the chief churches and halls. The bulk of the population, however, has moved. . . .

Since the marvelous development of Boston's street car service thousands of the better class of Negroes have bought homes in Cambridge, Roxbury, Dorchester, and Chelsea, and other places. These settlements are not usually in colonies, but the black families are scattered here and there among the whites, and the opposition which black neighbors at first aroused has largely died away, save, I believe, in the aristocratic suburb of Brookline. . . .

Economic conditions in Boston also show considerable difference from those in the other cities. The different environment, the less eager rush for wealth, and the New England ideals of home and society have plainly influenced the Negroes. Of those who work for a living only 60 per cent, a little over half, are servants and ordinary laborers—less than half of the men, and three-fourths of the working women. This is an unusually small proportion for a Negro population. At the same time, it renders the Negro a relatively unimportant part of the common labor force of Boston. . . .

In New York and Philadelphia the Negro is too largely handicapped by race prejudice to make much headway, but he has made some. In Boston the atmosphere has been more liberal, although by no means unbiased, and he has had correspondingly better success. The select laborers, as janitors, porters, messengers, draymen, etc., are an unusually trustworthy and respectable class in Boston. They form perhaps 15 per cent of the workers, and they are connecting links between menial labor and skilled labor or business.

In the skilled trades there are about 15 per cent of the colored workers, chiefly barbers, dressmakers, railway employes, tailors, carpenters, masons, painters, etc. In the mechanical industries which fill East Boston and South Boston there are few Negroes, although large concerns like the American Tool and Machine Company have a few colored apprentices.

There are quite a number of Negroes in the building trades, and they work side by side with whites on some jobs. Often they work for colored contractors. The Negro tailors are well represented and very skillful.

In the various lines of business enterprise will be found about 7 per cent of the colored people. This includes merchants, peddlers, clerks, salesmen, agents etc. . . .

Much more frequently than in the other two cities, Boston Negroes have gained positions in large mercantile establishments. Yet here the black boy's chance of promotion is nothing like the white boy's. The son of a prominent Negro, who had been graduated from a college of the first rank and had some capital of his own, wished a place in a mercantile establishment to learn business methods. He was promised several openings, but at last all frankly told him that their employees objected, and they could not take him. . . .

A little less than 3 per cent of the Boston Negroes are in the professions and Government service. There are twelve Negro lawyers, and nowhere else in the country, save in Chicago, are colored lawyers so successful. One is a Master in Chancery, and at least seven have a practice of $5,000 or more annually.

Their clients are largely white foreigners. One Negro held the position of Judge in the Charleston Court some years ago, but is now dead.

Among the medical men in Boston are nine general practitioners, four dentists, and one veterinary surgeon. . . .

In Boston and the immediate suburbs there is one Principal of a public school with white teachers and pupils, and there are five colored teachers in various other schools. In the governing bodies of the city and vicinity are two Aldermen and three Common Councilmen.

There have been several colored members of the Legislature and one Negro in the Governor's Council. One of the Aldermen mentioned was formerly the famous black class orator at Harvard in 1890. He has made an excellent record as a public servant.

It is noticeable that only 62 per cent of the Boston Negroes are in gainful occupations, a smaller proportion than in the other cities, showing a larger number of children in school and a larger number of mothers and daughters making and keeping homes. There are no very wealthy Negroes in Boston, but a large number of persons owning homes worth from $2,000 to $10,000.

There are in Boston a half dozen estates of $25,000 or more, ten or fifteen from $10,000 to $25,000, belonging to Negroes. Their total wealth is probably between two and three millions of dollars.

It would be wrong to suppose that beneath the fair conditions described there was not the usual substratum of crime and idleness. Seventy years ago the Negroes of Massachusetts furnished 14 per cent of the convicts. Just before the war they still furnished 11 per cent, although forming less than 1 per cent of the population.

Today, forming 2 per cent of the population, they furnish 2¼ per cent of the prisoners, 3½ per cent of the penitentiary convicts, and 1½ per cent of the paupers. While not ideal, this record is very encouraging.

On the whole Boston Negroes are more hopeful than those in

New York and Philadelphia. A prominent Negro author said recently in *The Boston Globe,* in answer to the question "Do Negroes expect to attain perfect equality with the whites?"

Contrast the changes which have taken place here during the last half century in relation to this question. What have we today in place of all that inequality and wrong?

Complete equality before the law, in the public schools, at the polls, and in public conveyances, and substantial equality in hotels, restaurants, and places of amusement, while on that self-same common from which colored boys were once driven by what seemed at the time a relentless race prejudice stands one of the noblest monuments of genius in America, erected to commemorate the heroic services to the Union of a regiment of black troops in the War of the Rebellion.

Some Conclusions

We have followed in some detail the history and condition of the colored people in the three chief cities of the Northeast, and there are some manifest conclusions which may here be gathered up and considered.

And first, in regard to the inner life of the Negroes, it is apparent that we have been dealing with two classes of people, the descendants of the Northern free Negroes and the freed immigrants from the South. This distinction is not always clear, as these two elements have mingled often so as to obliterate nearly all differences. . . .

The average Negro today knows the white world only from afar. His family and relatives are colored, his neighbors with few exceptions are colored, and his acquaintances are chiefly colored. He works with colored people, if not for them; he calls on colored people, attends meetings and joins societies of colored people, and goes to a colored church.

He reads the daily paper just as the whites read foreign news, chiefly for its facts relating to his interests; but for intimate local and social notes he reads *The Age* or *The Tribune* or *The Courant*— colored sheets. The chances are today that he is served by a colored physician, consults now and then a colored lawyer, and perhaps buys some of his supplies of colored merchants.

Thus the white world becomes to him only partially real, and then only at the points where he actually comes in contact with it —on the street car, in taking his employer's directions, and in a few of his amusements. This contact is least in New York and broadest in Boston, where it extends to restaurants, theaters, and churches.

Now there arises from such facts as these a peculiarly baffling question: Ought the black man to be satisfied with and encourage this arrangement, or should he be dissatisfied? In either case what ought he to do?

From the earliest times the attitude of the free Negroes has been opposed to any organization or segregation of Negroes as such. Men like Fortune, McCune, Smith, and Remond insisted that they were American citizens, not Negroes, and should act accordingly. On the other hand, the Southern immigrants had of necessity been used to herding together. When they came North the clan spirit prevailed, partly from instinct, chiefly because they felt their company was not desired and they dreaded refusals and rebuffs.

The free Negroes deeply resented this action; they declared it was voluntarily drawing the color line; that it showed cowardice, and that wherever the Negro withdrew his pretensions to being treated as a man among men, he lost ground and made himself a pariah. Notwithstanding all this opposition the new immigrants organized, slowly but surely, the best and only defense of the ostracized against prejudice. They built Negro churches, organized Negro societies, settled in Negro neighborhoods, and hired out to work in gangs.

They made a Negro world and then in turn taunted the free Negroes with wishing to escape from themselves, and being ashamed of their race and lineage. Here stood the paradox, and here it still stands to puzzle the best Negro thought. How can Negroes organize for social and economic purposes and not by that very organizing draw and invite the drawing of the color line? . . .

The problem of work, the problem of poverty, is today the central, baffling problem of the Northern Negro. It is useless and wrong to tell the Negro to stay South where he can find work. A certain sort of soul, a certain kind of spirit, finds the narrow repression and provincialism of the South simply unbearable. It sends the aspiring white man North, it sends also the Negro. It is a natural movement and should not be repressed.

And yet the surest way to pervert the movement and ruin good immigrants and encourage criminals is the policy of refusing Negroes remunerative work. That this is the case at present all evidence proves; the evidence of strain in domestic relations as shown by late marriage, deserted wives, children out of school, and unhealthful homes. Such strain falling as it does on the weakest spot in the Negro's social organization—the home—is a partial explanation of idleness and crime, while the encouragement of professional criminals and gamblers in our large cities furnishes whatever additional explanation is needed. . . .

To keep down the black men who are fit to rise costs the city something today and will cost more tomorrow. The black population of the North is growing. Despite the phenomenal increase in the white North the black North has silently kept abreast or been but little behind. It has doubtless increased more rapidly than the native whites and is still growing.

There can be no doubt of the drift of the black South northward. It is said that the Wilmington riot alone sent a thousand Negroes to Philadelphia. Every failure of the South, every oppressive act, every unlawful excess shifts the black problem northward. . . .

The black man who wants charity or protection in crime in the Quaker City can easily get it. But the black man who wants work will have to tramp the pavements many a day. Thus crime is encouraged, politics corrupted, energy and honesty discredited, and a reception prepared for simple-minded Negro immigrants such as Dunbar has so darkly painted in his *Sport of the Gods.*

What is the remedy? First, the Negroes must try to make the deserving and fit among them as numerous as possible. So long as the majority are mediocre workmen, and a considerable minority lazy and unreliable, those who seek to attack the race will have ample ammunition. Whatever, therefore, may be best as to Negro organization in many lines, certainly all must unite in keeping the blacks from succumbing to the present temptations of city life. Three lines of effort here seem advisable: first, systematic search for work; second, better homes; third, political reform.

There must be no idleness. Work, even if poorly paid and menial, is better than no work. Rebuffs and refusals, though brutal and repeated, should not discourage Negroes from continually and systematically seeking a chance to do their best.

Homes in respectable districts and healthful places should be had. No respectable Negro family should linger a week in the Tenderloin of New York or the Fifth Ward of Philadelphia, or in the worst parts of the West End in Boston.

Concerted, organized effort can bring relief here, even if it costs something in comfort and rent. The home training of children should be more strict even than that of whites. Social distinctions should be observed. A rising race must be aristocratic; the good cannot consort with the bad—nor even the best with the less good.

Negroes have an interest in honest government. They should not allow a few minor offices to keep them from allying themselves with the reform movements in city government. The police riot of New York is but one clear proof of this.

Finally the white people of these three great cities should [do their part]—but is it necessary here in the twentieth century to point out so plain a duty to fair-minded Americans?

Paul Laurence Dunbar

THE SPORT OF THE GODS

Paul Laurence Dunbar (1872–1906) was the first black man to achieve recognition as a man of letters. To achieve this recognition Dunbar wrote what his white audience expected, mostly trite and superficial prose and poetry. His best novel, The Sport of the Gods, *although it does not achieve greatness, is important because it is the first American novel to treat seriously black life in the North. The novel, based at least partially on the "plantation school concept," tells the story of the Hamilton family. Berry Hamilton, a long-time servant of a distinguished southern family, is wrongly charged with stealing a large sum of money. Because he is black and because of circumstantial evidence, he is found guilty and sentenced to ten years of hard labor. His wife Fannie and children, Joe and Kitty, flee to the North to hide their shame and to seek their livelihood. The novel portrays the impact of the city on the Hamilton family.*

To the provincial coming to New York for the first time, ignorant and unknown, the city presents a notable mingling of the qualities of cheeriness and gloom. If he have any eye at all for the beautiful, he cannot help experiencing a thrill as he crosses the ferry over the river filled with plying craft and catches the first sight of the spires and buildings of New York. If he have the right stuff in him, a something will take possession of him that will grip him again every time he returns to the scene and will make him long and hunger for the place when he is away from it. Later, the lights in the busy streets will bewilder and entice him. He will feel shy and helpless amid the hurrying crowds. A new emotion will take his heart as the people hasten by him—a feeling of loneliness, almost of grief, that with all of these souls about him he knows not one and not one of them cares for him. After a while he will find a place and give a sigh of relief as he settles away from the city's sights behind his cosy blinds. It is better here, and the city is cruel and cold and unfeeling. This he will feel, perhaps, for the first half-hour, and then he will be out in it all again. He will be glad to strike elbows with the bustling mob and be happy at their indifference to him, so that he may look

From Paul Laurence Dunbar, *The Sport of the Gods* (New York: Dodd, Mead and Company, 1902), pp. 81–95, 197–202, 207–209, 212–217.

at them and study them. After it is all over, after he has passed through the first pangs of strangeness and homesickness, yes, even after he has got beyond the stranger's enthusiasm for the metropolis, the real fever of love for the place will begin to take hold upon him. The subtle, insidious wine of New York will begin to intoxicate him. Then, if he be wise, he will go away, any place—yes, he will even go over to Jersey. But if he be a fool, he will stay and stay on until the town becomes all in all to him; until the very streets are his chums and certain buildings and corners his best friends. Then he is hopeless, and to live elsewhere would be death. The Bowery will be his romance, Broadway his lyric, and the Park his pastoral, the river and the glory of it all his epic, and he will look down pityingly on all the rest of humanity.

It was the afternoon of a clear October day that the Hamiltons reached New York. Fannie had some misgivings about crossing the ferry, but once on the boat these gave way to speculations as to what they should find on the other side. With the eagerness of youth to take in new impressions, Joe and Kitty were more concerned with what they saw about them than with what their future would hold, though they might well have stopped to ask some such questions. In all the great city they knew absolutely no one, and had no idea which way to go to find a stopping-place.

They looked about them for some colored face, and finally saw one among the porters who were handling the baggage. To Joe's inquiry he gave them an address, and also proffered his advice as to the best way to reach the place. He was exceedingly polite, and he looked hard at Kitty. They found the house to which they had been directed, and were a good deal surprised at its apparent grandeur. It was a four-storied brick dwelling on Twenty-seventh Street. As they looked from the outside, they were afraid that the price of staying in such a place would be too much for their pockets. Inside, the sight of the hard, gaudily upholstered instalment-plan furniture did not disillusion them, and they continued to fear that they could never stop at this fine place. But they found Mrs. Jones, the proprietress, both gracious and willing to come to terms with them.

As Mrs. Hamilton—she began to be Mrs. Hamilton now, to the exclusion of Fannie—would have described Mrs. Jones, she was a "big yellow woman." She had a broad good-natured face and a tendency to run to bust.

"Yes," she said, "I think I could arrange to take you. I could let you have two rooms, and you could use my kitchen until you decided whether you wanted to take a flat or not. I has the whole house myself, and I keeps roomers. But latah on I could fix things so's you could have the whole third floor ef you wanted to. Most o' my gent'men's railroad gent'men, they is. I guess it must 'a' been Mr. Thomas that sent you up here."

"He was a little bright man down at de deepo."

"Yes, that's him. That's Mr. Thomas. He's always lookin' out to send some one here, because he's been here three years hisself an' he kin recommend my house."

It was a relief to the Hamiltons to find Mrs. Jones so gracious and home-like. So the matter was settled, and they took up their abode with her and sent for their baggage.

With the first pause in the rush that they had experienced since starting away from home, Mrs. Hamilton began to have time for reflection, and their condition seemed to her much better as it was. Of course, it was hard to be away from home and among strangers, but the arrangement had this advantage—that no one knew them or could taunt them with their past trouble. She was not sure that she was going to like New York. It had a great name and was really a great place, but the very bigness of it frightened her and made her feel alone, for she knew that there could not be so many people together without a deal of wickedness. She did not argue the complement of this, that the amount of good would also be increased, but this was because to her evil was the very present factor in her life.

Joe and Kit were differently affected by what they saw about them. The boy was wild with enthusiasm and with a desire to be a part of all that the metropolis meant. In the evening he saw the young fellows passing by dressed in their spruce clothes, and he wondered with a sort of envy where they could be going. Back home there had been no place much worth going to, except church and one or two people's houses. But these young fellows seemed to show by their manners that they were neither going to church nor a family visiting. In the moment that he recognized this, a revelation came to him—the knowledge that his horizon had been very narrow, and he felt angry that it was so. Why should those fellows be different from him? Why should they walk the streets so knowingly, so independently, when he knew not whither to turn his steps? Well, he was in New York, and now he would learn. Some day some greenhorn from the South should stand at a window and look out envying him, as he passed, red-cravated, patent-leathered, intent on some goal. Was it not better, after all, that circumstances had forced them thither? Had it not been so, they might all have stayed home and stagnated. Well, thought he, it's an ill wind that blows nobody good, and somehow, with a guilty underthought, he forgot to feel the natural pity for his father, toiling guiltless in the prison of his native state.

Whom the Gods wish to destroy they first make mad. The first sign of the demoralization of the provincial who comes to New York is his pride at his insensibility to certain impressions which used to influence him at home. First, he begins to scoff, and there is no truth in his views nor depth in his laugh. But by and by, from mere pretending, it becomes real. He grows callous. After that he goes to the devil very cheerfully.

No such radical emotions, however, troubled Kit's mind. She too stood at the windows and looked down into the street. There was a sort of complacent calm in the manner in which she viewed the girls' hats and dresses. Many of them were really pretty, she told herself, but for the most part they were not better than what she had had down home. There was a sound quality in the girl's make-up that helped her to see through the glamour of mere place and recognize worth for itself. Or it may have been the critical faculty, which is prominent in most women, that kept her from thinking a five-cent cheesecloth any better in New York than it was at home. She had a certain self-respect which made her value herself and her own traditions higher than her brother did his.

When later in the evening the porter who had been kind to them came in and was introduced as Mr. William Thomas, young as she was, she took his open admiration for her with more coolness than Joe exhibited when Thomas offered to show him something of the town some day or night.

Mr. Thomas was a loquacious little man with a confident air born of an intense admiration of himself. He was the idol of a number of servant-girls' hearts, and altogether a decidedly dashing back-area-way Don Juan.

"I tell you, Miss Kitty," he burst forth, a few minutes after being introduced, "they ain't no use talkin', N' Yawk'll give you a shakin' up 'at you won't soon forget. It's the only town on the face of the earth. You kin bet your life they ain't no flies on N' Yawk. We git the best shows here, we git the best concerts—say, now, what's the use o' my callin' it all out?—we simply git the best of everything."

"Great place," said Joe wisely, in what he thought was going to be quite a man-of-the-world manner. But he burned with shame the next minute because his voice sounded so weak and youthful. Then too the oracle only said "Yes" to him, and went on expatiating to Kitty on the glories of the metropolis.

"D'jever see the Statue o' Liberty? Great thing, the Statue o' Liberty. I'll take you 'round some day. An' Cooney Island—oh, my, now that's the place; and talk about fun! That's the place for me."

"La, Thomas," Mrs. Jones put in, "how you do run on! Why, the strangers'll think they'll be talked to death before they have time to breathe."

"Oh, I guess the folks understan' me. I'm one o' them kin' o' men 'at believe in whooping things up right from the beginning. I'm never strange with anybody. I'm a N' Yawker, I tell you, from the word go. I say, Mis' Jones, let's have some beer, an' we'll have some music purty soon. There's a fellah in the house 'at plays 'Rag-time' out o' sight."

Mr. Thomas took the pail and went to the corner. As he left the room, Mrs. Jones slapped her knee and laughed until her bust shook like jelly.

"Mr. Thomas is a case, sho'," she said; "but he likes you all, an' I'm mighty glad of it, fu' he's mighty curious about the house when he don't like the roomers."

Joe felt distinctly flattered, for he found their new acquaintance charming. His mother was still a little doubtful, and Kitty was sure she found the young man "fresh."

He came in pretty soon with his beer, and a half-dozen crabs in a bag.

"Thought I'd bring home something to chew. I always like to eat something with my beer."

Mrs. Jones brought in the glasses, and the young man filled one and turned to Kitty.

"No, thanks," she said with a surprised look.

"What, don't you drink beer? Oh, come now, you'll get out o' that."

"Kitty don't drink no beer," broke in her mother with mild resentment. "I drinks it sometimes, but she don't. I reckon maybe de chillen better go to bed."

Joe felt as if the "chillen" had ruined all his hopes, but Kitty rose. The ingratiating "N' Yawker" was aghast.

"Oh, let 'em stay," said Mrs. Jones heartily; "a little beer ain't goin' to hurt 'em. Why, sakes, I know my father gave me beer from the time I could drink it, and I knows I ain't none the worse fu' it."

"They'll git out o' that, all right, if they live in N' Yawk," said Mr. Thomas, as he poured out a glass and handed it to Joe. "You neither?"

"Oh, I drink it," said the boy with an air, but not looking at his mother.

"Joe," she cried to him, "you must ricollect you ain't at home. What 'ud yo' pa think?" Then she stopped suddenly, and Joe gulped his beer and Kitty went to the piano to relieve her embarrassment.

"Yes, that's it, Miss Kitty, sing us something," said the irrepressible Thomas, "an' after while we'll have that fellah down that plays 'Rag-time.' He's out o' sight, I tell you."

With the pretty shyness of girlhood, Kitty sang one or two little songs in the simple manner she knew. Her voice was full and rich. It delighted Mr. Thomas.

"I say, that's singin' now, I tell you," he cried. "You ought to have some o' the new songs. D' jever hear 'Baby, you got to leave'? I tell you, that's a hot one. I'll bring you some of 'em. Why, you could git a job on the stage easy with that voice o' yourn. I got a frien' in one o' the comp'nies an' I'll speak to him about you."

"You ought to git Mr. Thomas to take you to the th'ater some night. He goes lots."

"Why, yes, what's the matter with tomorrer night? There's a good coon show in town. Out o' sight. Let's all go."

"I ain't nevah been to nothin' lak dat, an' I don't know," said Mrs. Hamilton.

"Aw, come, I'll git the tickets an' we'll all go. Great singin', you know. What d' you say?"

The mother hesitated, and Joe filled the breach.

"We'd all like to go," he said. "Ma, we'll go if you ain't too tired."

"Tired? Pshaw, you'll furgit all about your tiredness when Smithkins gits on the stage. Y' ought to hear him sing, 'I bin huntin' fu' wo'k'! You'd die laughing."

Mrs. Hamilton made no further demur, and the matter was closed.

Awhile later the "Rag-time" man came down and gave them a sample of what they were to hear the next night. Mr. Thomas and Mrs. Jones two-stepped, and they sent a boy after some more beer. Joe found it a very jolly evening, but Kit's and the mother's hearts were heavy as they went up to bed.

"Say," said Mr. Thomas when they had gone, "that little girl's a peach, you bet; a little green, I guess, but she'll ripen in the sun."

*   *   *

Five years is but a short time in the life of a man, and yet many things may happen therein. For instance, the whole way of a family's life may be changed. Good natures may be made into bad ones and out of a soul of faith grow a spirit of unbelief. The independence of respectability may harden into the insolence of defiance, and the sensitive cheek of modesty into the brazen face of shamelessness. It may be true that the habits of years are hard to change, but this is not true of the first sixteen or seventeen years of a young person's life, else Kitty Hamilton and Joe could not so easily have become what they were. It had taken barely five years to accomplish an entire metamorphosis of their characters. In Joe's case even a shorter time was needed. He was so ready to go down that it needed but a gentle push to start him, and once started, there was nothing within him to hold him back from the depths. For his will was as flabby as his conscience, and his pride, which stands to some men for conscience, had no definite aim or direction.

Hattie Sterling had given him both his greatest impulse for evil and for good. She had at first given him his gentle push, but when she saw that his collapse would lose her a faithful and useful slave she had sought to check his course. Her threat of the severance of their relations had held him up for a little time, and she began to believe that he was safe again. He went back to the work he had neglected, drank moderately, and acted in most things as a sound, sensible being. Then, all of a sudden, he went down again, and went down badly. She kept her promise and threw him over. Then he became a hanger-on at the clubs, a genteel loafer. He used to say in his sober moments that at last he was one of the boys that Sadness had spoken of. He did not work, and yet he lived and ate and was proud of his degradation. But he soon tired of being separated from Hattie, and straightened up again. After some demur she received him upon his former footing. It was only for a few months. He fell again. For almost four years this had happened intermittently. Finally he took a turn for the better that endured so long that Hattie Sterling again gave him her faith. Then the woman made her mistake. She warmed to him. She showed him that she was proud of him. He went forth at once to celebrate his victory. He did not return to her for three days. Then he was battered, unkempt, and thick of speech.

She looked at him in silent contempt for a while as he sat nursing his aching head.

"Well, you're a beauty," she said finally with cutting scorn. "You ought to be put under a glass case and placed on exhibition."

He groaned and his head sunk lower. A drunken man is always disarmed.

His helplessness, instead of inspiring her with pity, inflamed her with an unfeeling anger that burst forth in a volume of taunts.

"You're the thing I've given up all my chances for—you, a miserable, drunken jay, without a jay's decency. No one had ever looked at you until I picked you up and you've been strutting around ever since, showing off because I was kind to you, and now this is the way you pay me back. Drunk half the time and half drunk the rest. Well, you know what I told you the last time you got 'loaded'? I mean it too. You're not the only star in sight, see?"

She laughed meanly and began to sing, "You'll have to find another baby now."

For the first time he looked up, and his eyes were full of tears
—tears both of grief and intoxication. There was an expression of
a whipped dog on his face.

"Do'—Ha'ie, do'—" he pleaded, stretching out his hands to her.

Her eyes blazed back at him, but she sang on insolently, taunt-
ingly.

The very inanity of the man disgusted her, and on a sudden impulse she sprang up and struck him full in the face with the flat of
her hand. He was too weak to resist the blow, and, tumbling from
the chair, fell limply to the floor, where he lay at her feet, alternately
weeping aloud and quivering with drunken, hiccoughing sobs.

"Get up!" she cried; "get up and get out o' here. You sha'n't lay
around my house."

He had already begun to fall into a drunken sleep, but she shook
him, got him to his feet, and pushed him outside the door. "Now,
go, you drunken dog, and never put your foot inside this house
again."

He stood outside, swaying dizzily upon his feet and looking
back with dazed eyes at the door, then he muttered: "Pu' me out,
wi' you? Pu' me out, damn you! Well, I ki' you. See 'f I don't;" and
he half walked, half fell down the street. . . .

*   *   *

It was very late when he reached Hattie's door, but he opened it
with his latchkey, as he had been used to do. He stopped to help
himself to a glass of brandy, as he had so often done before. Then
he went directly to her room. She was a light sleeper, and his step
awakened her.

"Who is it?" she cried in affright.

"It's me." His voice was steadier now, but grim.

"What do you want? Didn't I tell you never to come here again?
Get out or I'll have you taken out."

She sprang up in bed, glaring angrily at him.

His hands twitched nervously, as if her will were conquering him
and he were uneasy, but he held her eye with his own.

"You put me out tonight," he said.

"Yes, and I'm going to do it again. You're drunk."

She started to rise, but he took a step toward her and she paused.

He looked as she had never seen him look before. His face was ashen and his eyes like fire and blood. She quailed beneath the look. He took another step towards her.

"You put me out tonight," he repeated, "like a dog."

His step was steady and his tone was clear, menacingly clear. She shrank back from him, back to the wall. Still his hands twitched and his eye held her. Still he crept slowly toward her, his lips working and his hands moving convulsively.

"Joe, Joe!" she said hoarsely, "what's the matter? Oh, don't look at me like that."

The gown had fallen away from her breast and showed the convulsive fluttering of her heart.

He broke into a laugh, a dry, murderous laugh, and his hands sought each other while the fingers twitched over one another like coiling serpents.

"You put me out—you—you, and you made me what I am." The realization of what he was, of his foulness and degradation, seemed just to have come to him fully. "You made me what I am, and then you sent me away. You let me come back, and now you put me out."

She gazed at him fascinated. She tried to scream and she could not. This was not Joe. This was not the boy that she had turned and twisted about her little finger. This was a terrible, terrible man or a monster.

He moved a step nearer her. His eyes fell to her throat. For an instant she lost their steady glare and then she found her voice. The scream was checked as it began. His fingers had closed over her throat just where the gown had left it temptingly bare. They gave it the caress of death. She struggled. They held her. Her eyes prayed to his. But his were the fire of hell. She fell back upon her pillow in silence. He had not uttered a word. He held her. Finally he flung her from him like a rag, and sank into a chair. And there the officers found him when Hattie Sterling's disappearance had become a strange thing. . . .

*   *   *

And so Sadness and all the club, with a muttered "Poor devil!" dismissed him. He was gone. Why should they worry? Only one more who had got into the whirlpool, enjoyed the sensation for a moment, and then swept dizzily down. There were, indeed, some who for an earnest hour sermonized about it and said, "Here is another example of the pernicious influence of the city on untrained Negroes. Oh, is there no way to keep these people from rushing away from the small villages and country districts of the South up to the cities, where they cannot battle with the terrible force of a strange and unusual environment? Is there no way to prove to them that woollen-shirted, brown-jeaned simplicity is infinitely better than broadclothed degradation?" They wanted to preach to these people that good agriculture is better than bad art—that it was better and nobler for them to sing to God across the Southern fields than to dance for rowdies in the Northern halls. They wanted to dare to say that the South has its faults—no one condones them—and its disadvantages, but that even what they suffered from these was better than what awaited them in the great alleys of New York. Down there, the bodies were restrained, and they chafed; but here the soul would fester, and they would be content.

This was but for an hour, for even while they exclaimed they knew that there was no way, and that the stream of young Negro life would continue to flow up from the South, dashing itself against the hard necessities of the city and breaking like waves against a rock —that, until the gods grew tired of their cruel sport, there must still be sacrifices to false ideals and unreal ambitions.

There was one heart, though, that neither dismissed Joe with gratuitous pity nor sermonized about him. The mother heart had only room for grief and pain. Already it had borne its share. It had known sorrow for a lost husband, tears at the neglect and brutality of a new companion, shame for a daughter's sake, and it had seemed already filled to overflowing. And yet the fates had put in this one other burden until it seemed it must burst with the weight of it.

To Fannie Hamilton's mind now all her boy's shortcomings became as naught. He was not her wayward, erring, criminal son. She only remembered that he was her son, and wept for him as such. She forgot his curses, while her memory went back to the sweetness of his baby prattle and the soft words of his tenderer youth. Until the last she clung to him, holding him guiltless, and to her thought they took to prison, not Joe Hamilton, a convicted criminal, but Joey, Joey, her boy, her first-born—a martyr.

The pretty Miss Kitty Hamilton was less deeply impressed. The arrest and subsequent conviction of her brother was quite a blow. She felt the shame of it keenly, and some of the grief. To her, coming as it did just at a time when the company was being strengthened and she more importantly featured than ever, it was decidedly inopportune, for no one could help connecting her name with the affair.

For a long time she and her brother had scarcely been upon speaking terms. During Joe's frequent lapses from industry he had been prone to "touch" his sister for the wherewithal to supply his various wants. When, finally, she grew tired and refused to be "touched," he rebuked her for withholding that which, save for his help, she would never have been able to make. This went on until they were almost entirely estranged. He was wont to say that "now his sister was up in the world, she had got the big head," and she to retort that her brother "wanted to use her for a 'soft thing.' "

From the time that she went on the stage she had begun to live her own life, a life in which the chief aim was the possession of good clothes and the ability to attract the attention which she had learned to crave. The greatest sign of interest she showed in her brother's affair was, at first, to offer her mother money to secure a lawyer. But when Joe confessed all, she consoled herself with the reflection that perhaps it was for the best, and kept her money in her pocket with a sense of satisfaction. She was getting to be so very much more Joe's sister. She did not go to see her brother. She was afraid it might make her nervous while she was in the city, and she went on the road with her company before he was taken away.

Miss Kitty Hamilton had to be very careful about her nerves and her health. She had had experiences, and her voice was not as good as it used to be, and her beauty had to be aided by cosmetics. So she went away from New York, and only read of all that happened when some one called her attention to it in the papers.

Berry Hamilton in his Southern prison knew nothing of all this, for no letters had passed between him and his family for more than two years. The very cruelty of destiny defeated itself in this and was kind.

Allan H. Spear

THE PHYSICAL AND THE INSTITUTIONAL GHETTO

As Allan H. Spear, a professor of history at the University of Minnesota, writes in the Preface to Black Chicago, *"every literate, socially conscious American has been made aware of the critical problems of the Negro ghetto." His study furthers this awareness by documenting the formation of the black ghetto in Chicago. It shows how in the relatively short period of time between 1890 and 1920 a stable black community became a ghetto. The Chicago ghetto came into being prior to, and not during, the Great Migration. Spear's study is primarily an examination of institutional developments—that is, a study of the structure of the ghetto.*

The Physical Ghetto

Between 1890 and 1915, the Negro population of Chicago grew from less than fifteen thousand to over fifty thousand. Although this growth was overshadowed by the massive influx of Negroes during and after World War I, this was nevertheless a significant increase. By the eve of World War I, although Negroes were still a minor element in the city's population, they were far more conspicuous than they had been a generation earlier. The population increase was accompanied by the concentration of Negroes into ever more constricted sections of the city. In the late nineteenth century, while most Negroes lived in certain sections of the South Side, they lived interspersed among whites; there were few all-Negro blocks. By 1915, on the other hand, the physical ghetto had taken shape; a large, almost all-Negro enclave on the South Side, with a similar offshoot on the West Side, housed most of Chicago's Negroes.

Migration was the major factor in the growth of the Negro community, and most migrants were coming from outside of the state. Over 80 per cent of Chicago's Negro population in 1900 was born in states other than Illinois. The largest portion of these migrants

Reprinted from *Black Chicago: The Making of a Negro Ghetto,* 1890–1920 by Allan H. Spear by permission of the University of Chicago Press and Allan H. Spear, pp. 11–12, 17–27, 91–102, 106–110. © 1967 by the University of Chicago. Footnotes in this and in following selections have been deleted.

originated in the border states and in the Upper South: Kentucky, and Missouri, in particular, had sent large groups of Negroes to Chicago. The states of the Deep South were, as yet, a secondary source of Chicago's Negro population; only 17 per cent had come from these states as opposed to 43 per cent from the Upper South. The states located directly south of Chicago supplied a larger segment of the population than the southeastern states, but there were sizable groups born in Virginia and Georgia.

From the beginning of Chicago's history, most Negroes had lived on the South Side. As early as 1850, 82 per cent of the Negro population lived in an area bounded by the Chicago River on the north, Sixteenth Street on the south, the South Branch of the river on the west, and Lake Michigan on the east. The famous South Side black belt was emerging—a narrow finger of land, wedged between the railroad yards and industrial plants just west of Wentworth Avenue and the fashionable homes east of Wabash Avenue. By 1900, the black belt stretched from the downtown business district as far south as Thirty-ninth Street. But there were also sizable Negro enclaves, usually of a few square blocks each, in several other sections of the city. . . .

Negro residential patterns for 1910 can be seen most clearly through the use of census tract data. Of 431 census tracts in the city, Negroes could be found in all but ninety-four; eighty-eight were at least 1 per cent Negro. Four tracts were over 50 per cent Negro, but no tract was more than 61 per cent Negro. Despite greater concentration, therefore, there were still few all-Negro neighborhoods in Chicago.

The eight or nine neighborhoods that had been distinguishable as areas of Negro settlement in 1900 remained the core of the Chicago Negro community in 1910. The principal South Side black belt was slowly expanding to accommodate the growing population. Not only did Negroes push steadily southward, but the narrow strip of land that made up the black belt began to widen as Negroes moved into the comfortable neighborhood east of State Street. By the end of the decade, Negroes could be found as far east as Cottage Grove Avenue.

Statistical data, then, reveal several definite trends in the pattern of Negro population in Chicago in the early twentieth century. The growth rate between 1900 and 1910 had decreased from the previous decade, but was still 50 per cent greater than that of whites. Most of the population increase was the result of migration, particularly from the nearby border states. Negroes could be found throughout much of the city and the Negro neighborhoods were by no means exclusively black. But the concentration of Negroes in two enclaves on the South and West Sides was increasing. As the population grew, Negroes were not spreading throughout the city but were becoming confined to a clearly delineated area of Negro settlement. . . .

The increasing physical separation of Chicago's Negroes was but one reflection of a growing pattern of segregation and discrimination in early twentieth-century Chicago. As the Negro community grew and opportunities for interracial conflict increased, so a pattern of discrimination and segregation became ever more pervasive. And perhaps the most critical aspect of interracial conflict came as the result of Negro attempts to secure adequate housing.

The South Side black belt could expand in only two directions in the early twentieth century—south and east. . . .

Negro expansion did not always mean conflict, nor did it mean that a neighborhood would shortly become exclusively black. In 1910, not more than a dozen blocks on the South Side were entirely Negro, and in many mixed areas Negroes and whites lived together harmoniously. But as Negroes became more numerous east of State and south of Fifty-first, friction increased and white hostility grew. When a Negro family moved into a previously all-white neighborhood, the neighbors frequently protested, tried to buy the property, and then, if unsuccessful, resorted to violence to drive out the interlopers. In many cases, the residents organized to urge real estate agents and property owners to sell and rent to whites only. The whites often succeeded in keeping Negroes out, at least temporarily. When their efforts failed, they gradually moved out, leaving the neighborhood predominantly, although rarely exclusively, Negro. . . .

The unwillingness of whites to tolerate Negroes as neighbors had far-reaching results. Because Negroes were so limited in their choice of housing, they were forced to pay higher rents in those buildings that were open to them. Real estate agents frequently converted buildings in marginal neighborhoods from white to Negro and demanded rents 10 to 15 per cent higher than they had previously received. Sophonisba Breckinridge of Hull House estimated that a Negro family "pays $12.50 for the same accommodations the Jew in the Ghetto received for $9 and the immigrant for $8." . . .

Living conditions in much of the black belt closely resembled conditions in the West Side ghetto or in the Stockyards district. Although Negroes could find some decent homes on the fringes of the Negro section, the core of the black belt was a festering slum. Here was an area of one- and two-story frame houses (unlike the older Eastern cities Chicago had, as yet, few large tenements), usually dilapidated with boarded-up porches and rickety wooden walks. Most of the buildings contained two flats and, although less crowded than houses in the Jewish, Polish, and Bohemian slums, they were usually in worse repair. The 1912 survey revealed that in a four-block area in the black belt, only 26 per cent of the dwellings were in good repair—as compared to 71 per cent in a similar sampling in a Polish neighborhood, 57 per cent among Bohemians, and 54 per cent in the ethnically mixed Stockyards district. "Colored tenants," the survey reported, "found it impossible to persuade their landlords either to make the necessary repairs or to release them from their contracts; . . . it was so hard to find better places in which to live that they were forced to make the repairs themselves, which they could rarely afford to do, or to endure the conditions as best they might."

White real estate agents, insensitive to class differences among Negroes, made no attempt to uphold standards in middle-class Negro neighborhoods as they did in comparable white districts. They persistently rented flats in "respectable" Negro neighborhoods to members of the "sporting element," thus forcing middle-class Negroes to move continually in search of decent areas to live and rear families. As a result, neighborhood stability was at best temporary. The streets east of State, which had become the mecca of the Negro middle class in the late 1890's, began to decline by 1905. A few years later the district was characterized by "men and women half clothed hanging out of a window," "rag-time piano playing . . . far into the night," and "shooting and cutting scrapes."

Municipal policy regarding vice further complicated the situation. City authorities, holding that the suppression of prostitution was impossible, tried to confine it to certain well-defined areas where it could be closely watched. The police frequently moved the vice district so as to keep it away from commercial and white residential areas. Invariably they located it in or near the black belt, often in Negro residential neighborhoods. The chief of police declared that so long as prostitutes confined their activities to the district between Wentworth and Wabash, they would not be apprehended. Neighborhood stability, then, was threatened not only by the influx of Negro "shadies," but by the presence of an officially sanctioned vice district catering primarily to whites.

Periodic attempts to clean up the red-light district received little support from Negro leaders who believed that such campaigns would merely drive the undesirables deeper into Negro residential neighborhoods. When legal prostitution was finally abolished in 1912, these fears were fully realized; vice in Chicago continued to be centered in the black belt. Fannie Barrier Williams, a prominent Negro civic leader, summed up the plight of the middle- and upper-class Negro: "The huddling together of the good and the bad, compelling the decent element of the colored people to witness the brazen display of vice of all kinds in front of their homes and in the faces of their children, are trying conditions under which to remain socially clean and respectable."

The pattern of Negro housing, then, was shaped by white hostility and indifference: limited in their choice of homes, Negroes were forced to pay higher rents for inferior dwellings and were frequently surrounded by prostitutes, panderers, and other undesirable elements. This, together with the poverty of the majority of Chicago Negroes, produced in the black belt the conditions of slum-living characteristic of American cities by the end of the nineteenth century.

The most striking feature of Negro housing, however, was not the existence of slum conditions, but the difficulty of escaping the slum. European immigrants needed only to prosper to be able to move to a more desirable neighborhood. Negroes, on the other hand, suffered from both economic deprivation and systematic racial discrimination. "The problem of the Chicago Negro," wrote Sophonisba Breckinridge,

> *is quite different from the white man and even that of the immigrants. With the Negro the housing dilemma was found to be an acute problem, not only among the poor, as in the case of the Polish, Jewish, or Italian immigrants, but also among the well-to-do. . . . Thus, even in the North, where the city administration does not recognize a "Ghetto" or "pale," the real estate agents who register and commercialize what they suppose to be a universal race prejudice are able to enforce one in practice.*

The development of a physical ghetto in Chicago, then, was not the result chiefly of poverty; nor did Negroes cluster out of choice. The ghetto was primarily the product of white hostility. Attempts on the part of Negroes to seek housing in predominantly white sections of the city met with resistance from the residents and from real estate dealers. Some Negroes, in fact, who had formerly lived in white neighborhoods, were pushed back into the black districts. As the Chicago Negro population grew, Negroes had no alternative but to settle in well-delineated Negro areas. And with increasing pressure for Negro housing, property owners in the black belt found it profitable to force out white tenants and convert previously mixed blocks into all-Negro blocks. The geographical dimensions of Black Chicago in the early twentieth century underwent no dramatic shift similar, for instance, to Negro New York, where the center of Negro life moved to previously all-white Harlem in less than a decade. Negroes in Chicago were not establishing new communities. But to meet the needs of a growing population, in the face of mounting white resistance, Negro neighborhoods were becoming more exclusively Negro as they slowly expanded their boundaries.

The Institutional Ghetto

The rise of the new middle-class leadership was closely interrelated with the development of Chicago's black ghetto. White hostility and population growth combined to create the physical ghetto on the South Side. The response of Negro leadership, on the other hand, created the institutional ghetto. Between 1900 and 1915, Chicago's Negro leaders built a complex of community organizations, institutions, and enterprises that made the South Side not simply an area of Negro concentration but a city within a city. Chicago's tightening color bar encouraged the development of a new economic and political leadership with its primary loyalty to a segregated Negro community. By meeting discrimination with self-help rather than militant protest, this leadership converted the dream of an integrated city into the vision of a "black metropolis."

The oldest and most stable Negro institution in Chicago was the church. The first Negro church in the city, Quinn Chapel A.M.E., was founded in 1847, just fourteen years after Chicago was incorporated. By the end of the century, Chicago had over a dozen Negro churches, and between 1900 and 1915 doubled this number. The majority of these churches were affiliated with the two largest Negro denominations—African Methodist Episcopal and Baptist—and were controlled and supported exclusively by Negroes from the beginning. New churches opened as the community grew and as perpetual dissension within the established congregations resulted in schisms. Most of the Baptist churches were offshoots of Olivet, the oldest and largest Negro Baptist church in the city, while the A.M.E. churches were generally founded by dissident parishioners from Quinn Chapel and Bethel Church. . . .

Yet the large, established churches were not able to attract all segments of the increasingly stratified Negro community. On the one hand, many sophisticated upper- and middle-class Negroes were no longer content with traditional Negro religion and sought other forms of religious expression. Julius F. Taylor expressed in exaggerated form the discontent that a growing minority felt about the churches. He wrote in one of his typical anticlerical tirades:

> *If we possessed the power, we would abolish or do away with Negro churches and establish in their stead ethical culture societies. . . . How long! Oh how long! will the Negro continue to erect costly and expensive temples unto the Gods, while his children are growing up in rags and tatters and in ignorance, and while poverty and squalor surrounds him on every hand.*

The old-line churches had even greater difficulty in holding the lowest stratum of Negro society—the poor and the ignorant and, especially, the recent migrants from the South. A survey of 398 persons in a lower-class precinct in 1901 showed that well over one-half had no church affiliations and a disproportionate number of those who belonged were women. Many poor Negroes could not afford church membership, while others were alienated by the predominantly middle-class outlook of the large churches. Although such churches as Quinn Chapel, Bethel, and Olivet continued to dominate Chicago Negro religious life down to 1915, they faced competition from churches appealing to special segments of the population.

During the late nineteenth century, some educated and relatively affluent Negroes gravitated to churches affiliated with the major white denominations—Presbyterian, Episcopalian, Methodist Episcopal, Congregational, and Roman Catholic—which offered more sophisticated worship services than the traditional Negro churches. . . .

Another unusual church that made a special appeal to Negroes dissatisfied with traditional forms of religious life was the Institutional Church and Social Settlement, founded in 1900 by Reverdy Ransom. Institutional, under Ransom and his successor, Archibald Carey, developed a full program of social services that went well beyond the welfare activities of Quinn Chapel, Olivet, and Bethel. Ransom called Institutional "the first social settlement in the world" for the race and said that it was "not a church in the ordinary sense . . . [but] a Hull House or Chicago Commons founded by Negroes for the help of people of that race." Some hostile Negro ministers told their congregations that Institutional was not a church at all and forbade them to take communion there. Institutional operated a day nursery, a kindergarten, a mothers' club, an employment bureau, a print shop, and a fully equipped gymnasium; it offered a complete slate of club activities and classes in sewing, cooking, and music; its Forum featured lectures by leading white and Negro figures; and its facilities were always available for concerts, meetings, and other civic functions. The church attempted to draw from both segments of the community that were alienated from the old-line congregations. The wide range of social activities was designed to attract lower-class Negroes without church affiliation and sophisticated Negroes who found Institutional's emphasis on a social gospel more appealing than the traditional preoccupation with sin and salvation. For a time, under Ransom and Carey, the church thrived and seemed to provide a meaningful answer to those who were critical of or indifferent to the Negro church. But it was unable to survive the World War I era. As secular agencies began to assume the social functions of Institutional, the church declined and eventually died.

Another solution to the problem of attracting the unchurched—one more portentous for the future—was the emergence of the Holiness and Spiritualist churches. These little storefront congregations with their uninhibited worship and informal atmosphere were not yet the potent force that they were to become during the migration era. But several were established in the first decade of the twentieth century. The Holy Nazarene Tabernacle Apostolic Church, for instance, was founded in 1908 by Mattie L. Thornton. It secured its own building in 1909, held camp meetings each summer, and even made an unsuccessful attempt to establish a branch in New York. By 1915, a Spiritualist congregation, the Church of Redemption of Souls, was operating on State Street.

The Negro churches of Chicago had from the beginning of their history exemplified the self-help philosophy. Since the mid-nineteenth century, Negroes had reacted against the hostility of most white churches by organizing separate congregations where they could manage their own affairs. The Negro churches, then, were already self-sufficient by the end of the century and underwent no sudden or unprecedented changes between 1890 and 1915. But certain trends were apparent. The churches were broadening their programs to include a wide range of social activities. The large churches, dominated by the middle class, were still the most important religious institutions in the community, but they now faced competition from new churches, designed to meet the special needs of those at the upper and lower reaches of the social and economic spectrum. The migrations of the World War I period would rapidly accelerate these trends and profoundly change the religious life of the South Side.

Secular institutions in the Negro community were of more recent origin than the churches. Provident Hospital, established in 1891, was Chicago's first Negro civic institution. By the eve of World

War I, the Chicago Negro community had perhaps a dozen social service institutions. Some of these were ephemeral while others became permanent fixtures of community life. Most were exclusively Negro institutions, operated by Negroes and intended for the use of the Negro community, although some received assistance from white philanthropists. Although the churches probably remained more important to the bulk of Chicago's Negroes, the secular institutions had become the major civic interest of Negro leaders by 1915.

Provident Hospital was the first and most ambitious Negro civic undertaking in Chicago and its history reveals in microcosm the major trends of community life on the South Side. Daniel Hale Williams, its proud and able founder, was continually rankled by the difficulties Negroes faced in the medical profession. Negro physicians found it almost impossible to secure internships and staff appointments at white hospitals, Negro women were unable to secure nurses' training courses, and Negro patients could not get private hospital rooms. But Williams, with his wide contacts among white medical men and his generally integrationist inclinations, did not want to establish a segregated Negro hospital. Such a project would separate Negroes from the mainstream of the medical profession and give white groups an additional reason for excluding Negroes from white hospitals and training schools.

In 1891, Williams called together a group of Negro community leaders and several of his white medical colleagues for the purpose of organizing the first interracial hospital in the United States. He reasoned that Negroes could operate a hospital just as European ethnic groups and religious denominations had sponsored hospitals in Chicago. Unlike any other hospital in the city, Provident would receive Negroes on an equal basis and provide opportunities for Negro doctors and nurses. But it would not be a hospital for Negroes alone. It would assemble an interracial staff drawn from the best medical talent in the city and admit patients of all races. Provident was to be a model, not of a Negro community institution, but of a venture in interracial cooperation. . . .

The thriving hospital of 1915, however, bore little resemblance to Dan Williams' original conception of a truly interracial hospital. Increasing racial tension and Negro race pride had profoundly influenced Provident's development. The doctors and nurses who came out of Provident's internship program and training school could not, despite their qualifications, find positions at white hospitals. Some left Chicago to help found Negro hospitals elsewhere, but many stayed on at Provident. By 1916, all of the nurses except the supervisor and almost all of the staff physicians were Negroes. Moreover, as Provident became a major focus of the civic and philanthropic life of the South Side, Negroes naturally came to regard it as their hospital. Despite the initial help of white philanthropists, Negro contributors provided an ever larger portion of Provident's operational expenses and 90 per cent of its endowment. As a result, many Negroes expected the hospital to provide positions for Negroes as a matter of duty, and Williams found it increasingly difficult to exclude from the staff Negroes whom he considered inadequately trained. The hospital continued to serve a sizable number of white patients, but while 65 per cent of the patients in the early years were white, that figure had dropped to less than 40 per cent by 1912. . . .

The Wabash Avenue Young Men's Christian Association was another important focus of community pride. Although still a young institution in 1915, its conception even antedated Provident. In 1889, several community leaders proposed the establishment of "a separate and distinct organization known as the Colored Young Men's Christian Association," but the suggestion aroused immediate opposition from the still dominant integrationists. The weekly *Appeal* declared itself "unalterably opposed to any scheme that draws about it the color line" and reminded its readers that "there is on Madison Street one of the finest Young Men's Christian Association organizations in the country to which all young men are cordially invited regardless of race or color." A protest meeting was held at Olivet Church and, within a month, the proposal was forgotten.

By the early twentieth century, however, the situation had changed. Negroes were no longer "cordially invited" to use the downtown YMCA; in fact, as Ida Barnett pointed out, neither the YMCA, YWCA, Salvation Army, or Mills Hotels admitted Negroes. Moreover many Negro community leaders believed that to serve the youth of the black belt, the YMCA must have an establishment located on the South Side. In 1910, a group of Negro leaders held a rally to raise funds for a YMCA. The voices that had protested in 1889 were now almost mute; no less an integrationist than Ferdinand Barnett led the campaign. Only Edward E. Wilson attacked the project as "the latest concrete example of jim-crowism." Most Negroes heartily approved the idea. As with Provident Hospital, white philanthropists made the project possible. At the end of 1910, Julius Rosenwald of Sears Roebuck and N. W. Harris, a prominent banker, each pledged $25,000 for a YMCA if the Negro community contributed an additional $50,000.

The fund-raising campaign that followed was conceived by both whites and Negroes as an experiment in Negro self-help. "The best help is self-help," the *Record-Herald* editorialized. "Such effort leads to increased self-respect and also to increased respect on the part of the community in general." Within three weeks, over $65,000 was raised—well over the necessary quota—and additional gifts from Cyrus McCormick and the central YMCA organization brought the total sum to the needed $190,000. In 1913, the Wabash Avenue YMCA opened as "the largest and finest Association building for colored men in the United States." Rosenwald was so pleased that he extended his offer of $25,000 to any Negro community in the United States that could raise the additional sum needed for a YMCA, and the Chicago organization became a prototype for many similar projects throughout the country.

The Colored Women's Club movement provided another example of Negro self-help in the face of mounting discrimination. The women's clubs gained nationwide support during the 1890's, and Chicago, the home of two of the movement's leading spokesmen—Fannie Barrier Williams and Ida Wells-Barnett—was in the vanguard. Even before the organization of the National Association of Colored Women in 1896, Chicago had its Ida Wells Club, dedicated to "civic and social betterment." By the turn of the century, the city had over a half-dozen women's clubs, which had banded together to form the Colored Women's Conference of Chicago. The clubs operated kindergartens, mothers' clubs, sewing schools, day nurseries, employment bureaus, parent-teacher associations, and a penny savings bank. . . .

Despite the flurry of civic activity, the South Side's social agencies were inadequate to meet the needs of the growing Negro community. In particular, as a city investigator reported in 1915, "a large district—the heart of the [second] ward—scarcely feels their influence"; the slum district in the northern end of the black belt still had few social agencies. Nevertheless, the interest in these institutions among Negro leaders reflected the growing belief that Negroes should themselves organize and manage community services in the black belt. Most of the institutions depended upon white financial support and a few used white personnel. But by 1915, Negro leaders had responded to discrimination in white institutions by establishing a wide range of Negro-operated community services. These activities had become a major focus of Negro civic life.

After 1900, the new institutions began to replace the older social and fraternal organizations as the center of communal activities. The lodges and fraternal orders in particular, which had flourished since the pre-Civil War era, began to decline in importance in the early twentieth century. Next to the churches, lodges had the longest history of any voluntary associations in Chicago. The Good Samaritans, a national Negro order, had a Chicago lodge as early as 1859, and by the 1880's over forty lodges—many with women's auxiliaries—were operating in the still small Negro community. Most important were the Prince Hall Masons, who, on the national level, traced their history back to the 1780's when a group of Boston Negroes, denied recognition by white Masons, received a charter from the Grand Lodge of England. The Illinois Grand Lodge organized in 1867, and by 1885, there were fifteen Masonic lodges in Chicago. Perhaps next in importance were the Odd Fellows who had six chapters in the city in the 1880's. The lodges included among their members many community leaders in the late nineteenth century: John Jones, Ferdinand Barnett, and Theodore Jones were all prominent Masons, while Edward Morris was one of the national leaders of the Odd Fellows. The politicians, in particular, found the lodges useful bases for political support: Ed Wright was an Odd Fellow and Robert R. Jackson, who belonged to almost all of the fraternal orders, had a special interest in the Knights of Pythias. Lodge social affairs were events of community-wide interest; over two thousand of the "best colored people" attended the Knights Templar Ball in 1900. The lodges also served a benevolent function, providing benefits for sickness or death in a period when few Negroes carried insurance.

But by the first decade of the twentieth century, the lodges were waning. Geared primarily for small, relatively homogeneous communities, the lodges found it difficult to compete for membership and prestige in a city with a wide variety of other institutions and activities and an increasingly differentiated social structure. The lodges found it difficult to maintain their benefit programs in the face of competition from commercial insurance companies. Moreover the social service institutions replaced the lodges as centers of civic activities, and social clubs appealing to particular strata in the community assumed their position as the focus of Negro social life.

By 1900, the social clubs had begun to reflect the growing delineation of class lines in the Negro community. The Ladies' Whist Club, for instance, which included in its membership Mesdames Edward Morris, Julius Avendorph, Edward Wilson, and Dan Williams, pointedly excluded Mrs. George Hall, while Dr. Hall was unable to gain admittance to the Chicago branch of Sigma Pi Phi, the most exclusive national Negro men's club. The class consciousness of the old elite was further reflected by the organization in 1902 of the Chicago Old Settlers' Club, "to keep the old settlers in touch with each other, and to cherish and keep fresh those memories of early colored life in Chicago." Closely related to the upper-class social clubs were the literary societies. The Prudence Crandall Club, organized in 1887 for "mutual improvement," included among its members the venerable Mrs. John Jones, widow of Chicago's pioneer Negro leader, Charles Bentley, James Madden, Ferdinand Barnett, and Lloyd Wheeler. A special type of social club that grew up before Chicago's biracial system had begun to harden was the Manasseh Society, an organization of Negro men with white wives. In 1892, the society boasted over five hundred members. Still active in 1912, it declined as interracial social contacts decreased.

Members of the new middle class, refused admittance to the most exclusive of the old clubs, began to form social organizations of their own. The Appomattox Club was founded in 1900 by Ed Wright as a rendezvous for the professional politicians, but it soon became a favorite of business and professional men as well and a center of Negro social life in general. Visiting dignitaries were invariably entertained in the club's comfortable quarters on Wabash Avenue, and the group's periodic balls and receptions were described in detail in the Negro press. By the 1920's, a Negro editor could state that "every man in Chicago who holds any kind of responsible position or occupies a big place politically, belongs to the Appomattox Club." In 1911, the Post Office employees, an important segment of the new Negro middle class, formed another prominent social organization—the Phalanx Forum. Founded for social, civic, and benevolent purposes, the Phalanx sponsored social affairs and safeguarded the interests of its members. The organization maintained close ties with the Appomattox Club and with the Republican political organization.

The development of secular institutions and organizations illustrated the major currents of prewar Negro community life. The changes in attitude toward such establishments as Provident Hospital and the YMCA reflected the trend toward separatism. The development of a wide range of social clubs catering to specific groupings in the community was a manifestation of increasing social differentiation. The growth of characteristically metropolitan institutions, such as social settlements and a YMCA, to challenge the traditional roles of the church and the lodge, indicated that the Chicago Negro community was developing an urban pattern of behavior. It could no longer rely upon the institutions that had dominated the civic life of rural and small town Negro communities. It now confronted urban problems that demanded urban solutions.

Gilbert Osofsky

THE MAKING OF A GHETTO

Gilbert Osofsky's book, Harlem: The Making of a Ghetto, Negro New York, 1890–1930, *appeared in 1965. In the first part of the book Osofsky describes the developments taking place in the nation and the city in the 1890's, relating these events to the black experience. The second part of the book details the process by which a white upper-middle-class neighborhood became a black ghetto. The final part shows how the ghetto became a slum. The following excerpt is taken from the second part of Osofsky's study. This excerpt provides an interesting comparison with the three earlier selections.*

Harlem life altered radically in the first decade of the twentieth century. The construction of new subway routes into the neighborhood in the late 1890s set off a second wave of speculation in Harlem land and property. Speculators who intended to make astronomic profits when the subway was completed bought the marshes, garbage dumps and lots left unimproved or undeveloped in the 1870s and 1880s. Between 1898 and 1904, the year that the Lenox Avenue line opened at One Hundred and Forty-fifth Street, "practically all the vacant land in Harlem" was "built over," the *Real Estate Record and Builders' Guide* noted in 1904. "The growth of . . . Harlem . . . has been truly astonishing during the last half dozen years." . . .

Speculation in West Harlem property led to phenomenal increases in the price of land and the cost of houses there—increases inflated out of all proportion to their real value. John M. Royall, Negro realtor, recalled that "from 1902 to 1905 real estate speculative fever seized all New York City. The great subway proposition . . . permeated the air. Real estate operators and speculators [imagined] becoming millionaires, and bought freely in the West Harlem district in and about the proposed subway stations. Men bought property on thirty and sixty day contracts, and sold their contracts . . . and made substantial profits. I have known buyers to pay $38,000 and $75,000 for tenements which showed a gross income of only

Abridgment of pp. 87, 90–93, 96, 99, 103–107, 109–123 in *Harlem: The Making of a Ghetto* by Gilbert Osofsky. Copyright © 1963, 1966 by Gilbert Osofsky. Reprinted by permission of Harper & Row, Publishers, Inc.

$2600 and $5000 a year. On they went buying, buying. . . ." Houses
continually changed hands. Each time a house was sold, Royall said,
it brought a higher price. In the urge to get rich quick on Harlem
property, few persons realized how artificial market values had become.

The inevitable bust came in 1904–1905. Speculators sadly realized
afterward that too many houses were constructed at one time. West
Harlem was glutted with apartments and "excessive building . . .
led to many vacancies." No one knew exactly how long it would
take to construct the subway and many houses built four and five
years in advance of its completion remained partly unoccupied. The
first of them to be inhabited by Negroes, for example, was never
rented previously. Rents were too high for the general population
($35–$45 per month) and precluded any great rush to West Harlem
even after the subway was completed. There was a widespread
"overestimation of . . . rental value," a contemporary remarked.
When the market broke, landlords competed with each other for
tenants by reducing rents, or offering a few months' rent-free occu-
pancy to them. Local realtors unsuccessfully attempted to eliminate
these cutthroat practices.

By 1905 financial institutions no longer made loans to Harlem
speculators and building-loan companies, and many foreclosed on
their original mortgages. The inflated prices asked for land and
property in West Harlem "solemnly settled beneath a sea of depreciated values." In the aftermath of the speculative collapse, and
as a consequence of the initiative of Negro realtors, large numbers
of colored people began to settle in West Harlem. . . .

The individuals and companies caught in Harlem's rapidly deflated real estate market were threatened with ruin. Rather than
face "financial destruction" some landlords and corporations opened
their houses to Negroes and collected the traditionally high rents
that colored people paid. Others used the threat of renting to Negroes to frighten neighbors into buying their property at higher than
market prices. Shrewder operators (contemporaries called them
"clever buyers" and "white blackmailers," present-day realtors refer
to them as "blockbusters") hoped to take advantage of the unusual
situation by "placing colored people in property so that they might
buy other parcels adjoining or in the same block [reduced in price

by] fear on the part of whites to one-half of the values then obtaining," John M. Royall noted. By using these techniques "a great number" of property owners were able "to dispose of their property or . . . get a . . . more lucrative return from rents paid by colored tenants," he concluded.

The existence of a loosely rooted Negro population ready to settle in Harlem was primarily the result of ever-increasing Negro migration to the city. Further, the destruction of many all-Negro blocks in the Tenderloin when Pennsylvania Station was built in the first decade of the twentieth century, part of a more general commercial expansion in midtown Manhattan, dislocated the Negro population. Negro businessmen who owned property in the Tenderloin made substantial fortunes by selling and moving uptown. Negro tenants, offered decent living accommodations for the first time in the city's history, "flocked to Harlem and filled houses as fast as they were opened to them."

This situation offered unusual money-making opportunities to a Negro realtor, Philip A. Payton, Jr. Payton was keenly aware of the housing needs of New York City's growing Negro population. His plan seemed foolproof, and guaranteed to satisfy Harlem's white landlords, the Negro people and himself. Payton offered to lease Harlem apartment houses from white owners and assure them a regular annual income. He, in turn, would rent these homes to Negroes and make a profit by charging rents ten per cent above the then deflated market price. Many Negroes were willing to scrimp to live in beautiful apartments in an exclusive section of the city and Payton's initial operations were highly successful. His name became a respected one in Negro New York. . . .

Payton's activities in Harlem real estate reached a high point in 1904 with his founding of the Afro-American Realty Company. The company had its genesis in a partnership of ten Negroes organized by Payton. This partnership specialized in acquiring five-year leases on Harlem property owned by whites and subsequently renting them to Negroes. In 1904, Payton conceived of reorganizing this small concern into a regular real estate corporation, capable of buying and constructing homes as well as leasing them. The company, incorporated on June 15, 1904, was permitted to "buy, sell, rent, lease, and sub-lease, all kinds of buildings, houses . . . lots, and other . . .

real estate in the City of New York. . . ." It was capitalized at
$500,000 and authorized to issue 50,000 shares at $10 each. Ten of
the eleven original members of the all-Negro Board of Directors
subscribed to 500 shares each. The company began with an estimated capital of $100,000. . . .

The Realty Company promised the world and delivered little. It
had hopefully been incorporated for fifty years, but folded after four.
During its short and hectic existence it was wracked with internal
dissension. In four years there were three major reorganizations of
its Board of Directors and officers. James C. Thomas and James E.
Garner severed connections with the company in its first year.
Wilford H. Smith was later influential in bringing suit against Payton
for fraud. The final reorganization, in 1906, left Payton as president
and general manager. It was formal recognition of the power he had
wielded since the founding of the corporation. . . .

The Afro-American Realty Company played a significant part in
opening homes for Negroes in Harlem. Philip A. Payton, Jr., owned
and managed apartment houses and brownstones in sections never
previously rented to Negro tenants. His holdings were scattered
throughout Harlem from One Hundred and Nineteenth to One Hundred and Forty-seventh Streets. When the company folded, white
realtors and mortgagors took over its property but the Negro tenants remained. The new owners continued to advertise the Negro
company's former houses in the colored press. The speculations of
Philip A. Payton, Jr., led to the downfall of the Afro-American Realty
Company, but they also helped lay the foundations of the largest
Negro ghetto in the world. . . .

The pressing need and desire for accommodations to house an
expanding Negro population made the founding of the Afro-American Realty Company possible. This need continued to exist with
greater intensity after the company's demise, and Negroes found
other means to buy or rent homes in Harlem. The "border line"
which separated whites and Negroes "rapidly receded" each year,
and by 1914 some 50,000 Negroes lived in the neighborhood.

But not all property owners were ready to open their houses to
colored people. It seemed unbelievable to some that theirs, one of
the most exclusive sections in the entire city, should become the
center of New York's most depressed and traditionally worst-housed

people. Some owners banded together in associations to repulse what they referred to as the Negro "invasion" or the Negro "influx." The language used to describe the movement of Negroes into Harlem—the words "invasion," "captured," "black hordes," "invaders," "enemy," for example, appear repeatedly in denunciations of Negroes—was the language of war. . . .

Most of the formal opposition to Negro settlement in Harlem centered in local associations of landlords. Some were committees representing individual blocks, others were community-wide in structure. . . .

Other community groups led by white realtors, businessmen, journalists, clergymen, members of the Board of Commerce and local citizens tried to hold back the Negro's "steady effort to invade Harlem." One realty company dealing in upper-Manhattan property was called the Anglo-Saxon Realty Corporation. Such organizations as the West Side Improvement Corporation, the West Harlem Property Owners' Association, the Save-Harlem Committee, the Committee of Thirty and the Harlem Property Owners' Improvement Corporation were formed. Each planned to arouse the interest of all white Harlemites in what they called "the greatest problem that Harlem has had to face."

The Harlem Property Owners' Improvement Corporation (HPOIC), active from 1910 to 1915, was the most forceful of these organizations. "We are approaching a crisis," its founder, John G. Taylor, said in 1913. "It is the question of whether the white man will rule Harlem or the Negro." Taylor hoped to organize the entire white community "to fight the common enemy." "We believe," he wrote on another occasion, "that real friends of the Negroes will eventually convince them that they should buy large tracts of unimproved land near the city and there build up colonies of their own." "Drive them out," Taylor shouted in an angry tirade at another time, "and send them to the slums where they belong. . . ."

The basic cause of the collapse of all organized efforts to exclude Negroes from Harlem was the inability of any group to gain total and unified support of all white property owners in the neighborhood. Without such support it was impossible to organize a successful neighborhood-wide restrictive movement. Landlords forming associations by blocks had a difficult time keeping people on individual streets united. There also continued to be speculators, Negro and white, who, as in 1904 and 1905, sought to exploit the situation for their own profit. They bought tenements and opened them to Negroes to try to force neighbors to repurchase them at higher prices. Nor was it possible, and this is the major point, to create a well-organized and well-financed movement of Negro restriction (the HPOIC plan called for the contribution of one-half of one per cent of the assessed valuation of all property to a community fund) in the disrupted and emotional atmosphere that pervaded Harlem in the first two decades of the twentieth century. The very setting in which whites were confronted with Negro neighbors for the first time led to less than level-headed reasoning. The first impulse of many "in a rather panicky state of mind" was to sell at whatever price their property would bring and move elsewhere. Realtors called this "panic selling" and, in spite of efforts to prevent it, it continued. Between 1907 and 1914, two-thirds of the houses in or near the Negro section were sold—practically all at substantial losses to the original owners. Since the already weak real estate market was flooded with property in a short time, and only a relatively few Negroes were wealthy enough to buy—"there was no market for real estate among the newcomers"—prices continued to depreciate rapidly: "realty values have tumbled by leaps and bounds." "The coming of Negroes to this locality without any financial backing brought about a decided change, as the colored people . . . were unable to adhere to the standard formerly observed by the whites," a Harlem banker wrote. "Hence there was a deterioration in values. . . ." In the 1870s and 1880s fortunes were made in soaring Harlem land prices; by 1917 white realtors tried to encourage interest in the neighborhood by advertising how cheap property had become: "Changes in the character of Harlem population," a member of the Harlem Board of Commerce wrote, have led "to remarkable bargains, both for rental and purchase. . . . Such properties in good condition can now be purchased at less than the assessed value of the land alone." In the 1920s, as will be shown, this situation changed radically. . . .

The creation of Negro Harlem was only one example of the general development of large, segregated Negro communities within many American cities in the years *preceding* and following World

War I. Harlem was New York's equivalent of the urban ghettos of the nation. "The Negroes are being relegated to the land of Goshen in all our great cities," Kelly Miller commented. "Niggertowns," "Buzzard's Alleys," "Nigger Rows," "Black Bottoms," "Smoketowns," "Bronzevilles," and "Chinch Rows" developed elsewhere, North and South, by 1913—and they would continue to emerge in the future. The District of Columbia was noted for its supposedly decadent Negro alleys: "Tin Can Alley," "Coon Alley," "Hog Alley," "Moonshine Alley," and "Goat Alley." (Life in "Goat Alley," was the subject of a play by that name in the 1920s.) "So closely have the terms Alleys and Negroes been associated," a historian of Washington's Negro section wrote, "that in the minds of the older citizens they are inseparable." "There is growing up in the cities of America a distinct Negro world," George Edmund Haynes said in 1913. These were neighborhoods "isolated from many of the impulses of the common life and little understood by the white world," he concluded.

Among these urban ghettos Harlem was unique. Initially, its name was a symbol of elegance and distinction, not derogation; its streets and avenues were broad, well-paved, clean and tree-lined, not narrow and dirty; its homes were spacious, replete with the best modern facilities, "finished in high-style." Harlem was originally not a slum, but an ideal place in which to live. For the first and generally last time in the history of New York City, Negroes were able to live in decent homes in a respectable neighborhood, "the best houses that they have ever had to live in": "It is no longer necessary for our people to live in small, dingy, stuffy tenements," The New York Age said in an editorial in 1906. Harlem was "a community in which Negroes as a whole are . . . better housed than in any other part of the country," an Urban League report concluded in 1914. "Those of the race who desire to live in grand style, with elevator, telephone and hall boy service, can now realize their cherished ambition." . . .

After the collapse of the Afro-American Realty Company, Negro churches played a more important role in the development of Harlem than all other institutions in the Negro community. The primary reason for this was that the church had traditionally been the most stable and wealthy Negro institution. As the Negro population expanded rapidly in the early twentieth century the influence and wealth of the church increased phenomenally. Membership in older churches doubled and trebled, and they continually moved to larger quarters; little missions which began in storefronts or in private homes became independent and built or bought stately structures in which to worship; new churches were founded. Mercy Street Baptist Church, for example, was organized in Harlem by seven Negroes at the turn of the century. At first the small congregation met in a house owned by the Baptist City Mission. By July 1907 the congregation, supported by eight hundred communicants, moved to a new building. Population pressure made these facilities inadequate—"Standing room is always at a premium"—and the congregation, under its new name, Metropolitan Baptist, negotiated the sale of a white Presbyterian church in 1918. Harlem Presbyterian had been "one of the finest church buildings in Harlem." Metropolitan Baptist has remained there ever since. . . .

Similar changes occurred throughout Harlem in the early twentieth century. Exclusive white denominations left the neighborhood and sold their property to Negro Baptists, Methodists and others. "Little Zion," the uptown branch of "Mother Zion," remained in a small wooden building on Harlem's east side for three-quarters of a century before it constructed a new church on the west side in 1911. "Not in seventy years has there been so much real enthusiasm in the Harlem A.M.E. Zion Church," one member commented. Ministers in all the churches preached in quarters inadequate to seat those who wished to attend, and some were forced to hold five or six services each Sunday. New Negro Moravian, Seventh Day Adventist, Roman Catholic and evangelical churches were established in Harlem prior to and after the First World War. Before all the downtown congregations moved to Harlem they too opened branch Sunday schools and Bible classes in public halls and theaters. Mass services were sometimes held in "gospel tents," "mammoth tents," pitched on Harlem's empty lots, as clergymen sought to "Harvest the Souls" of the ungodly.

Pastors of Negro churches, as they had done in the nineteenth century, planned to follow their congregations to the new Negro neighborhood. The Reverend Dr. Adam Clayton Powell, Sr., repeatedly preached his sermon "A Model Church," encouraging his congregation to move Abyssinian Baptist to Harlem and to purchase property there while prices were low. "It was apparent as early as 1911," he later wrote, "that Harlem would be the final destination of the Abyssinian Church." "On to Harlem" movements began in downtown churches and, prior to 1914, three of the oldest and most distinguished Negro churches, Bethel African Methodist Episcopal, African Methodist Episcopal Zion ("Mother Zion") and St. Philip's Protestant Episcopal Church moved into the section. By the early 1920's practically every established Negro church in Manhattan was located in Harlem, and most occupied exceptionally beautiful buildings.

But the Negro churches did more than simply follow their members to Harlem. Many were able to realize large profits by selling property in the midtown area at high prices and moving uptown where land and property had depreciated in value before World War I. The more important and wealthy congregations not only built new churches in Harlem, but invested heavily in local real estate. Negro churches became the largest Negro property owners in Harlem. St. Mark's Methodist Episcopal, Abyssinian Baptist, and "Mother Zion" owned houses in Harlem prior to 1915. After the war, they and other Negro churches continued to invest heavily in land and homes. Some of the houses purchased by churches were on blocks covered by restrictive covenants, but nothing could be done to prevent such transactions. By becoming landholders, Negro churches helped transform Harlem to a Negro section.

The Negro church most actively engaged in buying Harlem real estate was St. Philip's Protestant Episcopal Church. Throughout the nineteenth century St. Philip's was reputed to be the most exclusive Negro church in New York City. Its members were considered "the better element of colored people," and its services were dignified and refined. This reputation as a fashionable institution made membership in St. Philip's a sign of social recognition and many of the more prominent Negroes of the city were its communicants. It was the only Negro church in Manhattan with a "Pew System" in the nineteenth century—by which members outbid each other for choice seats in the chapel. St. Philip's was also recognized as the "wealthiest Negro church in the country," and this reputation has continued to the present.

The growth of St. Philip's was similar to that of many other important Negro churches. Founded by a small group of Negroes in the Five Points districts in 1809, it held its first formal services in 1819 in a wooden building, 60 feet by 50 feet, on what is now Centre Street. In 1856 St. Philip's moved to a former Methodist church on Mulberry Street and, in 1889, following the Negro population to the Tenderloin, it came to West Twenty-fifth Street. St. Philip's remained in the Tenderloin until 1910, when it moved to a newly constructed church in Harlem. . . .

The new St. Philip's, designed by Negro architects, as Madame Walker's mansion had been, was completed in Harlem in 1911. The church was always moderately wealthy, but it never before controlled the vast sums accumulated through the sale of its property in the Tenderloin. Taking advantage of the depressed condition of the real estate market, the decision was made to invest the church's capital in Harlem apartment houses. In 1911 St. Philip's bought a row of ten new apartment houses on West One Hundred and Thirty-fifth Street between Seventh and Lenox Avenues for $640,000—the largest single real estate transaction, involving Negroes, in the city's history at that time. Before the sale, signs which hung in renting offices of the white realtors who managed these buildings read:

The agents promise their tenants that
these houses will be rented only to
white people.

Shortly after the transfer of this property to St. Philip's and after its remaining white tenants were evicted, a new sign was displayed, telling prospective Negro tenants to contact colored real estate agents:

For Rent, Apply to Nail and Parker

The success that Nail and Parker achieved was typical of many other Negro realtors. As each year passed it became more evident that Harlem was to become a Negro section permanently: "The colored [people] are in Harlem to stay, and they are coming each year by the thousands." White landlords and corporations hired Negro managers to deal with their new Negro tenants. By 1914, 37 per cent of the Negro tenements in Harlem were managed by "colored agents," although less than five per cent of these houses were owned by Negro landlords. In 1920 there were twenty-one Negro real estate firms with offices in Harlem, specializing in uptown property, and real estate dealers composed the largest single Negro professional group at the time of the 1930 census.

Compared with holdings of white landlords, insurance companies and business firms, Negro ownership of Harlem property was, and always remained, limited. After 1914, however, when houses were made available to Negroes in larger numbers, a significant increase in the amount of Negro capital invested in the area took place. Negro businessmen from the South and other sections of the country, smelling success and opportunity in Harlem, sent agents there. Local realtors, like the dogged Philip A. Payton, Jr., closed deals involving more than a million dollars. A month before his death, in August 1917, Payton and his associates, many of them Negro businessmen from the South, bought six elevator apartment houses, "the last word in high-class apartment house construction," and immediately opened them to Negroes:

The World's Finest Housing Proposition
Catering Exclusively to
Refined Colored Tenants

Each house bore the name of a distinguished Negro, and at the center of every hall was a picture of the dignitary: Toussaint, Wheatley, Attucks, Dunbar, Washington, Douglass. . . .

Practically every major Negro institution moved from its downtown quarters to Harlem by the early 1920's: the United Order of True Reformers; Odd Fellows, Masons, Elks, Pythians and other fraternal orders; the Music School Settlement; the Coachmen's Union League; the African Society of Mutual Relief; *The New York Age;* West Fifty-third Street YMCA and YWCA; almost all the Negro social service agencies, including local offices of the Urban League and NAACP; the AME Home and Foreign Missionary Society; all the major churches. The virtual monopoly *The New York Age* had for generations as the city's only leading Negro journal was broken, and two other weeklies were established: the *New York News* and the *Amsterdam News* ("boasting local sheets," the *Age* called them). The *Age* continued to be a staid newspaper in the tradition of nine-

teenth-century journalism, although it too began to change in the
1920s. Its competitors were tabloids whose blaring and sensational
headlines appealed to mass audiences and mirrored the highly successful white dailies. P.S. 89, on Lenox Avenue, three-quarters Negro by 1915, opened a night school, reading room and a community center for Negro youth. Within a short time it became one
of the most run-down public schools in the city. P.S. 68, the former
"Silk Stocking" school, was now noted for its regular skirmishes
between white and Negro pupils. The *Harlem Home News* moved to
the Bronx in 1913. A historic landmark of an earlier Harlem, Watt
Mansion, was first transformed into a cafeteria, "the Lybia," and
finally torn down. The famous Pabst Restaurant became a Kress
five-and-ten-cent store in 1920, and Horton's Ice Cream Parlor, a
well-known meeting place owned by the "Grand Old Man" of white
Harlem, was transformed into a shoestore. The most famous institution of white Harlem, Collegiate Reformed Church (Second Dutch
Reformed Church), held out against the inevitable longer than most
—in 1930, however, it became the Negro Ephesus Seventh Day
Adventist Church, and has remained that to the present. . . .

The larger the Negro population became, the more often businessmen spoke of their community as "Greater Harlem"—an undefined
term which apparently included surrounding white areas. In the
1920s, when Americans came to know Harlem as the "Negro Capital
of the World," *Harlem Magazine* argued the impression was "erroneous." Negroes occupied only "a small fraction of *Greater Harlem*," it maintained. By 1932 the Harlem Board of Commerce gave
up its mirage. It changed its name, and the name of its journal.
"While the decision of the Board to adopt a new name . . . is certain
to cause deep regret," the final issue of *Harlem Magazine* editorialized, "it must be apparent to all . . . that such a step was inevitable. [Harlem has] a new and entirely different meaning to the
present generation." "How our old Dutch burghers would writhe,"
an old resident commented, "if they could be reincarnated for just
long enough to grasp the modern idea of what once was their cherished 'Nieuw Haarlem!' "

In 1914 Negroes lived in some 1,100 different houses within a
twenty-three-block area of Harlem. After a house-to-house survey in
that year, the Urban League estimated Harlem's population at

49,555—the entire Negro population of Manhattan in 1910 was 60,534. *Prior to World War I,* the neighborhood was already the "largest colony of colored people, in similar limits, in the world"— and it continued to expand. By 1920 the section of Harlem bordered approximately by One Hundred and Thirtieth Street on the south, One Hundred and Forty-fifth Street on the north and west of Fifth to Eighth Avenue was predominantly Negro—and inhabited by some 73,000 people. Two-thirds of Manhattan's Negro population lived there in 1920. "If my race can make Harlem," one man said "good lord, what can't it do?" Harlem had become "the Mecca of the colored people of New York City."

II THE GHETTO AS PROMISED LAND

The Chicago Commission on Race Relations
THE MIGRATION OF NEGROES
FROM THE SOUTH

The Great Migration began during World War I and continued virtually uninterrupted until the Depression. The excerpt included here details the reasons for the Great Migration, not only to Chicago but also to the industrial North. It discusses the "push" from the South and the "pull" of the North. A major "pull" was the portrayal by the black press, especially the Chicago Defender, *of the northern city as the "promised land." This selection is taken from* The Negro in Chicago: A Study of Race Relations and a Race Riot in 1919, *the exhaustive report by the Chicago Commission on Race Relations. This commission, appointed by Governor Frank O. Lowden in the wake of the Chicago riot of 1919, made a thorough study of the causes and conditions underlying the riot. As a part of their report the commission interviewed hundreds of blacks seeking to determine the reasons for the Great Migration. The commission's findings are as follows.*

During the period 1916–18 approximately a half-million Negroes suddenly moved from southern to northern states. This movement, however, was not without a precedent. A similar migration occurred in 1879, when Negroes moved from Mississippi, Louisiana, Texas, Alabama, Tennessee, and North Carolina to Kansas. The origin of this earlier movement, its causes, and manner resemble in many respects the one which has so recently attracted public attention.

The migration of 1916–18 cannot be separated completely from the steady, though inconspicuous, exodus from southern to northern states that has been in progress since 1860, or, in fact, since the operation of the "underground railway." In 1900 there were 911,025 Negroes living in the North, 10.3 per cent of the total Negro population, which was then 8,883,994. Census figures for the period 1900–1910 show a net loss for southern states east of the Mississippi of 595,703 Negroes. Of this number 366,880 are found in northern states. Reliable estimates for the last decade place the increase of northern Negro population around 500,000.

The 1910–20 increase of the Negro population of Chicago was from 44,103 to 109,594, or 148.5 per cent, with a corresponding increase in the white population of 21 per cent, including foreign immigration. According to the Census Bureau method of estimating natural increase of population, the Negro population of Chicago unaffected by the migration would be 58,056 in 1920, and the increase by migration alone would be 51,538.

The relative 1910–20 increases in white and Negro population in typical industrial cities of the Middle West, given in [the table], illustrate the effect of the migration of southern Negroes.

	Negroes		Percentage of Negro Increase, 1910–1920	Percentage of White Increase, 1910–1920
	1910	1920		
Cincinnati, Ohio	19,639	29,636	50.9	8.0
Dayton, Ohio	4,842	9,029	86.5	28.0
Toledo, Ohio	1,877	5,690	203.1	42.5
Fort Wayne, Ind.	572	1,476	158.0	34.3
Canton, Ohio	291	1,349	363.6	71.7
Gary, Ind.	383	5,299	1,283.6	205.1
Detroit, Mich.	5,741	41,532	623.4	106.9
Chicago, Ill.	44,103	109,594	148.5	21.0

A series of circumstances acting together in an unusual combination both provoked and made possible the migration of Negroes from the South on a large scale. The causes of the movement fall into definite divisions, even as stated by the migrants themselves. For example, one of the most frequent causes mentioned by southern Negroes for their change of home is the treatment accorded them in the South. Yet this treatment of which they complain has been practiced since their emancipation, and fifty years afterward more than nine-tenths of the Negro population of the United States still remained in the South. "Higher wages" was also commonly stated as a cause of the movement, yet thousands came to the North and to Chicago who in the South had been earning more in their professions and even in skilled occupations than they expected to receive in the North. These causes then divide into two main classes:

(1) economic causes, (2) sentimental causes. Each has a bearing on both North and South.

1. ECONOMIC CAUSES OF THE MIGRATION

A. The South

Low wages.   Wages of Negroes in the South varied from 75 cents a day on the farms to $1.75 a day in certain city jobs, in the period just preceding 1914. The rise in living costs which followed the outbreak of the war outstripped the rise in wages. In Alabama the price paid for day labor in the twenty-one "black belt" counties averaged 50 and 60 cents a day. It ranged from 40 cents, as a minimum, to 75 cents, and, in a few instances, $1.00 was a maximum for able-bodied male farm hands.

The boll weevil.   In 1915 and 1916 the boll weevil cotton pest so ravaged sections of the South that thousands of farmers were almost ruined. Cotton crops were lost, and the farmers were forced to change from cotton to food products. The growing of cotton requires about thirty times as many "hands" as food products. As a result many Negroes were thrown out of employment. The damage wrought by the boll weevil was augmented by destructive storms and floods, which not only affected crops but made the living conditions of Negroes more miserable.

Lack of capital.   The "credit system" is a very convenient and common practice in many parts of the South. Money is borrowed for upkeep until the selling season, when it is repaid in one lump sum. The succession of short crops and the destruction due to the boll weevil and storms occasioned heavy demands for capital to carry labor through the fall and early winter until a new crop could be started. There was a shortage of capital, and as a result there was little opportunity for work. During this period many white persons migrated from sections of the South most seriously affected.

"Unsatisfactory" living conditions.   The plantation cabins and segregated sections in cities where municipal laxity made home surroundings undesirable have been stated as another contributing cause of the movement.

Lack of school facilities. The desire to place their children in good schools was a reason often given by migrants with families for leaving the South. School facilities are described as lamentably poor even by southern whites.

B. The North

The cessation of immigration. Prior to the war the yearly immigration to the United States equaled approximately the total Negro population of the North. Foreign labor filled the unskilled labor field, and Negroes were held closely in domestic and personal-service work. The cessation of immigration and the return of thousands of aliens to their mother-country, together with the opening of new industries and the extension of old ones, created a much greater demand for American labor. Employers looked to the South for Negroes and advertised for them.

High wages. Wages for unskilled work in the North in 1916 and 1917 ranged from $3.00 to $8.00 a day. There were shorter hours of work and opportunity for overtime and bonuses.

Living conditions. Houses available for Negroes in the North, though by northern standards classed as unsanitary and unfit for habitation, afforded greater comforts than the rude cabins of the plantation. For those who had owned homes in the South there was the opportunity of selling them and applying the money to payment for a good home in the North.

Identical school privileges. Co-education of whites and Negroes in northern schools made possible a higher grade of instruction for the children of migrants.

2. SENTIMENTAL CAUSES OF THE MIGRATION

The causes classed as sentimental include those which have reference to the feelings of Negroes concerning their surroundings in the South and their reactions to the social systems and practices of certain sections of the South. Frequently these causes were given as the source of an old discontent among Negroes concerning the South. Frequently they took prominence over economic causes, and they were held for the most part by a fairly high class of Negroes. These causes are in part as follows:

Lack of protection from mob violence. Between 1885 and 1918, 2,881 Negroes were lynched in the United States, more than 85 per cent of these lynchings occurring in the South. In 1917, 2,500 Negroes were driven by force out of Dawson and Forsythe counties, Georgia.

The Chicago Urban League reported that numbers of migrants from towns where lynchings had occurred registered for jobs in Chicago very shortly after lynchings. . . .

Injustice in the courts. An excerpt from one of the newspapers of that period illustrates the basis of this cause:

> *While our very solvency is being sucked out from underneath we go out about affairs as usual—our police officers raid poolrooms for "loafing Negroes," bring in twelve, keep them in the barracks all night, and next morning find that many of them have steady, regular jobs, valuable assets to their white employers, suddenly left and gone to Cleveland, "where they don't arrest fifty niggers for what three of 'em done"* [Montgomery *(Alabama)* Advertiser *(white), September 21, 1916*].

Inferior transportation facilities. This refers to "Jim Crow cars," a partitioned section of one railway car, usually the baggage car, and partitioned sections of railway waiting-rooms, poorly kept, bearing signs, "For colored only." . . .

Other causes stated are (*a*) the deprivation of the right to vote, (*b*) the "rough-handed" and unfair competition of "poor whites," (*c*) persecution by petty officers of the law, and (*d*) the "persecution of the Press." . . .

The enormous proportions to which the exodus grew obscure its beginning. Several experiments had been tried with southern labor in the Northeast, particularly in the Connecticut tobacco fields and in Pennsylvania. In Connecticut, Negro students from the southern schools had been employed during summers with great success. Early in 1916, industries in Pennsylvania imported many Negroes from Georgia and Florida. During July one railroad company stated that it had brought to Pennsylvania more than 13,000 Negroes. They wrote back for their friends and families, and from the points to which they had been brought they spread out into new and "labor slack" territories. Once begun, this means of recruiting labor was used by hard-pressed industries in other sections of the North. The reports of high wages, of the unexpected welcome of the North, and of unusually good treatment accorded Negroes spread throughout the South from Georgia and Florida to Texas.

The stimuli of suggestion and hysteria gave the migration an almost religious significance, and it became a mass movement. Letters, rumors, Negro newspapers, gossip, and other forms of social control operated to add volume and enthusiasm to the exodus. Songs and poems of the period characterized the migration as the "Flight Out of Egypt," "Bound for the Promised Land," "Going into Canaan," "The Escape from Slavery," etc.

The first movement was from Southeast to Northeast, following main lines of transportation. Soon, however, it became known that the Middle West was similarly in need of men. Many industries advertised for southern Negroes in Negro papers. The federal Department of Labor for a period was instrumental in transporting Negroes from the South to relieve the labor shortage in other sections of the country, but discontinued such efforts when southern congressmen pointed out that the South's labor supply was being depleted. It was brought out in the East St. Louis riot inquiry that plants there had advertised in Texas newspapers for Negro laborers.

Chicago was the logical destination of Negroes from Mississippi, Arkansas, Alabama, Louisiana, and Texas, because of the more direct railway lines, the way in which the city had become known in these sections through its two great mail-order houses, the Stock Yards, and the packing-plants with their numerous storage houses scattered in various towns and cities of the South. It was rumored in these sections that the Stock Yards needed 50,000 men; it was said that temporary housing was being provided by these hard-pressed industries. Many Negroes came to the city on free transportation, but by far the greater numbers paid their own fare. Club rates offered by the railroads brought the fare within reach of many who ordinarily could not have brought their families or even come themselves. The organization into clubs composed of from ten to fifty persons from the same community had the effect, on the one hand, of adding the stimulus of intimate persuasion to the movement, and, on the other hand, of concentrating solid groups in congested spots in Chicago.

A study of certain Negro periodicals shows a powerful influence on southern Negroes already in a state of unsettlement over news of the "opening up of the North."

The *Chicago Defender* became a "herald of glad tidings" to southern Negroes. . . .

Articles and headlines carrying this special appeal which appeared in the *Defender* are quoted:

FROZEN DEATH BETTER

To die from the bite of frost is far more glorious than that of the mob. I beg of you, my brothers, to leave that benighted land. You are free men. Show the world that you will not let false leaders lead you. Your neck has been in the yoke. Will you continue to keep it there because some "white folks Nigger" wants you to? Leave to all quarters of the globe. Get out of the South. Your being there in the numbers you are gives the southern politician too strong a hold on your progress.

LEAVING FOR THE NORTH

Tampa, Fla., Jan. 19.—J. T. King, supposed to be a race leader, is using his wits to get on the good side of the white people by calling a meeting to urge our people not to migrate North. King has been termed a "good nigger" by his pernicious activity on the emigration question. Reports have been received here that all who have gone North are at work and pleased with the splendid conditions in the North. It is known here that in the North there is a scarcity of labor, mills and factories are open to them. People are not paying any attention to King and are packing and ready to travel North to the "promised land."

Denunciation of the South. The idea that the South is a bad place, unfit for the habitation of Negroes, was "played up" and emphasized by the *Defender*. Conditions most distasteful to Negroes were given first prominence. In this it had a clear field, for the local southern Negro papers dared not make such unrestrained utterances. . . .

It is probably no exaggeration to say that the *Defender's* policy prompted thousands of restless Negroes to venture North, where they were assured of its protection and championship of their cause. Many migrants in Chicago attribute their presence in the North to the *Defender's* encouraging pictures of relief from conditions at home with which they became increasingly dissatisfied as they read.

St. Clair Drake and Horace R. Cayton
THE FAT YEARS

Black Metropolis: A Study of Negro Life in a Northern City appeared in 1945. It represents the labors of a WPA project in Chicago and the scholarship of two leading black intellectuals. The study of black Chicago began as an investigation of general conditions of life on Chicago's South Side. But it ended as a detailed "description and analysis of the structure and organization of the Negro community, both internally, and in relation to the metropolis of which it is a part." Although the study is just of Chicago, the conclusions reached by the authors are applicable to the Black North. This excerpt deals with the period of the 1920s. To the black middle class in Chicago these were indeed the "Fat Years."

The Black Belt became the Black Metropolis in the twenty years between the close of the First World War and the beginning of the Second. The fifty or sixty thousand Negroes who came to the city during the Great Migration had no intention of returning to the South. Despite bombs and riots they insisted upon a place to live within the city, and upon room for friends and relatives who followed them North and for the children who would be born in Midwest Metropolis. By 1925, the city had adjusted itself to the obvious fact that a rapidly growing Negro community was there to stay. Negroes had secured a foothold.

Although Negroes had to fight block-by-block for houses during the war years, they did not have any trouble getting jobs. With the close of the war they found themselves in a precarious position. Returning soldiers wanted their old jobs or better ones. As industries retrenched, Negroes were either fired outright or asked to work at very low wages. White workers became apprehensive over a large pool of unorganized Negroes that could be used to keep wages low. Three years after the war a minor depression wiped out most of the gains which Negro women had made in light manufacturing and in the garment industry. The same year Negroes were used to break a stockyards strike and although they became permanently established in that industry they earned the bitter antagonism of Irish,

Polish and Italian workers. In 1924, another recession resulted in widespread unemployment among Negroes. By 1925, however, a boom was under way and racial conflict in industry as well as unemployment subsided. Gangsters replaced Negroes in the civic consciousness as Social Problem No. 1.

*　　　*　　　*

"Behold now the days of super-speed, of super-brilliance, of super-power," wrote Henry Justin Smith, referring to the Twenties in Chicago; "American energy not only had survived the war, but apparently had been redoubled by it. . . . Chicago caught the pace —the amazing, dazzling, even perilous pace of the third decade." This is the Chicago of popular imagination—the Chicago of Al Capone and Jim Colosimo; of Mayor Thompson and Samuel Insull; the Chicago of the great building boom, when the sound of riveting hammers alternated with the fire of sub-machine guns; of skyscrapers and factories thrusting themselves up through a subsoil of slums and speakeasies. People made money in the Twenties and they spent it freely—sometimes with calculation, often with recklessness.

The new white-collar middle class and thousands of frugal skilled and semi-skilled workers rushed to buy or build homes in the suburbs, seeking fresh air and avoiding high taxes. They left the heart of the city to the poor, the newer immigrants, the underworld, the corrupt political machine, and the Negroes. Thousands of other middle-class people stayed within the city limits to stew in bitterness over the foreign-born workers and Negroes who rented and bought the homes of their neighbors who had moved to the outskirts. Among those who stayed within the corporate limits "there arose a diverse community feeling, rather than a civic unity, all up and down the long stretch of city. . . . New centers everywhere— new groups of stores, theaters, churches, garages, and all that the ordinary man needs, with houses clustering about, neighborhood interests developing, improvement-associations, parent-teacher clubs, art and literary societies. More than a hundred Chicagos, there were, within the one Chicago."

And among the "hundred" was Black Metropolis.

The five years from 1924 to 1929 were no doubt the most prosperous ones the Negro community in Chicago had ever experienced. A professional and business class arose upon the broad base of over seventy-five thousand colored wage-earners, and was able for a brief period to enjoy the fruits of its training and investment. Throughout the Twenties, additional migrants from the rural South swelled the size of the Black Belt market. The Fat Years were at hand.

The Negroes spread along the once fashionable South Parkway and Michigan Boulevard, closing up the pocket which existed in 1920 . . . , taking over the stone-front houses and the apartments, buying the large church edifices and opening smaller churches in houses and stores, establishing businesses, and building a political machine as they went. By 1925 the Black Belt business center had shifted two miles southward, and those who could afford to do so were trying to move from the slums into more stable residential areas. The masses flowed along persistently as the Black Belt lengthened.

Occasionally a white community resisted this expansion violently. In 1921, for instance, the Chicago *Whip,* a militant Negro newspaper, assailed Mayor Thompson for refusing to see a delegation of Negroes who wanted to protest against several bombings. "[He] has only yelped something about five-cent fares," the paper charged almost hysterically, "while our property was blown into smithereens, while our sleeping babes have been torpedoed from their mothers' arms. . . . The City Council laughs at the 'floor leader's' [a Negro] jokes while the poor black people who put him into office toss in troubled slumber with nightmares of bursting bombs."

In one block on Michigan Avenue, a synagogue bought by a Negro Baptist congregation was repeatedly bombed in 1925. (The colored congregation ultimately took out an insurance policy against bombing.) But bombings became rarer and rarer, and finally ceased. To deny living space to Negroes, law-abiding Chicagoans developed something more subtle than a "pineapple" tossed by a "gorilla" hired by a respectable "neighborhood improvement association." In the spring of 1928, the Hyde Park *Herald,* a neighborhood newspaper, reported a speech proclaiming the efficacy of a new device for locking Negroes within the Black Belt [italics are Drake's and Cayton's]:

> . . . *Judge* —— *of the Chicago Real Estate Board, before the Ki-wanis Club of Hyde Park at the Windemere East, in summarizing the earnest and conscientious work of the Board for the last twelve months . . . proceeded to explain the fine network of contracts that like a marvelous delicately woven chain of armor is being raised from the northern gates of Hyde Park at 35th Street and Drexel Boulevard to Woodlawn, Park Manor, South Shore, Windsor Park, and all the far-flung white communities of the South Side. And of what does this armor consist?* It consists of a contract which the owner of the property signs not to exchange with, sell to, or lease to any member of a race not Caucasian.

The tensions of the Riot period gradually subsided, but the migration left a residue of antagonism toward Negroes. There were definite restrictions on the activities of Negroes—restrictions due to deeply laid habit patterns which white Chicagoans shared with other Americans. Most Negroes took the matter philosophically, if not fatalistically—unless they were pushed too hard. Then they were likely to direct a storm of invective or blows at any denial of their rights. Usually they avoided trouble spots and enjoyed the city in situations where they didn't have to bother with white folks.

There were stores and restaurants that didn't like to serve Negroes. To walk into certain downtown hot-spots was unthinkable. To run for any state office higher than Senator from the Black Belt just wasn't done. To hope for a managerial or highly skilled job in industry was ridiculous. To buy or rent a house out of the Black Belt precipitated a storm. But after all, Chicago was in America, not in France or Brazil. It was certainly different from slavery sixty years ago, or from the South today. Negroes liked Midwest Metropolis.

There were evidences on every hand that "the Race was progressing." Here were colored policemen, firemen, aldermen, and precinct captains, state Representatives, doctors, lawyers, and teachers. Colored children were attending the public schools and the city's junior colleges. There were fine churches in the Negro areas, and beautiful boulevards. It seemed reasonable to assume that this development would continue with more and more Negroes getting ahead and becoming educated. There were prophets of doom in the Twenties, but a general air of optimism pervaded the Black Belt, as it did the whole city.

On eight square miles of land a Black Metropolis was growing

in the womb of the white. Negro politicians and business and professional men, barred by color from competing for the highest prizes
in Midwest Metropolis, saw their destiny linked with the growth of
Black Metropolis. Negroes were making money in the steel mills,
stockyards, and garment factories, in the hotels and kitchens, on
the railroads, and in a hundred other spots. "Why," the leaders
asked, "should these dollars be spent with white men or wasted in
riotous living? If white men are so determined that Negroes must
live separate and apart, why not beat them at their own game?"

What did it matter if white men snubbed black men socially? Negroes were building an attractive home life and "society" of their
own. They did not need white intimates.

What did Negro ministers care if white Christians sealed themselves off in Jim Crow congregations? They would take the church
or the synagogue that white worshipers abandoned as they fled from
contact with their black brothers, and turn it into a worthy house of
the Lord (when they had finished paying off the mortgage).

Why should Negro doctors and dentists give a damn that most
white folks would rather die than let skilled black fingers repair
their vital organs? The Negro masses were gradually learning to
trust their own professional men and would some day scorn to en-
rich white physicians at the expense of their own.

Why beg white stores and offices to rescue educated colored
girls from service in the white folks' kitchens and factories? Negroes
were learning to support their own businesses, and some day
colored entrepreneurs would own all the stores and offices in the
Black Belt; cash registers and comptometers and typewriters would
click merrily under lithe brown fingers.

If Negroes wanted to pay two cents a day for white papers that
stigmatized the group as a menace, picturing them as rapists and
buffoons, let them do so—but more and more of them were spending
an additional dime each week for a colored paper, where they could
read about themselves and their own accomplishments and applaud
the verbal body-blows that colored journalists slammed at American
race prejudice.

Negroes who, a few years before, had been disfranchised, were
voting for Negroes to represent them in the councils of city, state
and nation. In 1928, Black Metropolis won the acclaim of Negroes

throughout America when it succeeded in electing a colored Congressman—the first Negro to occupy a seat in the House of Representatives since 1901. If Negroes used their political power wisely they could bargain for unlimited concessions from the two parties bidding for their votes.

This was the dream of Black Metropolis, not yet fully realized, but on the way—a hope kept alive by press and pulpit.

To some the dream was inspiring. To many it was a makeshift dream, a substitute for the real American Dream of complete integration into American life. To some who watched Negroes inherit the city's slums, crowded together amid squalor and vice, where schemers, white and black, battened on their blood, the dream seemed a fraud and a delusion. "How can we build a metropolis," they asked, "when we not not control the industries that employ the Negro masses? How can we build the good society when we can't get enough decent houses to live in?"

To others, the development of a greater Black Metropolis was a tactical maneuver within the framework of a broad strategy for complete equality. The very preacher, editors, and politicians who did the most to keep the dream of Black Metropolis alive only half believed in its ultimate realization. They knew that unless the ordinary Negro could have a steady income and could share more fully in the wave of prosperity, their own careers would always be insecure. "But," they reasoned, "if Negroes could support their own business and professional class, if they would rally about their politicians, some day their leaders might teach them how to throw their weight in such a way as to win the respect of the white world." Negroes had votes and they were accumulating money. If they used both skillfully, they could force the city to grant them more room in which to live, better jobs and, some day, perhaps, *full* equality. In the meantime, successful individuals would become living examples of what all Negroes could do if they got a chance. Gradually the city would begin to accept Negroes in high places as people, and not as Negroes. The Jews had done it—why couldn't Negroes?

Symbolic of this era of optimism was a colored banker, Jesse Binga, who in 1893 had come to Chicago penniless. Within thirty-five years he had risen from Pullman porter to real-estate speculator and then to banker. A feature writer for a Chicago daily sought him out in 1928 to get his story of Black Metropolis. Binga talked of the forty million dollars which Negroes had to their credit in Chicago's banks; of the four billion dollars' worth of property on which they paid taxes; of the two million dollars they had contributed to charity that year.

He also spoke with pride of "a new generation of business and professional men, coming to the fore"; of the seven big insurance companies "managed by colored people for colored policy holders —$1,000,000 in premiums a year." He dwelt at length upon the hope which Negro businessmen had of eventually controlling the Negro market and providing jobs for young men and women as clerks, salesmen, cashiers, and managers. He cited as examples the two colored banks, one of them his own. Five years before, these banks had been entrusted with less than a hundred and fifty thousand dollars; now, between them they handled four of the forty million dollars that Chicago Negroes had on deposit.

The Black Belt was experiencing the Fat Years. When Jesse Binga saw an unending vista of progress and profit in the Negroes' future, if only they would support their business and professional men, he was voicing the confident hope of thousands.

Robert Bone

THE BACKGROUND OF THE NEGRO RENAISSANCE

One of the reasons for the optimism of the black middle class in the 1920s was the Harlem Renaissance. Harlem became the cultural capital of black America and the Harlem cabarets became America's answer to Paris. The prose and poetry of black authors were in demand. Young blacks broke with tradition by insisting on interpreting black culture rather than pleading the cause of racial justice. Their novels dealt with black life rather than the race relations. Robert Bone discusses the background of the Harlem Renaissance in this selection taken from The Negro Novel in America.

The Great Migration

Alain Locke has described the Negro Renaissance as "the mass movement of the urban immigration of Negroes, projected on the plane of an increasingly articulate elite." The Great Migration to which Locke refers was the most important event in the history of the American Negro since his emancipation from slavery. In the course of this migration, centuries of historical development were traversed in a few decades. It was not merely a movement of the colored population from South to North, or from country to city; it was the sudden transplanting of a debased feudal folk from medieval to modern America.

From 1890 to 1920, while the business and professional class was fighting for the right to rise, the base of the Negro social pyramid was shifting from a peasantry to an urban proletariat. In these decades more than 2,000,000 Negroes left the farm for the factory. As growing numbers of Negro sharecroppers were pushed off the land by erosion and drought, by an exhausted soil, and by the mechanical cotton-picker, they were drawn to the cities by the demands of American industry for cheap labor. Competition from the European immigrant was conveniently eliminated by World War I and by the immigration laws of 1924. At the same time, the war encouraged a vast expansion of American industry, creating a labor

Reprinted from *The Negro Novel in America* by Robert Bone, by permission of Yale University Press, Inc. Copyright 1958, 1965 by Yale University. This selection is taken from pages 53–55, 57–64.

market for thousands of black workers. Under these circumstances, the urbanization of the American Negro took place at an unprecedented rate.

The Great Migration brought the Negro masses into contact with the quickened pulse of the modern city. There they were faced with a mass of strange experiences which forced them to revise their traditional ways of thinking. The crowded ghetto, unlike the isolated farm, provided a basis for a vigorous group life. A rising standard of living and better educational opportunities fostered new attitudes of self-respect and independence. In a word, the Negro's urban environment lifted him to a new plane of consciousness. Such a profound transformation could hardly occur among the masses without reverberations in the world of letters. The new group experience called for a new literary movement to interpret it.

It was a foregone conclusion that Harlem should become the center of the new movement. The largest Negro community in the world, Harlem was itself a product of the Great Migration. Doubling its population from 1900 to 1920, it was wrested from the whites by sheer weight of numbers. As it grew to metropolitan proportions, it gradually acquired the character of a race capital. Negroes from Africa and the West Indies, from North and South, and from all classes and backgrounds poured into the crucible of dark Manhattan. Harlem thus provided the Negro artist with an infinite variety of human subjects, as well as an opportunity to observe urban life at its maximum intensity.

Moreover, this black metropolis evolved within the womb of a city which was the literary, musical, and theatrical capital of America. Harlem meant proximity to Broadway, to the little magazines and the big publishing houses, to Greenwich Village and its white intellectuals, to avant-garde literary groups and successful, established writers. It offered a unique, cosmopolitan milieu, where artists and intellectuals of all kinds could find mutual stimulation. Under the circumstances, it is hardly surprising that Harlem became the cultural center of Negro America. . . .

The New Negro Movement

The term "New Negro" presents certain difficulties, for it has been used to describe both a racial attitude and a literary movement.

The extension of the term from its original meaning was the work of Alain Locke, who in 1925 published an anthology of younger writers entitled *The New Negro*. The title struck a responsive chord, and it soon became the accepted designation of the new literary movement. From the standpoint of literary history this was unfortunate. "New Negro" is not a descriptive term in any literary sense; basically it indicates a rejection of racial conservatism on the part of those who employ it. It is nonetheless of considerable subjective importance that Renaissance writers should think of themselves as "New Negroes." To establish the primary meaning of the term may therefore cast additional light on the period.

The New Negro, with his uncompromising demand for equal rights, was the end product of a long historical process which began when the Negro middle class emerged from slavery and entered upon a new kind of social relations. As the patriarchal relations of slavery were replaced by the contractual relations of bourgeois society, a corresponding psychological transformation took place. Feudal attitudes of servility and dependence were abandoned in favor of the sturdy bourgeois virtues of initiative and self-reliance. This psychological transformation crystallized politically when DuBois challenged the "accommodating" leadership of Booker T. Washington in the name of universal manhood suffrage. Manhood suffrage, the basic aim of DuBois' Niagara Movement, became a symbol of the new spirit which animated the Negro middle class. This sense of manhood, greatly enhanced by the Negro's participation in World War I, was passed on to the Renaissance generation as part of its spiritual heritage.

There is a direct line from the Niagara Movement of the early 1900s to the New Negro Movement of the 1920s. The descent may be traced through Negro defense organizations such as the NAACP and the National Urban League, and more precisely through their house organs, *Crisis* and *Opportunity.* These two periodicals and their editors, Jessie Fauset and Charles S. Johnson, did yeoman's work for the Negro Renaissance. They encouraged new talent, opened their pages to young writers, and offered cash prizes for outstanding literary achievement. In this manner, as well as through overt patronage, the Negro middle class made a substantial contribution to the birth of the New Negro Movement. Whether they were prepared to acknowledge the lusty and sometimes ungrateful infant which they sired is another matter.

As the Negro Renaissance gained momentum and its break with the tradition of Chesnutt and Dunbar became apparent, the term "New Negro" began to take on an additional connotation of modernism. As a result, it became intellectually fashionable to declare oneself a member of the New Negro coterie. Yet if the New Negro slogan created something of a vogue, it also provided the literary movement of the 1920s with a unifying idea. "New Negro" literary societies sprang up in several large cities; New Negro magazines were founded by avant-garde writers; and one novelist playfully christened his first-born "the New Negro"! This self-consciousness, this sense of belonging to a movement, made for a high group morale, and for an atmosphere which encouraged literary effort. Moreover, in its own way the New Negro Movement expressed that determination to ring out the old and ring in the new which was the central theme of the decade.

Cultural Collaboration in the Jazz Age

The years following World War I were marked by a sudden upsurge of interest in Negro life and culture among the white intelligentsia. Manifestations of this interest were numerous and varied. Throughout the 1920s books on the Negro by white authors appeared in ever-increasing numbers. *Survey Graphic* came out with an issue devoted entirely to Harlem, while Albert and Charles Boni offered a prize of $1,000 for the best novel written by an American Negro. Musical reviews which featured Negro performers broke downtown box-office records, and nightly throngs of white "tourists" invaded Harlem, drawn to night club and cabaret by colored celebrities of musical and theatrical fame. By the mid-1920s the Negro had become a national pastime.

What had happened to change the intellectual climate from hostility and indifference to sympathetic, if often misguided, interest? For one thing the Jazz Age, which derived its very character from the Negro's music, was in full swing. With "flaming youth" leading the way, a popular uprising was in progress against the stuffiness and artificial restraint of the Victorian era. These were the years of postwar catharsis—of Freud and the sexual revolution, of heavy drinking in defiance of authority, of a wild dance called the Charleston, and of a wilder music which made its way from the bordellos of New Orleans to the night clubs of Chicago and New York. Somewhat to his surprise and not entirely to his liking, the Negro suddenly found himself called upon to uphold a new stereotype: he became a symbol of that freedom from restraint for which the white intellectual longed so ardently.

In the sophisticated art centers of Europe and America, interest in the Negro focused around the cult of the primitive. Insofar as it idealizes simpler cultures, primitivism is a romantic retreat from the complexities of modern life. Reflecting the writings of Sigmund Freud, it exalts instinct over intellect, Id over Super-Ego, and is thus a revolt against the Puritan spirit. For such an artistic movement the Negro had obvious uses: he represented the unspoiled child of nature, the noble savage—carefree, spontaneous, and sexually uninhibited. The discovery of primitive African sculpture and the ascendancy of jazz reinforced the development of this new stereotype.

Like all previous stereotypes, that of the primitive Negro exercised a coercive effect on the Negro novelist. As in the past, the degree of accommodation was astonishing; with few exceptions the Negro intelligentsia accepted this exotic image of themselves. Perhaps they found in primitivism a useful support for the cultural dualism which they espoused during the Renaissance period. In any event, the younger Negro writers were quite carried away. Langston Hughes wrote ecstatically of jazz as "the tom-tom of revolt," while Countee Cullen discovered "elemental" religion in a Harlem revival meeting. Claude McKay glorified the instinctive Negro in all of his novels, and proudly proclaimed the "primitive sexuality" of the Negro race. Jean Toomer, perhaps the most authentic exponent of Renaissance primitivism, wrote in a sophisticated vein of "the zoo-restrictions and keeper-taboos" of modern civilization.

Whatever its excesses, primitivism provided the common ground for a fruitful period of cultural collaboration. Works like Eugene O'Neill's *The Emperor Jones* (1920) and *All God's Chillun Got Wings* (1924), Waldo Frank's *Holiday* (1923), Sherwood Anderson's *Dark Laughter* (1925), DuBose Heyward's *Porgy* (1925) and *Mamba's*

Daughters (1929), and Carl Van Vechten's *Nigger Heaven* (1926), acted as a spur to Negro writers and created a sympathetic audience for the serious treatment of Negro subjects. Personal association with white authors meant an end of cultural isolation and provincialism, and an immense gain in technical maturity for the Negro writer. In economic terms alone, considerable patronage and sponsorship occurred, while publishing forts and editorial desks capitulated in the face of a growing market for novels of Negro life. In the forefront of these developments, consciously promoting this cultural exchange, was a white *littérateur* named Carl Van Vechten.

Van Vechten's role in furthering the Negro Renaissance was unique. His literary salons provided a warm atmosphere in which artists and intellectuals of both races could break down their taboos against personal association. His one-man "know the Negro" campaign was eminently successful in overcoming prejudice and awkwardness among his white contemporaries. His efforts on behalf of individual Negro writers and artists were indefatigable, and were amply rewarded in later years when many of his former protégés entrusted their literary effects to his care.

A more questionable contribution, at least in the eyes of some Negro critics, was Van Vechten's *Nigger Heaven,* a novel which appeared in 1926 and quickly ran through several editions. Emphasizing the bawdy and exotic aspects of Harlem life, and heavily influenced by primitivistic conceptions, *Nigger Heaven* shattered the complacency of the Negro intelligentsia by threatening to steal their literary thunder. For most of the Negro middle class the title of the novel was enough. Bitterly attacked in some quarters as a slander against the race, *Nigger Heaven* has been ably defended by James Weldon Johnson, and requires no apologia here. It is sufficient to acknowledge its role in creating an audience for the exotic novel of Harlem life, and its influence on certain members of the so-called Harlem School.

The influence of white intellectuals on the Negro Renaissance ought not to be overestimated. Some Negro critics have charged the New Negro Movement with white domination, but a sober appraisal leaves no doubt of its indigenous character. The New Negro Movement was not a "vogue" initiated by white "literary faddists," but a serious attempt by the Negro artist to interpret his own group life.

There were excesses, to be sure, for which the whites must bear their share of responsibility. Insofar as the Negro novelist adopted a pose in response to the "primitive" effusions of the white intellectual, it produced a certain shallowness in his work, and a legitimate suspicion that his novels, like his cabarets, were designed to entertain the white folks. In the long run, however, the Negro novelist outgrew his primitive phase; meanwhile it helped him to discover unsuspected values in his own folk culture.

The Essence of the Negro Renaissance

There is a phase in the growth of a derivative literature which corresponds to the adolescent rebellion in an individual—a time when it must cut loose from the parent literature and establish an independent existence. This phase occurred in American literature during the flowering of New England; it was highlighted by Emerson's famous Phi Beta Kappa address, in which he protests, "We have listened too long to the courtly Muses of Europe." The Negro Renaissance represents a similar impulse toward cultural autonomy on the part of the American Negro.

The Negro Renaissance was essentially a period of self-discovery, marked by a sudden growth of interest in things Negro. The Renaissance thus reversed the assimilationist trend of the prewar period, with its conscious imitation of white norms and its deliberate suppression of "racial" elements. The motivation for this sudden reversal was not primarily literary but sociological. The Negro Renaissance, as E. Franklin Frazier has observed, reflects a pattern of adjustment common to all ethnic minorities in America: "At first the group attempts to lose itself in the majority group, disdaining its own characteristics. When this is not possible, there is a new valuation placed upon these very same characteristics, and they are glorified in the eyes of the group."

The discovery of autonomous "racial" values by the Renaissance generation was prompted by a wave of Negro nationalism which swept over the colored community in the wake of World War I. As a direct result of his war experience the American Negro became bitterly disillusioned with the promises of the white majority. Discrimination in the armed forces, brutal attacks on returning veterans, and the bloody riots of the summer of 1919 convinced the Negro that his sacrifices for the nation would be acknowledged only by renewed oppression. With every avenue of assimilation apparently closed, a strongly nationalistic reflex occurred on all levels of Negro society.

Among the Negro masses this reflex took the form of recruitment to Marcus Garvey's "Back to Africa" movement. Garvey's program, in spite of its utterly Utopian content, deserves the closest scrutiny, for it stirred the imagination of the Negro masses as never before or since. Garvey held that the Negro must renounce all hope of assistance or understanding from American whites, leave the country, and build a new civilization in Africa. His secessionist movement preyed upon a dissatisfaction so deep that it amounted to despair of ever achieving a full life in America. His immense popularity stands as a sober warning to all who would underestimate the nationalism of the Negro masses.

Meanwhile the logic of events forced the Negro middle class to adopt what might be called a tactical nationalism. As the fluid patterns of the post-Reconstruction period hardened into a rigid and unyielding color line, it became increasingly clear to the Talented Tenth that they could never hope to breach this caste barrier as a special class of "white" Negroes. The war years in particular convinced them that they could not succeed short of an all-out assault on Jim Crow. Abandoning their former strategy, they turned to the Negro masses for support in the coming struggle.

This *rapprochement* with the black masses could not be consummated without great psychological effort. The habit of emphatically differentiating themselves from the "lower classes" was not easily relinquished by the Talented Tenth. Race leaders perceived at once that they would have to cultivate a mild nationalism in order to achieve a decent show of racial solidarity. One of their number, Jessie Fauset, has preserved this insight for posterity in her novel *Plum Bun:*

> *Those of us who have forged forward are not able as yet to go our separate ways apart from the unwashed, untutored herd. We must still look back and render service to our less fortunate, weaker brethren. And the first step toward making this a workable attitude is the acquisition not so much of a racial love as a racial pride. A pride that*

enables us to find our own beautiful and praiseworthy, an intense chauvinism that is content with its own types, that finds completeness within its own group, that loves its own as the French love their country.

The nationalist reflex of the Negro intelligentsia consisted of a withdrawal of allegiance from the values of the dominant culture, and a search for alternative values within their own tradition. Unlike the nationalism of the masses or of the middle class, that of the intelligentsia was not based on racial considerations alone. It was motivated by factors larger than, but including, race—factors related to the universal revolt of the modern artist from bourgeois civilization. The Negro intellectual of the 1920s shared fully in the spiritual alienation of the Lost Generation. Like the white expatriate, he rejected the chromium plate of American culture. His alienation as an artist caused him in turn to alter his goals as a Negro. Instead of advocating blind assimilation into a hopelessly materialistic culture, he began to think in terms of preserving his racial individuality.

The search for a distinctive tradition led in many directions. The alienated Negro intellectual fell back predominantly on the folk culture, with its antecedents in slavery, its roots in the rural South, and its final flowering on the city pavements. Where the folk culture seemed inadequate to his needs, he turned to the cult of African origins, and to primitivism. At the same time, a new concept of the Negro's manifest destiny arose, to replace the old faith in race progress. Along with a sophisticated critique of (white) European civilization, the thesis was advanced that certain enduring qualities in the racial temperament would redeem the decadent and enervated West. The sum and substance of these explorations was an unequivocal cultural dualism—a conscious attempt to endow Negro literature with a life of its own, apart from the dominant literary tradition.

The frank espousal of cultural dualism by the Negro intelligentsia was viewed with great alarm by the Negro middle class, whose long-range strategy called for eradicating cultural differences. Even at the peak of Renaissance nationalism the middle-class writer could never muster more than token enthusiasm for a distinctive Negro culture. The issues posed by cultural dualism therefore divided the

novelists of the period into two schools. The Harlem School, pur-
suing the nationalist impulse to its logical conclusion, turned to the
black masses for literary material. The Old Guard, still intent upon
portraying "respectable" Negroes, remained prisoners of the Genteel
Tradition.

James Weldon Johnson

HARLEM: THE CULTURE CAPITAL

James Weldon Johnson (1871–1938) was a very active and versatile black spokesman in the early twentieth century. During his life he was a teacher, lawyer, diplomat, song writer, executive secretary of the NAACP, poet, novelist, and historian. Robert Bone describes Johnson "as the only true artist among the early Negro novelists." His novel, The Autobiography of an Ex-Colored Man, *marked him as a forerunner of the Harlem Renaissance. Although Johnson's age and his position as executive secretary of the NAACP made it impossible for him to be an active member of the Harlem Renaissance, he was certainly a leader of the New Negro Movement. The following selection, which appeared in Alain Locke's* The New Negro, *offers a naive and romantic vision of the Harlem of the twenties. This essay, supported by other writings on Harlem during the twenties, bolstered the middle-class view of the city as the "promised land."*

In the history of New York, the significance of the name Harlem has changed from Dutch to Irish to Jewish to Negro. Of these changes, the last has come most swiftly. Throughout colored America, from Massachusetts to Mississippi, and across the continent to Los Angeles and Seattle, its name, which as late as fifteen years ago had scarcely been heard, now stands for the Negro metropolis. Harlem is indeed the great Mecca for the sightseer, the pleasure-seeker, the curious, the adventurous, the enterprising, the ambitious and the talented of the whole Negro world; for the lure of it has reached down to every island of the Carib Sea and has penetrated even into Africa.

In the make-up of New York, Harlem is not merely a Negro colony or community, it is a city within a city, the greatest Negro city in the world. It is not a slum or a fringe, it is located in the heart of Manhattan and occupies one of the most beautiful and healthful sections of the city. It is not a "quarter" of dilapidated tenements, but is made up of new-law apartments and handsome dwellings, with well-paved and well-lighted streets. It has its own churches, social and civic centers, shops, theaters and other places of amusement. And it contains more Negroes to the square mile than any other spot on earth. A stranger who rides up magnificent Seventh Avenue on a bus or in an automobile must be struck with surprise at the transformation which takes place after he crosses One Hundred and Twenty-fifth Street. Beginning there, the population suddenly darkens and he rides through twenty-five solid blocks where the passers-by, the shoppers, those sitting in restaurants, coming out of theaters, standing in doorways and looking out of windows are practically all Negroes; and then he emerges where the population as suddenly becomes white again. There is nothing just like it in any other city in the country, for there is no preparation for it; no change in the character of the houses and streets; no change, indeed, in the appearance of the people, except their color. . . .

. . . Following the outbreak of the war in Europe Negro Harlem received a new and tremendous impetus. Because of the war thousands of aliens in the United States rushed back to their native lands to join the colors and immigration practically ceased. The result was a critical shortage in labor. This shortage was rapidly increased as the United States went more and more largely into the business of furnishing munitions and supplies to the warring countries. To help meet this shortage of common labor Negroes were brought up from the South. The government itself took the first steps, following the practice in vogue in Germany of shifting labor according to the supply and demand in various parts of the country. The example of the government was promptly taken up by the big industrial concerns, which sent hundreds, perhaps thousands, of labor agents into the South who recruited Negroes by wholesale. I was in Jacksonville, Florida, for a while at that time, and I sat one day and watched the stream of migrants passing to take the train. For hours they passed steadily, carrying flimsy suit cases, new and shiny, rusty old ones, bursting at the seams, boxes and bundles and impedimenta of all sorts, including banjos, guitars, birds in cages and what not. Similar scenes were being enacted in cities and towns all over that region. The first wave of the great exodus of Negroes from the South was on. Great numbers of these migrants headed for New York or eventually got there, and naturally the majority went up into Harlem. But the Negro population of Harlem was not swollen by migrants from the South alone; the opportunity for Negro labor exerted its pull upon the Negroes of the West Indies, and those islanders in the course of time poured into Harlem to the number of twenty-five thousand or more.

These newcomers did not have to look for work; work looked for them, and at wages of which they had never even dreamed. And here is where the unlooked for, the unprecedented, the miraculous happened. According to all preconceived notions, these Negroes suddenly earning large sums of money for the first time in their lives should have had their heads turned; they should have squandered it in the most silly and absurd manners imaginable. Later, after the United States had entered the war and even Negroes in the South were making money fast, many stories in accord with the tradition came out of that section. There was the one about the colored man who went into a general store and on hearing a phonograph for the first time promptly ordered six of them, one for each child in the house. I shall not stop to discuss whether Negroes in the South did that sort of thing or not, but I do know that those who got to New York didn't. The Negroes of Harlem, for the greater part, worked and saved their money. Nobody knew how much they had saved until congestion made expansion necessary for tenants and owner-ship profitable for landlords, and they began to buy property. Persons who would never be suspected of having money bought property. The Rev. W. W. Brown, pastor of the Metropolitan Baptist Church, repeatedly made "Buy Property" the text of his sermons. A large part of his congregation carried out the injunction. The church itself set an example by purchasing a magnificent brownstone church building on Seventh Avenue from a white congregation. Buying property became a fever. At the height of this activity, that is, 1920–21, it was not an uncommon thing for a colored washerwoman or cook to go into a real estate office and lay down from one thousand to five thousand dollars on a house. "Pig Foot Mary" is a character in Harlem. Everybody who knows the corner of Lenox Avenue and One Hundred and Thirty-fifth Street knows "Mary" and her stand, and has been tempted by the smell of her pigsfeet, fried chicken and hot corn, even if he has not been a customer. "Mary," whose real name is Mrs. Mary Dean, bought the five-story apartment house at the corner of Seventh Avenue and One Hundred and Thirty-seventh Street at a price of $42,000. Later she sold it to the YWCA for dormitory purposes. The YWCA sold it recently to Adolph Howell, a leading colored undertaker, the price given being $72,000. Often companies of a half dozen men combined to buy a house—these combinations were and still are generally made up of West Indians —and would produce five or ten thousand dollars to put through the deal.

When the buying activity began to make itself felt, the lending companies that had been holding vacant the handsome dwellings on and abutting Seventh Avenue decided to put them on the market. The values on these houses had dropped to the lowest mark possible and they were put up at astonishingly low prices. Houses that had been bought at from $15,000 to $20,000 were sold at one-third those figures. They were quickly gobbled up. The Equitable Life Assurance Company held 106 model private houses that were designed by Stanford White. They are built with courts running straight through the block and closed off by wrought-iron gates. Every one of these houses was sold within eleven months at an aggregate price of about two million dollars. Today they are probably worth about 100 per cent more. And not only have private dwellings and similar apartments been bought but big elevator apartments have been taken over. Corporations have been organized for this purpose. Two of these, The Antillian Realty Company, composed of West Indian Negroes, and the Sphinx Securities Company, composed of American and West Indian Negroes, represent holdings amounting to approximately $750,000. Individual Negroes and companies in the South have invested in Harlem real estate. About two years ago a Negro institution of Savannah, Georgia, bought a parcel for $115,000 which it sold a month or so ago at a profit of $110,000.

I am informed by John E. Nail, a successful colored real estate dealer of Harlem and a reliable authority, that the total value of property in Harlem owned and controlled by colored people would at a conservative estimate amount to more than sixty million dollars. These figures are amazing, especially when we take into account the short time in which they have been piled up. Twenty years ago Negroes were begging for the privilege of renting a flat in Harlem. Fifteen years ago barely a half dozen colored men owned real property in all Manhattan. And down to ten years ago the amount that had been acquired in Harlem was comparatively negligible. Today Negro Harlem is practically owned by Negroes.

The question naturally arises, "Are the Negroes going to be able to hold Harlem?" If they have been steadily driven northward for the past hundred years and out of less desirable sections, can they hold this choice bit of Manhattan Island? It is hardly probable that Negroes will hold Harlem indefinitely, but when they are forced out it will not be for the same reasons that forced them out of former quarters in New York City. The situation is entirely different and without precedent. When colored people do leave Harlem, their homes, their churches, their investments and their businesses, it will be because the land has become so valuable they can no longer afford to live on it. But the date of another move northward is very far in the future. What will Harlem be and become in the meantime? Is there danger that the Negro may lose his economic status in New York and be unable to hold his property? Will Harlem become merely a famous ghetto, or will it be a center of intellectual, cultural and economic forces exerting an influence throughout the world, especially upon Negro peoples? Will it become a point of friction between the races in New York?

I think there is less danger to the Negroes of New York of losing out economically and industrially than to the Negroes of any [other] large city in the North. In most of the big industrial centers Negroes are engaged in gang labor. They are employed by thousands in the stockyards in Chicago, by thousands in the automobile plants in Detroit; and in those cities they are likely to be the first to be let go, and in thousands, with every business depression. In New York there is hardly such a thing as gang labor among Negroes, except among the longshoremen, and it is in the longshoremen's unions, above all others, that Negroes stand on an equal footing. Employment among Negroes in New York is highly diversified; in the main they are employed more as individuals than as non-integral parts of a gang. Furthermore, Harlem is gradually becoming more and more a self-supporting community. Negroes there are steadily branching out into new businesses and enterprises in which Negroes are employed. So the danger of great numbers of Negroes being thrown out of work at once, with a resulting economic crisis among them, is less in New York than in most of the large cities of the North to which Southern migrants have come.

These facts have an effect which goes beyond the economic and industrial situation. They have a direct bearing on the future character of Harlem and on the question as to whether Harlem will be a point of friction between the races in New York. It is true that Harlem is a Negro community, well defined and stable; anchored to its fixed homes, churches, institutions, business and amusement places; having its own working, business and professional classes. It is experiencing a constant growth of group consciousness and community feeling. Harlem is, therefore, in many respects, typically Negro. It has many unique characteristics. It has movement, color, gayety, singing, dancing, boisterous laughter and loud talk. One of its outstanding features is brass band parades. Hardly a Sunday passes but that there are several of these parades of which many are gorgeous with regalia and insignia. Almost any excuse will do —the death of an humble member of the Elks, the laying of a cornerstone, the "turning out" of the order of this or that. In many of these characteristics it is similar to the Italian colony. But withal, Harlem grows more metropolitan and more a part of New York all the while. Why is it then that its tendency is not to become a mere "quarter"?

I shall give three reasons that seem to me to be important in their order. First, the language of Harlem is not alien; it is not Italian or Yiddish; it is English. Harlem talks American, reads American, thinks American. Second, Harlem is not physically a "quarter." It is not a section cut off. It is merely a zone through which four main arteries of the city run. Third, the fact that there is little or no gang labor gives Harlem Negroes the opportunity for individual expansion and individual contacts with the life and spirit of New York. A thousand Negroes from Mississippi put to work as a gang in a Pittsburgh steel mill will for a long time remain a thousand Negroes from Mississippi. Under the conditions that prevail in New York they would all within six months become New Yorkers. The rapidity with which Negroes become good New Yorkers is one of the marvels to observers.

These three reasons form a single reason why there is small probability that Harlem will ever be a point of race friction between the races in New York. One of the principal factors in the race riot in

Chicago in 1919 was the fact that at that time there were 12,000 Negroes employed in gangs in the stockyards. There was considerable race feeling in Harlem at the time of the hegira of white residents due to the "invasion," but that feeling, of course, is no more. Indeed, a number of the old white residents who didn't go or could not get away before the housing shortage struck New York are now living peacefully side by side with colored residents. In fact, in some cases white and colored tenants occupy apartments in the same house. Many white merchants still do business in thickest Harlem. On the whole, I know of no place in the country where the feeling between the races is so cordial and at the same time so matter-of-fact and taken for granted. One of the surest safeguards against an outbreak in New York such as took place in so many Northern cities in the summer of 1919 is the large proportion of Negro police on duty in Harlem.

To my mind, Harlem is more than a Negro community; it is a large scale laboratory experiment in the race problem. The statement has often been made that if Negroes were transported to the North in large numbers the race problem with all of its acuteness and with new aspects would be transferred with them. Well, 175,000 Negroes live closely together in Harlem, in the heart of New York—75,000 more than live in any Southern city—and do so without any race friction. Nor is there any unusual record of crime. I once heard a captain of the 38th Police Precinct (the Harlem precinct) say that on the whole it was the most law-abiding precinct in the city. New York guarantees its Negro citizens the fundamental rights of American citizenship and protects them in the exercise of those rights. In return the Negro loves New York and is proud of it, and contributes in his way to its greatness. He still meets with discriminations, but possessing the basic rights, he knows that these discriminations will be abolished.

I believe that the Negro's advantages and opportunities are greater in Harlem than in any other place in the country, and that Harlem will become the intellectual, the cultural and the financial center for Negroes of the United States, and will exert a vital influence upon all Negro peoples.

III THE PROMISED LAND QUESTIONED

Elliott M. Rudwick
PATTERNS IN RACE RIOTS

World War I brought about a nationalizing of the race issue. Although there had been an ever-increasing migration from the rural South to the urban North prior to the war, the demand for unskilled labor during the war caused the Great Migration. As blacks entered the cities they slowly pushed out the boundaries of the ghetto. To many of the black middle class, expansion meant progress. But to whites it meant confrontation and, at times, violence. Race riots were not new to the North, but major outbreaks had been few and far between after 1863. In the earlier part of the twentieth century, racial clashes had occurred in both the North and the South. These were usually isolated and of short duration. But the 1917 race riot in East St. Louis opened a new chapter in race relations. The intensity of the hatred, the amount of damage, and the number of deaths and injuries made the East St. Louis riot a forerunner of things to come rather than a continuation of the violence of earlier times. Elliott Rudwick, a professor of sociology at Kent State University, wrote in the early sixties a monograph examining in detail the violence and brutality that occurred in July, 1917. The events in East St. Louis plus the riots that followed cast a serious shadow over the optimism of the twenties. It is quite true that race violence did not occur on the same level of intensity after the riots of 1919. Yet there were enough instances of individual acts of violence to cause the black middle class to feel somewhat insecure with their vision of the North as the "promised land." In this selection Rudwick compares the East St. Louis riot with the Chicago riot of 1919 and the Detroit riot of 1943.

If seriousness of a race riot is measured by its death toll, the East St. Louis riot, which took the lives of nine whites and about thirty-nine Negroes, was the most serious one in the United States during the twentieth century. Next were the Chicago riot of 1919 (fifteen whites and twenty-three Negroes) and the Detroit riot of 1943 (nine whites and twenty-five Negroes). In the three cities the racial violence resulted from: threats to the security of whites brought on by the Negroes' gains in economic, political, and social status; Negro resentment of the attempts to "kick him back into his place"; and

Reprinted from Elliott M. Rudwick, "A Summary of Patterns in Race Riots: East St. Louis, Chicago, Detroit," in *Race Riot at East St. Louis, July 2, 1917.* Copyright © 1964 by Southern Illinois University Press. Reprinted by permission of Southern Illinois University Press.

the weakness of the "external forces of constraint"—the city government, especially the police department.

During the years immediately preceding its race riot each city experienced large increases in Negro population primarily because of an influx from the South. Between 1910 and 1917 the East St. Louis Negro community grew from nearly 6,000 to perhaps as many as 13,000. In Chicago there were nearly 110,000 Negroes in 1920 compared to 44,000 a decade earlier. Detroit in 1940 had about 160,000 Negro residents, but three years later there were an estimated 220,000 Negroes. The numerical increases in East St. Louis seem small compared with Chicago and Detroit, but largely as a result of the migration, the percentage of Negroes in the total East St. Louis population rose from 10 per cent to perhaps 18 per cent. Consequently, white East St. Louisans, to a greater degree than was true of whites in Chicago or Detroit, feared being overrun by Negroes.

In all three cities, unskilled whites manifested tension after they considered their jobs threatened by Negroes. There was also concern because migrants had overburdened the housing and transportation facilities. Everywhere, efforts of Negroes to improve their status were defined as arrogant assaults, and whites insisted on retaining competitive advantages enjoyed before the Negro migration.

Economic conflict was inevitable because the industrial corporations had employed Negroes not only to supplement white labor but also to crush strikes and destroy unions. Negroes had helped to break the 1904 and 1916 strikes in the Chicago stockyards, and a generation later near Detroit, a strike erupted at the Ford River Rouge plant where Negro and white workers were "pitted against each other." However, nowhere was the relationship between labor strife and race rioting more clearly and directly evident than in East St. Louis. The July violence occurred shortly after the Aluminum Ore Company workers lost a strike that began when union sympathizers were replaced by Negroes.

Of course, labor leaders might have combatted industrialists by conducting an aggressive campaign to encourage Negro unionization. Until the late 1930's such gestures were insignificant because of Negro prejudice against unions as well as union prejudice against

Negroes. By inclination and pressure the migrants trusted employer paternalism to protect them against the hostility of lower class whites. Even in the 1940's, many whites were unable to surrender their "depression psychology" and their fears that Negroes would displace them. For example, shortly before the Detroit race riot, there were several strikes when Negroes were hired, and at the Packard plant, 3,000 whites walked off their jobs in protest against the upgrading of three colored assembly line workers.

The East St. Louis and Detroit riots erupted in wartime, and the Chicago riot occurred in an immediate postwar period when even substandard housing was scarce. Landlords raised rents, playing off one race against the other. Whites also resented increased contacts with Negroes after the black ghetto gradually expanded or "invasions" took place. Improvement Associations held indignation meetings, and, when warnings were ignored, violent measures were sometimes taken. During the two years before the Chicago riot, bombs wrecked an average of one Negro dwelling a month.

Slum neighborhoods were (and are) deficient in recreational facilities; this inadequacy became critical as a result of the migration. Disputes occurred when Negroes attempted to use parks, playgrounds, or bathing beaches which were controlled by whites. Frequently, before the conflicts subsided, adult participants became involved. The Chicago riot began at a bathing beach and the Detroit riot started in an amusement park. Of the communities under study, only at East St. Louis were recreational facilities unimportant as sites of pre-riot clashes. In East St. Louis Negroes evidently still "knew their place" in regard to these facilities and had not yet challenged their complete exclusion from parks, playgrounds and theaters.

In all three cities, public transit systems were overtaxed. Crowded, uncomfortable streetcars were responsible for many incidents which, in the absence of racial prejudice, would have been endured with good humor or only perfunctory grumbling. Jammed vehicles, with their jerking and jolting motions, furnished an excuse for hostile and tense passengers of both races to interpret unintentional pushes or shoves as racial insults. Many whites were annoyed that they were obliged to stand, particularly when any Negroes occupied seats. Shortly before the East St. Louis riots, a sixty-six year old

Negro was beaten into insensibility by an embryonic race riot mob after refusing to give his seat, it was stated, to an elderly lady.

Whites also complained that migrants took advantage of Northern freedom by refusing to follow segregation patterns prevalent in the region from which they came. It was said that dirty Negroes sat all over the car, smelled of body odor, and exhibited loud or boisterous behavior. Interestingly, in East St. Louis, Chicago, and Detroit, there were almost no complaints that Negro passengers molested white women, although the Chicago Commission on Race Relations learned of cases where white males allegedly molested Negro women.

Many whites charged that the Negroes' challenge of the old social order was caused by their political power, which increased as a direct result of migration and residential segregation. There was resentment that at close elections (the mayoralty races in East St. Louis in 1915 and in Chicago four years later), the Negro bloc was the deciding factor. Race prejudice was used as a political weapon: during the colonization controversy preceding the 1916 Presidential election, East St. Louis and Chicago Democrats employed it as a stick to insure a large turnout of supporters at the polls gaining extra white supremacy votes and to intimidate colored migrants from casting ballots.

Whites resented sharing political rewards with Negroes, invariably exaggerating the number of important political jobs allocated to colored people. Despite a bargaining advantage Negroes were actually slow to exploit their voting power. White politicians flattered them by occasionally attending colored meetings or calling Negroes to City Hall for "consultations," and even these innocuous actions, in seeming to suggest equal treatment, angered some whites. Politicians were blamed for Negro "arrogance." Before the riots, whites charged that because of the ballot, Negroes had transformed from a subordinate to an insubordinate race. Critics even suggested that if the North had denied political participation to Negroes, the migration would never have occurred.

Another accusation was that Negroes were responsible for large-scale vice and obtained protection through political influence. Unquestionably, at least in East St. Louis and Chicago, certain Negroes supported corrupt municipal administrations but so did other groups. Negroes had their "gambling dens" and houses of prostitution, but a considerable portion of the organized vice in Negro neighborhoods (or in close proximity to these districts) was operated by whites for other whites, under the protection of municipal officials and the police.

Negro participation in politics, while of limited practical value until World War II, was an important propaganda weapon which Negro organizations used in their conscious campaign to teach members of their race a new conception of self. This new image challenged the traditional ideology of white supremacy and race inequality. It was no coincidence that the major race riots occurred in the World War I and World War II periods when equal rights agencies, such as the NAACP, and militant race newspapers, such as the *Chicago Defender,* encouraged Negroes to reject their role of a biologically and socially inferior caste and refuse to accommodate themselves to a subordinated, dominated, and isolated status.

There is no doubt that this self-conception motivated some Negroes to test the availability of first class citizenship by "creating incidents." The new teachings, almost as much as the presence of Negroes, provoked "violence-proneness" and tensions among whites, who complained that migrants were "intoxicated by new Northern freedom." At least in East St. Louis, several of the Negroes arrested after the riot were political leaders known to be vigorous advocates of equal rights. For whites, this was an erroneous doctrine which, in creating discontent, was a prelude to race war.

In East St. Louis, Chicago, and Detroit, each race riot was preceded by "a series of irritating events that dramatized race frictions upon a rising crescendo." Before the East St. Louis riot, Negro workers at the Aluminum Ore plant were repeatedly beaten. In late May, a "preliminary riot" erupted after a union-sponsored meeting protesting the migration. A rise in the number of robberies committed by Negroes was also reported (and magnified by the press); at least some of these crimes may have been counterattacks motivated by revenge.

In Chicago, many pre-riot incidents erupted in playgrounds and trolley cars. Negroes returning from work were also repeatedly waylaid by white gangs, and five weeks before the holocaust, two colored men, each traveling alone, were murdered without provocation.

After the killings, signs began appearing all over the South Side, announcing that the whites "intended to get all the niggers on July 4." These two crimes and the notices stimulated Negro efforts to prepare for the impending explosion.

In Detroit, a year before the riot, a serious conflict occurred at the Sojourner Truth Housing Project when Negro tenants attempted to move into the development which had been constructed for them. Subsequent to this outbreak, fights between Negro and white teen-agers increased in intensity near several high schools, and these events were followed by: a "battle" between white soldiers and Negroes; the strikes at the Packard plant protesting Negro hiring and upgrading; and clashes between white and Negro youths at the Eastwood Amusement Park.

According to sociologists Alfred M. Lee and Norman Humphrey, ". . . with respect to the symptoms of approaching riot, the incidents are not as significant in themselves as is the inescapable fact that they begin to increase in (a) frequency, (b) boldness, and (c) violence." In East St. Louis and Chicago, observers, after examining the quality and quantity of these incidents, forecast the explosions. Similarly, over a year before the Detroit race riot, the Federal Office of Facts and Figures (later renamed the Office of War Information) issued a memorandum containing such a prediction.

At each of these cities, the incidents both reflected and reenforced the tensions among Negroes and whites until the spontaneous occurrence of the event which actually provoked the riot:

> *It may be submitted that given a sufficient level of social tension and/or a sufficiently low level of efficiency in the agencies of external control [primarily the police], any one of a large variety of types of incidents can provide the spark that sets off a major eruption of social violence.*

In East St. Louis, white detectives were shot by a Negro mob after being, in all likelihood, mistaken for a group of whites who had fired into a Negro neighborhood earlier that evening. The riot erupted the following morning when whites learned about the killing. In Chicago, several Negroes were ejected from a beach which by tacit understanding had been reserved for whites; within less than an hour, a Negro teenager drowned after being attacked in the swimming area. A white policeman refused to arrest a white man allegedly involved in the drowning, and in anger and protest, a large group of Negroes crossed the imaginary line from their bathing area two blocks away. One of them was arrested by the same policeman who had failed to take any action a few moments earlier. The riot began after the officer was mobbed.

The Detroit riot also erupted in a recreation area, when white and Negro teenagers clashed at the Belle Isle Amusement Park. According to sociologist Allen Grimshaw, "some of the Negro boys who attacked whites in the initial battles of that day were themselves reacting directly to their own exclusion several days earlier from Eastwood Park, a commercial recreation facility dominated by whites." At Belle Isle, members of both races disseminated the rumor that persons of the other group had attacked a woman and her baby; after this false information was relayed to a Negro night club, the patrons there were told "to take care of a bunch of whites who killed a colored woman and her baby at Belle Isle Park."

Rumors contributed to the violence in all three cities. During periods of tension and crisis, when "people were jittery and willing to believe almost anything," rumors were manufactured, rapidly circulated, and of course accepted uncritically by many citizens. Grimshaw commented, a rumor "reaches individuals who are already prejudiced and reinforces rather than changes or molds attitudes. This reinforcement may tend to raise the level of social tension and violence-proneness." . . .

There is no doubt that during all three riots, newspapers contributed to social tension and "violence proneness" by publishing inflammatory rumors. For example, in Chicago, metropolitan newspapers reported that Negroes slaughtered a defenseless white woman carrying a child in her arms. The *Chicago Defender* erroneously announced the killing of a Negro woman and her baby. It has already been noted that a generation later, the same story helped to extend the Detroit riot. The *Detroit Times* also reported that a Negro had murdered a white police sergeant, although the officer actually survived the assault.

The three race riots occurred in warm weather during the summer months—Detroit in late June and East St. Louis and Chicago in July—when large crowds of people congregated out of doors. In each case the precipitating incident took place on a Sunday. According to the typical riot pattern, a gathering crowd provided "the media through which hysterical, inciting rumors travel." During the overwrought confusion participants stimulated each other, raising the level of excitement. Although the crowds were large, most persons were spectators or bystanders furnishing encouragement and a sense of anonymity for the attacking gangs. The Chicago Commission on Race Relations noted, "without the spectators mob violence would probably have stopped short of murder in many cases." The actual rioting gangs were small, usually containing far less than fifty persons in each group (typically composed of teenagers or young men).

During the riots, all three cities exhibited similar ecological patterns. Regardless of where the precipitating event occurred, considerable violence broke out in downtown business sections, where whites invariably outnumbered Negroes. In these areas, the largest crowds of East St. Louis, Chicago, and Detroit gathered. In each city, a small active nucleus was encouraged to attack isolated Negroes without risking immediate retaliation. Police were both unable and unwilling to protect the victims. At various transfer points in these districts, Negroes were stranded waiting for streetcars to return them to the safety of their neighborhoods, and some who were fortunate enough to board trolleys were pulled off, beaten, or killed.

Violence invariably occurred in Negro slum neighborhoods. Principally in the early stages of the riots, Negro gangs in the black belt of East St. Louis and Chicago killed a few isolated whites. In Detroit's Paradise Valley, stones were hurled at cars driven by whites (who did not realize there was a race riot). Negro gangs also roamed the area, stopping streetcars and beating whites. Other Negro mobs broke into white stores, looting and destroying property. Particularly in Chicago and Detroit, small groups of whites in automobiles made a few raids through Negro neighborhoods, firing into homes; the residents were prepared and returned the fire. Most police contingents were assigned to the black belt where gun battles took place between lawmen and the Negro mobs.

Whites, fearing a counterattack, did not make invasions into the heart of Negro territory. In Detroit, although a large mob was supposedly prepared to penetrate, they were actually not anxious to face an angry multitude of armed Negro residents. Most violence occurred on the edges of Negro territory and in a boundary zone separating a colored residential district from a lower class white area. In Detroit there were many casualties along Woodward Avenue, the main north-south thoroughfare, where isolated members of one race were beset by gangs of the other racial group. In East St. Louis, white mobs invaded Negro homes at Fourth and Broadway, near the downtown business district, and the residents who died there were isolated from other members of their race. The Negro victims at Eighth and Broadway in East St. Louis, which was "burned to an ash heap," lived on the edge of a colored neighborhood.

In Chicago, Wentworth Avenue was the boundary line separating the two races, and although there were clashes on that thoroughfare, most Negro casualties occurred farther west in the white-dominated stockyards residential district. In that respect, the ecological pattern represented a special case because Negroes passed through a violently hostile Irish neighborhood to go from their homes to their jobs in the stockyards. During the first day of the riot, streetcars carrying colored passengers were attacked, and on the second day, after a strike suspended public transportation facilities, white gangs assaulted Negroes walking through hostile territory to the black belt. According to Grimshaw, "If in Chicago, it had not been for the transportation strike, it is doubtful that so large an amount of total social violence would have occurred within the stockyards area. More likely, a pattern similar to that of other cities would have occurred in which battles were concentrated along boundary lines between the two areas."

In all three riots, more Negroes than whites were killed and seriously injured. The number of wounded Negroes was underreported, since many were afraid to seek hospitalization and risk arrest for rioting. Nevertheless, the majority of persons arrested were Negroes. Since there was obviously greater riot activity on the part of whites, prejudicial police attitudes accounted for the conclusion that "whites were not apprehended as readily as Negroes."

The law enforcement officers invariably interfered when Negroes assaulted whites, but when Negroes were attacked, police frequently left the scene or adopted the role of interested spectators. Sometimes they were even participants. There is no way of knowing how many police bullets killed Negroes during the violence of East St. Louis, but as many as seven Chicago Negroes and seventeen or eighteen Detroit Negroes were shot down by law enforcement officers. Municipal authorities adjudged such cases "justifiable homicides," and a portion undoubtedly were, i.e., where colored mobs looted property or fired on the police. However, the race prejudices of police officers inflated the Negro death toll. . . .

During the months before the riots, police partisanship was obvious to both whites and Negroes. MacClay Hoyne, the Cook County State's Attorney, frankly described a situation which characterized all cities experiencing major race riots: "There is no doubt that a great many police officers were grossly unfair in making arrests. They shut their eyes to offenses committed by white men while they were very vigorous in getting all the colored men they could get." At East St. Louis, police were unavailable to protect Negroes subjected to nightly attacks by white gangs. In Chicago when Negroes were excluded from recreation facilities, patrolmen were frequently on the scene—to encourage the whites. The police never apprehended persons responsible for bombing Negro homes. Nor did the law enforcement officers make an arrest when a white woman identified the man who murdered a Negro without provocation shortly before the riot. In Detroit, at the Sojourner Truth Housing Project disturbance, police encouraged white mobs by pointing guns at colored tenants trying to move into their new homes.

It was for reasons such as these that Grimshaw, in his *Study in Social Violence,* suggested "that the occurrence or non-occurrence of violence depends less on the degree of social tension . . . than on the strength and attitude of police forces. . . . In every case where major rioting has occurred the social structure of the community has been characterized by weak patterns of external control."

In East St. Louis, Chicago, and Detroit, military forces were sent to quell the riots. In Chicago (and to a lesser extent Detroit), there was an unconscionable delay before municipal authorities asked for military assistance. At Detroit and East St. Louis, even after requests by the Mayor, the troops were not available for duty until many lives were lost. With the exception of East St. Louis, when the soldiers finally arrived, they took vigorous action to stop the disorders and preserve the peace.

In Chicago, the police chief readily admitted that his men were inadequate to meet the emergency, but claiming that inexperienced militiamen would make the situation worse, he opposed requesting military re-enforcements. He was supported by Mayor Thompson until mounting pressure forced the latter to call the governor for help three days after the outbreak at the bathing beach.

In Detroit, federal troops were on duty approximately twenty-four hours after the opening violence at Belle Isle. However, over thirty persons had already been killed. The delay was due to bureaucratic bungling. By half-past six on the morning after the Belle Isle disorders several persons had lost their lives, but the mayor considered "the situation under control." By nine o'clock, he overcame initial reluctance to ask for troops, but two hours later he learned that in the absence of martial law, no military assistance would be given. The governor refused to suspend state and local laws, and by four o'clock that afternoon, he and the mayor were in conference exploring the possibilities of employing federal troops without declaring "full" martial law. The debates were interminable and more hours passed; by late evening someone discovered that only President Roosevelt could issue the proclamation calling out the troops.

At East St. Louis, the mayor requested the aid of militiamen almost immediately after the slaying of Sergeant Coppedge, but during the following seventeen hours, while the Negro death toll rose, only about 160 guardsmen arrived. Inexperienced, biased soldiers were commanded by an incompetent officer lacking any knowledge of riot control measures. He refused to call for reenforcements and there was no interference with the mobs "as long as they killed nobody but Negroes."

In each city, after the violence was over, whites sought justification by blaming Negroes. More Negroes than whites were indicted and convicted for felonies growing out of the rioting. Everywhere there were widespread rumors that Negroes were plotting a drive for revenge, while whites freely threatened "to finish the job next time."

Even among white and Negro community leaders a breakdown in communication resulted. The pattern was seen most clearly at East St. Louis where several Negro professional men were arrested. In Detroit social work agencies "were forced to sharply curtail their activities . . . and their effectiveness, particularly in the case of inter-racial agencies, suffered a sharp decline." In Chicago, "after the restoration of order community activities were superficially the same as before the riot, but under the surface there remained a deepened bitterness of race feeling. . . ."

However, despite the alienation, a reaction occurred when white community leaders realized the serious threat to law and order and the bad publicity that would result from another riot. Newspapers which had previously increased social tensions made concerted efforts to prevent a recurrence of the disorders. Governors' commissions of inquiry were appointed in all three cities in addition to the Congressional Committee which investigated in East St. Louis.

The Military Board of Inquiry at East St. Louis ignored the conduct of the militiamen. The Detroit investigation was even more biased —conducted by the Detroit prosecuting attorney, the Attorney General of Michigan, the Commissioner of the Michigan State Police, and the Detroit Police Commissioner. Blaming the riot on Negro leaders, the report whitewashed the activities of law enforcement agencies and government officials. The East St. Louis Congressional investigation and the Chicago inquiry were serious efforts to examine the background of the riots. The legislators' relatively short report on East St. Louis—containing some errors—has long been forgotten. However, *The Negro in Chicago,* the volume published in 1922 by the Chicago Commission on Race Relations, is still "without question the best single source on social racial violence in the United States and quite likely is the best sociological study of a single case of social violence which is available."

Race riots have led to some limited social reforms; for example, Mayors' commissions on interracial relations were established at Detroit and Chicago, and there were small improvements in Negro living conditions. . . .

Gunnar Myrdal discussed race riots in *An American Dilemma,* writing that because of "their devastation and relative fewness" they were "landmarks in history." The violence in East St. Louis, Chicago, and Detroit, resulting from the status struggle between Negroes and whites, demonstrated how far from realization were the ideals Myrdal described as "the American creed." Yet it must not be forgotten that the last major race riot took place over two decades ago, and since then there have been far-reaching demands for a redefinition in the relations between Negroes and whites. The Negro protest for equal status, although generating controversy, recrimination, and even conflict, has thus far occurred without a major race riot. This is itself a landmark of significance in American race relations.

Constance McLaughlin Green
THE TWENTIES: THE NEW NADIR

In Black Metropolis, *St. Clair Drake and Horace Cayton discussed the reasons for the optimism of the black middle class in Chicago during the twenties. Prosperity covered a multitude of weaknesses within the social system and rapid growth provided the necessary excuse for the weaknesses that were visible. Optimism was greatest where growth was greatest. But the experience of the black middle class in Washington, D.C., should have sounded a warning to blacks in other northern cities. Washington, prior to 1914, had a large black population and a rather substantial middle class. Until the 1920s the nation's capital was the educational and the cultural center of black America. Here black society had a solid base on which either to build an autonomous society or to unite with white society. Black gains in the twenties should have been more impressive in Washington than elsewhere. This did not occur. Constance McLaughlin Green examines why the black middle class not only failed to gain but actually lost ground during the twenties. Green, author of a two-volume history of Washington, as well as a noted urban historian, wrote her work on the history of race relations in the nation's capital in the early sixties. Her title,* The Secret City, *reflects the realization of that time that blacks were indeed invisible to white America. She writes that black Washington "was psychologically a secret city all but unknown to the white world around it" (vii).*

In the autumn of 1919, while colored Washingtonians wondered whether they had gained more than they lost by the race riots, white business leaders worried briefly about whether the outburst had given the city a bad reputation for uncontrolled racial violence and for being a hotbed of Negro radicalism. But a large part of white Washington soon ceased to think about the riots at all. Senate ratification or rejection of the Versailles Treaty, plans, quickly quashed, for a District policemen's union affiliated with the American Federation of Labor, wage strikes that threatened Washington's white building trades, and the intensifying conflict throughout the United States between capital and industrial labor preempted white men's

Selections from Constance McLaughlin Green, *The Secret City: A History of Race Relations in the Nation's Capital* (copyright © 1967 by Princeton University Press; Princeton Paperback, 1969), 196–199, 201–204, 206–207, 209–210, 213–214. Reprinted by permission of Princeton University Press. Documenting footnotes in this selection have been omitted.

attention. Although, like Americans everywhere, people here were frightened by the bogey of red infiltration into the ranks of organized labor, in a predominantly white-collar city fear of a red-infected local black proletariat had relatively little to feed upon. Neither the local business community nor federal officials could link Washington's race riots to labor radicalism. Although nine men had lost their lives in the street fights and more than thirty men later died from injuries, Congress saw no cause to investigate. Thus reassured, whites banished from memory the uncomfortable events of July as representing no more than an unfortunate episode best forgotten as quickly as possible. The wish to forget the unpleasantness of "the intense, restless, disturbed year," as a Board of Trade committee described 1919, nevertheless had long-lasting consequences; it gradually reinforced white prejudices, deepened the obliviousness of much of white Washington to the needs of a biracial city, and for nearly two decades defeated the attempts of an enlightened minority to collaborate with Negro citizens.

During 1920 and early 1921, however, neither Negro nor most of white Washington foresaw a worsening of race relations. On the contrary, racial toleration seemed to be regaining some of the headway lost after the Reconstruction era. Two biracial organizations came into being in 1920, Community Services, Inc., a group of civic-spirited volunteers, and the Council of Social Workers, composed of white and colored professionally trained employees of the police department, the Juvenile Court, the U.S. Public Health Service, the Visiting Nurse Association, the Associated Charities, the white and colored YMCA's, the NAACP, the Boy Scouts, and a half-dozen more. By exchanging information on common problems and meeting sociably over the luncheon table from time to time, social workers hoped to breach the color line. Community Services planned to open neighborhood recreation centers which white and colored people could enjoy together. Unfortunately, to archconservatives fearful of social change, such proposals smacked of Bolshevism; the Board of Trade considered them dangerously radical. Community Services, Inc., thus denied businessmen's financial support, withered before it was well started, and the Council of Social Workers within a matter of months became a small, rather ineffectual colored gathering as white members dropped out. Still Negroes refused to believe that racism would strengthen after Warren G. Harding became President. The campaign rumor that he had Negro blood in his veins had some currency in the colored community and not improbably increased colored men's faith in the President-elect. Joyfully they heard him announce in his inaugural address that American Negroes "have earned the full measure of citizenship bestowed; that their sacrifice in blood on the battlefields of the Republic has entitled them to all freedom and opportunity, all sympathy and aid that the American spirit of fairness and justice demands." With those words ringing in its ears, colored society celebrated that night with a large reception and a dance.

Although government offices had dismissed some 16,000 wartime employees, the city's permanent population between 1917 and the end of 1920 had increased about 25 per cent; the building trades were booming in consequence, and the Red Scare fizzled out in the spring of 1921. When a business recession accompanied by wage cuts and unemployment overtook the capital in mid-summer, Negroes, letting hope triumph over experience, still counted on the new administration to set its face against the racial discrimination and segregation that had taken root under Woodrow Wilson. True, Harding's North Carolina-born commissioner of public buildings and grounds had recently decreed that colored people could use the new golf course in East Potomac Park and the tennis courts on the Washington Monument grounds only on Tuesdays. True also, the President delayed month after month to name Negroes to the federal offices they had expected of him. But in November, when the capital welcomed Marshal Foche, French hero of the Marne, and Howard University conferred upon him a honorary degree while "scores of veterans of colored regiments who had served under the French military leader in the World War stood at attention," Negroes half believed that white onlookers had been sufficiently impressed to prod the President into keeping his promises to colored Americans.

It was a year after the inauguration before politically naive colored people admitted that they had been leaning on a man of straw. In that twelve-month Harding had assigned only three Negroes to appointive posts in Washington; Negroes in the civil service were

of lower-class whites. Whatever the reason, whites chose to build
an invisible wall about all colored Washington and then strove to
forget about what a contributor to *Crisis* called the Secret City. Its
inhabitants unexpectedly gained two infinitesimal advantages from
:his sedulous ignoring—a slight decline in white bullying and an
companying reduction of newspaper talk about Negro crime.

⸱ᴵ   ᴱnd of 1926 the *Tribune,* by then Washington's principal
      ᵉr, declared that segregation had "grown to the dimen-
      ᶦonal policy." It was in full force in the government
      d "it remains only to observe that the Negroes
      ᵇbout reached the stage of acquiescence in the
      ᶦvil service employees, fearful of losing their
      ᵒmplaints, leaving NAACP officials without
      ᵗest. The major gratification the colored
      ar was the Howard University trustees'
      ᵈent, Mordecai Johnson. What had begun
      long ago become wholly Negro. . . .
      ᵗon's upper-class Negroes a peculiarly
      ᵗ their liberties had only recently received
      e Court when a ruling of 1926 upheld the
      ᵢants among white property-owners aimed
      rom purchasing or occupying houses in
      e battle against restrictive municipal ordi-
      efore the war in a case originating in Balti-
      ᶜompacts seemingly negated that victory and
      all Negroes in the capital to a true ghetto.
      covenants displayed as much passion as the
      to halt them. . . .
      at colored Washington underwent in these years
      despair was forced upon it by white laws, white bigotry, or
      ᵗhoughtlessness and stupidity, citizens of the Secret City
      ᶦlves determined part of their fate, bad and good. The
      ies and quarrels that had splintered the community before
      ᵗain took command. If the fight against the housing covenants
      ᵈd a measure of unity, it did not reach down to families whose
      ᵖoverty precluded their trying to live in comfortable white neighbor-
      ᵗoods. Certainly Washington's high yellow society did not recapture

more fully segregated and all Negroes more rigidly excluded from the city's public recreational facilities than during the Wilson regime; neither Congress nor the white press had demurred at the forming of a District Ku Klux Klan; white newspapers had allotted two lines at most to the "silent parade" of 1,500 Negroes in wordless protest against lynchings in the South. Full realization of the situation came at the dedication of the Lincoln Memorial on Decoration Day 1922. Dr. Robert Moten, president of Tuskegee Institute, invited to speak at the unveiling of the statue of the G pator, but, instead of being placed on the speake was relegated along with other distinguished color all-Negro section separated by a road from the and the language of the ill-tempered M "niggers" into their seats caused well-bred indignation as the segregated seating i later explanation that the arrangement ha failed to modify colored Washington's v to be treated as a full-fledged Americ White House, Congress, and the overwhe white residents looked upon him as a c

That state of affairs underwent little Coolidge. . . .

Had the ratio of Negro to white inhabit and after the war, the tightening of segr might be easier to explain. Between 1910 an Detroit's colored populations had grown resp and six times as fast as their white, and the c less pronounced in four or five other Northern confronted an unfamiliar social and economic p ington a large Negro population was no novelty. Here, mc the proportion of Negroes to white had dropped since 19 with the exception of 1920, the 27.1 per cent of 1930 was be figure shown in any census since the Civil War. White fears of swamped in a black metropolis therefore had little validity. sibly Negroes' slightly improved economic position threatene lessen the supply of cheap domestic and unskilled labor and, b enlarging the Negro middle class, to jeopardize the social status

ıe
in
., had been
ıreat Emanci-
r's platform, he
ed people to an
ıest of the audience;
ıarine who herded the
ı colored people as much
ıself. Chief Justice Taft's
d not had official sanction
ıew: no Negro could hope
ıan citizen as long as the
lming majority of the city's
eature apart and inferior.
change under President

ants risen sharply during
egation in Washington
ıd 1920 Chicago's and
ɔectively nearly seven
hange had been only
cities. All of them
ɔroblem. For Wash-
ɔreover,
10 and,
ow the
being
Pos-
d to

ac

A the e
colored pape
sions of a nat
departments, an
themselves have a
practice." Colored c
jobs, refused to lodge c
provable grounds for pro
intelligentsia had that ye
selection of a Negro presid
as a biracial institution had

In the eyes of Washing
invidious new restriction on
the blessing of the Suprem
legality of voluntary cover
at preventing Negroes f
white neighborhoods. Th
nances had been won b
more; now voluntary c
threatened to confine
Whites endorsing the
Negroes who sought

While most of wh
of near
white t
themse
jealous
1915 a
create
p
h

more fully segregated and all Negroes more rigidly excluded from the city's public recreational facilities than during the Wilson regime; neither Congress nor the white press had demurred at the forming of a District Ku Klux Klan; white newspapers had allotted two lines at most to the "silent parade" of 1,500 Negroes in wordless protest against lynchings in the South. Full realization of the situation came at the dedication of the Lincoln Memorial on Decoration Day in 1922. Dr. Robert Moten, president of Tuskegee Institute had been invited to speak at the unveiling of the statue of the Great Emancipator, but, instead of being placed on the speakers platform, he was relegated along with other distinguished colored people to an all-Negro section separated by a road from the rest of the audience; and the language of the ill-tempered Marine who herded the "niggers" into their seats caused well-bred colored people as much indignation as the segregated seating itself. Chief Justice Taft's later explanation that the arrangement had not had official sanction failed to modify colored Washington's view: no Negro could hope to be treated as a full-fledged American citizen as long as the White House, Congress, and the overwhelming majority of the city's white residents looked upon him as a creature apart and inferior.

That state of affairs underwent little change under President Coolidge. . . .

Had the ratio of Negro to white inhabitants risen sharply during and after the war, the tightening of segregation in Washington might be easier to explain. Between 1910 and 1920 Chicago's and Detroit's colored populations had grown respectively nearly seven and six times as fast as their white, and the change had been only less pronounced in four or five other Northern cities. All of them confronted an unfamiliar social and economic problem. For Washington a large Negro population was no novelty. Here, moreover, the proportion of Negroes to white had dropped since 1910 and, with the exception of 1920, the 27.1 per cent of 1930 was below the figure shown in any census since the Civil War. White fears of being swamped in a black metropolis therefore had little validity. Possibly Negroes' slightly improved economic position threatened to lessen the supply of cheap domestic and unskilled labor and, by enlarging the Negro middle class, to jeopardize the social status of lower-class whites. Whatever the reason, whites chose to build an invisible wall about all colored Washington and then strove to forget about what a contributor to *Crisis* called the Secret City. Its inhabitants unexpectedly gained two infinitesimal advantages from his sedulous ignoring—a slight decline in white bullying and an accompanying reduction of newspaper talk about Negro crime.

At the end of 1926 the *Tribune,* by then Washington's principal colored paper, declared that segregation had "grown to the dimensions of a national policy." It was in full force in the government departments, and "it remains only to observe that the Negroes themselves have about reached the stage of acquiescence in the practice." Colored civil service employees, fearful of losing their jobs, refused to lodge complaints, leaving NAACP officials without provable grounds for protest. The major gratification the colored intelligentsia had that year was the Howard University trustees' selection of a Negro president, Mordecai Johnson. What had begun as a biracial institution had long ago become wholly Negro. . . .

In the eyes of Washington's upper-class Negroes a peculiarly invidious new restriction on their liberties had only recently received the blessing of the Supreme Court when a ruling of 1926 upheld the legality of voluntary covenants among white property-owners aimed at preventing Negroes from purchasing or occupying houses in white neighborhoods. The battle against restrictive municipal ordinances had been won before the war in a case originating in Baltimore; now voluntary compacts seemingly negated that victory and threatened to confine all Negroes in the capital to a true ghetto. Whites endorsing the covenants displayed as much passion as the Negroes who sought to halt them. . . .

While most of what colored Washington underwent in these years of near despair was forced upon it by white laws, white bigotry, or white thoughtlessness and stupidity, citizens of the Secret City themselves determined part of their fate, bad and good. The jealousies and quarrels that had splintered the community before 1915 again took command. If the fight against the housing covenants created a measure of unity, it did not reach down to families whose poverty precluded their trying to live in comfortable white neighborhoods. Certainly Washington's high yellow society did not recapture its wartime zeal to "close ranks" with its social inferiors. On the contrary, civic-minded Negroes encountered among their educated fellows the same kind of indifference to the welfare of the black masses as public-spirited white people met with in high white society. Altruism did not flourish in the "Age of the Golden Calf."

The Washington NAACP was no longer powerful. Some Negroes thought it too radical, others too conservative and too prone to appease; a good many gave it no thought at all. With a few rare exceptions, young men upon whom leadership might logically have fallen lacked the will or had lost faith in their capacity to win a respected place for their people. Negro real estate brokers and firms building Negro apartment houses made some money, and the National Life Insurance Company with three hundred employees in its home office on U Street paid a 10 per cent dividend in 1928, but confidence in other Negro enterprises waned. When a Harvard graduate after a distinguished but heartbreaking career in the AEF became a convert to the necessity of never-ending Negro militance, he started the Washington *Daily American,* the second Negro daily in the United States; despite its excellence, the paper was unable to get enough advertising to survive. The *Tribune* absorbed it. Between the lines of newspaper exhortations to "buy Negro," give to Negro charities, and build up a self-sufficient community ran hints that calls for racial solidarity fell on deaf ears.

Upper-class families, tired of making common cause with needy blacks, washed their hands of every group but their own. Lightness of color was necessarily a bond, for where light-skinned people could move about in a white world with some freedom, the acceptance of a dark-skinned person into the group circumscribed the activities of all. It was a fact of life white people never had to face. Whites prone to think Negro social distinctions absurd lost sight of the obvious truth that the cultivated Negro had no more in common with the lower-class black than the white society leader with the white ditchdigger. The creed of the high yellow elite ran: let the uninformed masses applaud Marcus Garvey, "the Black Moses," or gather adoringly about "Papa Divine." Let the vulgar loaf on 7th Street, that "bastard of Prohibition and the War," where, sang Jean Toomer,

Money burns the pocket, pocket hurts,
Bootleggers in silken shirts,
Ballooned, zooming Cadillacs,
Whizzing, whizzing down the streetcar tracks. . . .

At the end of the 1920s Langston Hughes, grandson of colored Washington's idol of the 1870s and 1880s, lashed out at the city's high yellow elite. Poems sketching the porter "climbing a great big mountain of Yes Sirs," the "Black Gal" crying "I hate them rinney yaller gals," and the "loud laughers in the hand of Fate" had won him some literary fame, but the disregard of his Washington neighbors angered him. They overlooked talent; they objected to Jean Toomer's *Cane* and Rudolph Fisher's *City of Refuge* because the main characters in both books were so "black." Many of the "best people" were newly rich, and many were not cultured at all. A true picture would reveal their "pseudoculture, their slavish devotion to Nordic standards, their snobbishness, their detachment from the Negro masses and their vast sense of importance to themselves."

Other gifted young men also found the atmosphere surrounding "the best people" stifling. As the "Harlem Renaissance" gained momentum about 1925, writers and musicians aspired to leave Washington for New York, where they would not be throttled by the dead hand of a past, imagined or real. If relatively few followed the example of a Jean Toomer, a Duke Ellington, and a Louis Armstrong in making names for themselves in the North, and more felt obliged simply to forget their artistic ambitions, by the mid-1920's Washington had nevertheless lost most of the attraction she had once held for the creative Negro. Unlike Harlem, the Secret City remained "undiscovered" by the rest of the world, partly because there was less talent to discover here. Thirty years later the city had still not recaptured the prestige she had commanded in the colored world at the turn of the century. Howard University drew exceptionally able students in law, medicine, and sociology, and colored scholars in many fields were glad to teach at this, one of the two or three institutions of higher learning that could offer them chances of professional advancement. Men of the caliber of Kelly Miller, the young economist Abram Harris, the eloquent Alain Locke, apostle of the "New Negro," and Ralph Bunche, in 1928 starting the university's first political science courses, lent the faculty distinction. But undergraduates entering from high schools outside the District all too often received from classmates native to Washington the same kind of patronizing treatment as cave-dwelling parents accorded older outsiders. . . .

Where white people placed in the circumstances surrounding colored Washington might have either soon sunk into sullen despair or resorted to open warfare, Negroes managed to find pleasure in their own society, mutual jealousies and envy notwithstanding. With their gift for laughter, they got genuine amusement out of the antics of the complacent white—his stiff-jointed contortions, for example, in trying to master the rhythms of the Charleston, that import from Cat Fish Alley, or his manifest expectation of a cordial welcome of a Sunday when he visited a revivalist colored church in order to be entertained by the breast-beating and hallelujahs of repenting sinners. While crap games and evenings in a black speakeasy offset some of the frustrations of "low-life" Negroes, people further up the economic and social ladder turned to music and dancing for recreation. Jazz bands, in demand for white debutante balls, generally played with greater abandon and artistry in the colored dance halls. Certainly Washington's "reputation for syncopation" did not stem from whites. Music, in fact, whether popular, classical, or spiritual, was a cultural bond in the Secret City. The passerby might hear as much singing and merrymaking in a Negro neighborhood as in the purlieus of the most affluent and carefree whites.

Yet every Negro in the District of Columbia felt hemmed in. The pattern of the late 1920s closely resembled that of the years following the collapse of Reconstruction, but this time disillusionment bit deeper and carried a kind of dreadful finality. In the 1880s and 1890s the federal government still offered colored people chances in Washington. Indeed they pinned their future on political preferment until the Wilson administration knocked that prop out from under them. Thereupon anger, abetted by the indignation of white liberals, had pumped adrenalin into the colored community creating a solidarity that promised to produce noteworthy results. Patriotism and patience during and after the war for a time had held out further prospects which survived even a race riot. Then piece by piece the edifice of hope had crumbled. The national government took the line of the Deep South, and white people as private persons

now looked upon Negroes scarcely as citizens at all. Negro en-
deavors to break into Washington's business world had largely
failed. Skilled Negro craftsmen had found themselves nosed out of
job after job and occupation after occupation until their skills had
all but atrophied. The higher a Negro's place in the colored social
hierarchy the more pronounced his resentment at banging his head
on the underside of the lid that ceiled him in. Better no doubt to
be at the top than farther down within the caste, but was the difference in elevation worth much, where head space was at best so
cramped? The courage that had enabled men of fortitude to rise
above the bitter defeats of a generation before and undertake a
second assault on the bastion of prejudice now appeared to have
exhausted itself. Hope deferred maketh the heart sick. Hope
annihilated meant the death of every ambition.

E. Franklin Frazier

SOME EFFECTS OF THE DEPRESSION ON THE NEGRO IN NORTHERN CITIES

E. Franklin Frazier (1894–1962) was a major American sociologist whose studies on the black family and race relations have provided points of departure for further study. Frazier spent most of his adult life at Howard University, graduating in 1916 and returning to teach there in 1932, after taking a Ph.D. at the University of Chicago. At Chicago Frazier came under the influence of the great men in sociology: Robert E. Park, Ernest W. Burgess, Louis Wirth. Later, because of his own work, he became one of the great men of his field. His major works include The Negro Family in the United States *(1939) and* Black Bourgeoisie *(1957). In these and other works Frazier analyzed the effects of increasing urbanization on the black family. He believed that the isolation of the black American produced serious flaws in his institutions and affected his own self-conception. The isolation of blacks increased with urbanization. Urbanization produced the ghetto which, according to Frazier, was a pathological phenomenon. Frazier argued that the only hope for blacks was full integration, but an integration based on a sense of racial identity. In this article, written in 1938, Frazier discusses not only the effects of the depression on blacks in general but also on the middle class in particular.*

Since the migration of thousands of Negroes to the metropolitan areas of the North during and following the World War, there has been a growing tendency to view the problems of the Negro in relationship to the dominant social and economic currents in American life. As an example of this shift in viewpoint, one might mention Professor Frank A. Ross's study of the urbanization of the Negro population which views the cityward movement of the Negro as a part of the whole process of urbanization in America. Viewed from this standpoint, the Negro migrations to northern industrial centers are seen in their relation to changes in southern agriculture and the cessation of European immigration coupled with a demand for cheap unskilled labor. Consequently, it was not by accident, but because of certain fundamental economic forces in American life

From E. Franklin Frazier, "Some Effects of the Depression on the Negro in Northern Cities," *Science and Society*, II (Fall, 1938), pp. 489–499. (Originally a paper read before the annual meeting of the Eastern Sociological Society, Vassar College, April 16, 1938.) Reprinted by permission of *Science and Society*.

that New York, Chicago, Philadelphia, and Detroit became the chief goals of the migrating black masses. Within the metropolitan districts of these four cities, there were, in 1930, 1,185,530 Negroes or about a half of the entire Negro population in the North. The remainder of the Negro population in the North, excluding less than 300,000 rural dwellers, was concentrated in smaller industrial centers where there was a demand for cheap labor. The social consequences of the shift of these peasant folk to the industrial centers of the North has been the subject of a vast literature. But concerning the effects of the depression on these newcomers to modern industrial society very little systematic information is available. In this paper, an attempt will be made to bring together and interpret the available information which we have been able to secure from various sources.

Concerning the volume of unemployment and relief in the Negro population in northern cities, our information is about as reliable as that for the whites. In fourteen of the sixteen northern and western cities included in the unemployment census of 1931, the percentage of Negroes unemployed was higher than that of either native or foreign-born whites. This was true for women as well as men. For example, in Chicago, 40.3 per cent of the employable Negro men and 55.4 of the women were reported unemployed, whereas only 24.6 per cent of the foreign-born white men and 12.0 per cent of the foreign-born white women; and 23.4 per cent of the native white men and 16.9 per cent of native white women were reported unemployed. Klein, in his recent survey of Pittsburgh, reported that in February 1934, "48 per cent of the employable Negroes were entirely without employment . . . while only 31.1 per cent of the potential white workers were unemployed." That this situation was generally true in regard to Negro women was indicated in a study of fluctuations in the employment of women from 1928 to 1931 in Bridgeport, Buffalo, Syracuse, and Philadelphia. According to this study, "the proportion of Negro women unemployed ordinarily was greater than their share in the total woman population or among those in gainful employment."

Although there is a rather general but uncritical acceptance of the belief that the "Negro is the last to be hired and the first to be fired," it is difficult to make any generalization concerning practices during the depression in northern cities. In a paper read before the Conference on the Economic Status of the Negro held in Washington, D.C., in May 1933, it was reported that in the meat packing industry, "Reductions in the working force due to the depression have in general left these Negro workers in relatively larger proportions than other workers." On the other hand, Dr. Joseph H. Willits of the University of Pennsylvania, in a study of unemployment among several groups in Philadelphia, found the following situation during the years 1929 to 1933. "In 1929 when 9.0 per cent of all white employables were unemployed, 15.7 per cent of the Negroes were unemployed. In 1930 it was 13.8 per cent for whites and 19.4 per cent for Negroes; in 1931 it was 24.1 per cent for whites and 35.0 per cent for Negroes; and in 1932 it was 39.7 per cent for whites and 56.0 per cent for Negroes." It is likely that these figures are typical of northern cities since the vast majority of Negro workers are employed on jobs which are generally susceptible to fluctuations in industry.

We are on much surer ground when we consider the incidence of relief. When the unemployment relief census was taken in 1933, there was in New York, Chicago, Philadelphia, and Detroit, a total of 78,027 Negro families on relief or 32.5 per cent of the Negro families in these four cities. Measured in terms of population, New York with 23.9 per cent and Detroit with 27.6 per cent had smaller percentages of Negroes on relief than Chicago and Philadelphia in each of which cities 34 per cent of the Negro population was on relief. The situation was even worse in Pittsburgh and Cleveland each with 43 per cent and Akron, Ohio, with 67 per cent of the Negro population on relief. After the census of 1933 was taken, the situation in these cities undoubtedly became worse. For example, by February 1935, "practically three out of every five Negroes in Allegheny County," where Pittsburgh is located, were on the relief rolls. A study of the situation in the Harlem area of New York City in 1935 revealed that 24,293 or 43.2 per cent of 56,157 Negro families were receiving relief. In addition to these relief families, 7,560 unattached Negro men had registered with the Emergency Relief Bureau over a period of four years.

There is good reason for believing that as the depression lifted momentarily, Negroes were not reabsorbed into industry to the same extent as white workers. According to a report of the FERA on Baltimore, Bridgeport, Connecticut, Chicago, Detroit, Omaha, St. Louis, Mo., and Paterson, N.J., as late as May 1935, Negroes were "being added to the relief population in greater proportions of total intake than they existed in the general population (1930 Census)." The report ventured the explanation that it reflected in part "a tendency for employers to favor unemployed white persons as compared with Negro workers." In Pittsburgh, two of the largest employers of Negroes in the steel industry who claimed that they had brought hundreds of Negroes north would not guarantee the reemployment of Negroes because, in their opinion, Negro workers had been demoralized by relief and had become radical. Although there is some evidence that Negroes have been displaced by white workers in northern cities, the question has not been studied systematically. The 1930 census indicated that for the country as a whole the Negro was being pushed back into domestic and personal service. However, in an analysis of the occupational statistics for individual cities, it was found that this was true in southern rather than in northern cities. But, it appears from statistics on relief that Negro domestic workers in northern cities have become unemployed as the depression has become worse. In New York State, there were 26,359 unemployed Negro domestic workers on relief in 1935.

Negro workers who have not lost their jobs have suffered a reduction in earning power. In Kiser's study of 2,061 Negro households in a section of Harlem in New York City, it was found that the median income of skilled workers had declined from $1,955 in 1929 to $1,003 in 1932 or 48.7 per cent. The decline in the incomes of semi-skilled and unskilled workers was slightly less or 43 per cent. This study also gave information on the effect of the depression on the earning power of the Negro middle class which had rapidly emerged in response to the varied demands of large Negro communities in northern cities. It was found that among the white collar workers, who comprised 16 per cent of the households studied, "the income decreases were 35 per cent in the professional class, 44 per cent in the proprietary class and 37 per cent among clerical and kindred workers." First hand observations and reports of college students indicate that this was representative of the Negro middle class throughout the North. Their savings and incomes, and investments from business, which gave this class a favored position in the Negro community, were largely wiped out and even Negro doctors were forced to seek relief.

Concerning the effects of the depression upon the Negro family in the northern city, the void in our knowledge is not illumined even by one shining exception such as Cavan and Ranck have provided in their study of one hundred white families. However, it appears that among Negroes, just as these authors found among white families, "well organized families met the depression with less catastrophic consequences than families that were already disorganized." That this was true of upper-class Negro families was revealed in the documents furnished by college students who come from the more stabilized elements in the Negro population. Although in many cases, savings were lost or consumed, homes were mortgaged or lost, and the children had to delay their college education for one to three years, these families maintained their solidarity and by pooling their resources were able to achieve some of their major family objectives. But since family disorganization among the masses has been one of the main problems resulting from the migration of the Negro to the northern city, it is not unreasonable to assume that family disorganization increased as a result of the depression. First, among the consequences of reduction or loss of income was the seeking of cheaper living quarters or the crowding of families and relatives in a single household. We have a record of a case of mass housing in Chicago, where 67 families were permitted to move into an old apartment building that had been partially destroyed by fire and was without heat and light. For heat, they used coal stoves such as are used in the rural districts, and for light, they burned kerosene lamps. The owners of the building operated the house through a committee of Negroes and collected rents from those families who were able to pay. In some cases, the men in the families made payments in terms of various services. Although thousands of Negro families in northern cities, who had constantly lived close to the margin of existence, had been crowded into slum areas, the depression made their condition worse and reduced thousands of others to their level. An analysis of deserted "under care" families of the Charity Organization Society of New York City revealed that the number of families with one or more relatives had increased significantly during the depression. Although even under normal conditions from 10 to 30 per cent of Negro families in northern cities have women heads, it is probable that the number increased during the depression. Among the relief families in Chicago, Detroit, New York, and Philadelphia, we find that only from 29 per cent (in Chicago) to 50 per cent (in New York City), were normal family groups; i.e., man, wife, and children. Among the relief families in these same cities, a fifth to a fourth of the families had a woman head. Moreover, it is also significant that a relatively larger number of Negro dependents than white dependents were unattached women. It is because of this fact that the FERA views the rehabilitation of Negroes as less a problem of the aged than a problem of female dependency often involving children. . . .

We turn, finally, to those changes in the Negro's philosophy and outlook on life which may reasonably be attributed to the depression. First, among these changes, one might mention the disillusionment of the Negro middle class. Probably no section of the middle class in America had such high hopes as the Negro middle class during the years of prosperity. Their dream of reaping the rewards of individual thrift and foresight which had had only a partial fulfillment in the South seemed to have come true in the northern city. The Negro professional and business man had prospered upon the earnings of the black masses in northern cities. Moreover, the political power of the Negro had opened the way to political patronage and the civil service held out a substantial living for many educated Negroes. Then, suddenly, the purchasing power and savings of the masses began to melt. Doctors' and lawyers' fees dwindled and finally ceased, and the hothouse growth of Negro business behind the walls of segregation shrivelled and died, often swallowing up the savings of the black masses. Fine homes and cars and other forms of conspicuous consumption were given up. In their disillusionment, some of the very professional men in New York who had laughed at the small group of radical intellectuals now formed a class to study Marx. But disillusionment did not breed radicalism among a very large group. It appears that more often, they turned to racial chauvinism as a way of realizing their dreams. In Chicago, those of the middle class who had laughed at Garvey's grandiose ideas of a back to Africa movement began to talk of a Forty-ninth State which according to their specifications would be a Black Utopia where the black middle class could exploit the black workers without white competition. In New York City, small Negro business men pointed to the Jewish merchant as the cause of their failures and began to demand that Harlem be reserved as their field of exploitation.

Closely associated with the chauvinistic aims of many members of the middle class have been the efforts of Negroes in a number of northern cities to organize cooperatives as a solution of the Negro's economic problems. However, little or no success has attended these efforts which tended in some instances to nurture if not encourage racial chauvinism. Another movement of greater significance so far as it reflects the growth of militancy directed toward immediate economic ends, has been the picketing and boycotting of stores in order to enforce the employment of Negro workers, usually as clerks. In Columbus, Ohio, the Housewives League assumed the leadership in this movement. Although in some cities white storekeepers have made concessions to the demands of the Negroes, they secured relief for a time through court injunctions. But the recent ruling of the United States Supreme Court on a case in the District of Columbia has removed legal barriers against this type of picketing. Inasmuch as the demands for employment in stores where Negroes were the chief customers involved the employment of Negroes as clerks and salesmen, it implied a demand for status, which redounded also to the economic advantage of the middle class.

Although the middle class Negro intellectuals and business men tried to arouse the Negro masses to support their chauvinistic aims, the militancy of the Negro masses did not flow in a single channel. Much of the militancy was unorganized and without an ideology. There were rent strikes to force lowering of rentals. When tenants were evicted for non-payment of rent, crowds often gathered and returned the belongings of the evicted family to the house. In one of these battles in Chicago, several were killed. It has often been charged that white radicals were responsible for the militancy on the part of the Negroes. It seems nearer to the truth to say that white radicals attempted to give direction to these more or less spontaneous outbursts and to provide Negroes with the ideology of the class struggle. This was undoubtedly true of the spontaneous outburst in Harlem in March 1935. This riot, which began during a time of severe economic stress and when there was much complaint against the Home Relief Bureau, flared up when a flimsy rumor was circulated that a boy had been murdered in a five and ten cent store for stealing a pocket knife. Although the riot at first had a racial character, under the stimulation, if not the direction of white radicals, it became a riot against property rather than persons. The influence of radical white leadership was probably most effective in the various unemployed councils in which Negroes participated on a basis of equality. Perhaps, one of the chief effects of the depression in northern cities upon the thinking of the Negro has been the spread of radical ideas among working class Negroes through cooperation with white workers. Probably at no time in the past have the Negro masses had so many white allies as in their present struggle for work and relief. This newly developed sympathy and cooperation between the two races has even extended to white collar workers especially in the relief agencies.

In summing up the effects of the depression on the Negro in northern cities, one can say, first, that the depression has laid bare the general economic insecurity of the Negro masses. It has tended to destroy the high hopes that were kindled during the War period when it appeared that the Negro, though at the bottom of the industrial ladder, had secured a firm foothold in the industries of the North. From a position of increased earning power, unequalled during his career in America, the Negro has become the ward of the community with from a third to a half of his numbers dependent upon relief. His family life, which had been shattered by the impact of the modern metropolis upon his simple folk life, had scarcely had time to recover and reorganize itself before the shock of the depression shattered it once again. The struggle for survival, always precarious and in doubt became even more uncertain, though relief has probably enabled children to survive who otherwise would have died. Naturally, the crisis produced a tremendous change in the Negro's evaluation of his position in American life. Many conflicting currents of thought were set in motion. Though the fatuous philosophy of racial chauvinism supported by a segregated black economy, advocated by many of the middle class, did not succeed in winning the masses, they, as a whole, have not accepted a radical definition of their problems. But, at least, it seems certain that the Negro in the northern city with his back to the wall and cut off from retreat because of the collapse of southern agriculture will fight rather than starve and that he has found allies among whites, especially those who find themselves in similar circumstances.

Ralph Ellison

RIOT

Ralph Ellison's Invisible Man *is thought by many to be the finest novel ever written by a black writer in America. Ellison, born in Oklahoma, and educated at Tuskegee, left home at the end of his junior year to seek his fame in New York City. An accomplished musician, an artist as well as a writer, he showed himself worthy of the fame he sought. Through his friendship with Richard Wright and other black writers he became involved in radical politics. After losing interest in politics in 1943, Ellison began work on* Invisible Man, *which took him until the early fifties to finish. In the novel Ellison attempts to incorporate the myth and literature of the western world into the experience of the black American. Being influenced by Dostoevsky, James, Melville, Eliot, Faulkner, and Wright, Ellison produced one of the best novels of the twentieth century. The novel is a surrealistic presentation of the odyssey of a southern black to the city and his search for identity. In the following selection, Ellison portrays the fury of a violent riot in Harlem during the Depression. Ellison's description of the riot is a fitting epitaph to the disappearance of the "promised land." It also is a prophetic description of the black rage of the sixties.*

The crowd was working in and out of the stores like ants around spilled sugar. From time to time there came the crash of glass, shots; fire trucks in distant streets.

"How you feel?" the man said.

"Still fuzzy," I said, "and weak."

"Le's see if it's stopped bleeding. Yeah, you'll be all right."

I saw him vaguely though his voice came clear.

"Sure," I said.

"Man, you lucky you ain't dead. These sonsabitches is really shooting now," he said. "Over on Lenox they was aiming up in the air. If I could find me a rifle, I'd show 'em! Here, take you a drink of this good scotch," he said, taking a quart bottle from a hip pocket. "I got me a whole case stashed what I got from a liquor store over there. Over there all you got to do is breathe, and you drunk, man. Drunk! Hundred proof bonded whiskey flowing all in the gutters."

I took a drink, shuddering as the whiskey went down but thankful for the shock it gave me. There was a bursting, tearing movement of people around me, dark figures in a blue glow.

"Look at them take it away," he said, looking into the dark action of the crowd. "Me, I'm tired. Was you over on Lenox?"

"No," I said, seeing a woman moving slowly past with a row of about a dozen dressed chickens suspended by their necks from the handle of a new straw broom . . .

"Hell, you ought to see it, man. Everything is tore up. By now the womens is picking it clean. I saw one ole woman with a whole side of a cow on her back. Man, she was 'bout bent bowlegged trying to make it home—Here come Dupre now," he said, breaking off.

I saw a little hard man come out of the crowd carrying several boxes. He wore three hats upon his head, and several pairs of suspenders flopped about his shoulders, and now as he came toward us I saw that he wore a pair of gleaming new rubber hip boots. His pockets bulged and over his shoulder he carried a cloth sack that swung heavily behind him.

"Damn, Dupre," my friend said, pointing to his head, "you got one of them for me? What kind is they?"

Dupre stopped and looked at him. "With all them hats in there and I'm going to come out with anything but a *Dobbs?* Man, are you *mad?* All them new, pretty—colored *Dobbs?* Come on, let's get going before the cops git back. Damn, look at that thing blaze!"

I looked toward the curtain of blue fire, through which vague figures toiled. Dupre called out and several men left the crowd and joined us in the street. We moved off, my friend (Scofield, the others called him) leading me along. My head throbbed, still bled. . . .

"How did all this get started?" I said.

Scofield seemed surprised. "Damn if I know, man. A cop shot a woman or something."

Another man moved close to us as somewhere a piece of heavy steel rang down.

"Hell, that wasn't what started it," he said. "It was that fellow, what's his name . . . ?"

"Who?" I said. "What's his name?"

"That young guy!"

"You know, everybody's mad about it . . ."

Clifton, I thought. It's for Clifton. A night for Clifton.

"Aw man, don't tell me," Scofield said. "Didn't I see it with my own eyes? About eight o'clock down on Lenox and 123rd this paddy slapped a kid for grabbing a Baby Ruth and the kid's mama took it up and then the paddy slapped her and that's when hell broke loose."

"You were there?" I said.

"Same's I'm here. Some fellow said the kid made the paddy mad by grabbing a candy named after a white woman."

"Damn if that's the way I heard it," another man said. "When I come up they said a white woman set it off by trying to take a black gal's man."

"Damn *who* started it," Dupre said. "All I want is for it to last a while."

"It was a white gal, all right, but that wasn't the way it was. She was drunk—" another voice said.

But it couldn't have been Sybil, I thought; it had already started.

"You wahn know who started it?" A man holding a pair of binoculars called from the window of a pawnshop. "You wahn really to know?"

"Sure," I said.

"Well, you don't need to go no further. It was started by that great leader, Ras the Destroyer!"

"That monkey-chaser?" someone said.

"Listen, bahstard!"

"Don't nobody know how it started," Dupre said.

"Somebody has to know," I said.

Scofield held his whiskey toward me. I refused it.

"Hell, man, it just exploded. These is dog days," he said.

"*Dog* days?"

"Sho, this hot weather."

"I tell you they mad over what happen to that young fellow, what's-his-name . . ."

We were passing a building now and I heard a voice calling frantically, "Colored store! Colored store!"

"Then put up a sign, motherfouler," a voice said. "You probably rotten as the others."

"Listen at the bastard. For one time in his life he's glad to be colored," Scofield said.

"Colored store," the voice went on automatically.

"Hey! You sho you ain't got some white blood?"

"No, *sir!*" the voice said.

"Should I bust him, man?"

"For what? He ain't got a damn thing. Let the motherfouler alone."

A few doors away we came to a hardware store. "This is the first stop, men," Dupre said.

"What happens now?" I said.

"Who you?" he said, cocking his thrice-hatted head.

"Nobody, just one of the boys—" I began.

"You sho you ain't somebody I know?"

"I'm pretty sure," I said.

"He's all right, Du," said Scofield. "Them cops shot him."

Dupre looked at me and kicked something—a pound of butter, sending it smearing across the hot street. "We fixing to do something what needs to be done," he said. "First we gets a flashlight for everybody . . . And let's have some organization, y'all. Don't everybody be running over everybody else. Come on!"

"Come on in, buddy," Scofield said.

I felt no need to lead or leave them; was glad to follow; was gripped by a need to see where and to what they would lead. And all the time the thought that I should go to the district was with me. We went inside the store, into the dark glinting with metal. They moved carefully, and I could hear them searching, sweeping objects to the floor. The cash register rang.

"Here some flashlights over here," someone called.

"How many?" Dupre said.

"Plenty, man."

"Okay, pass out one to everybody. They got batteries?"

"Naw, but there's plenty them too, 'bout a dozen boxes."

"Okay, give me one with batteries so I can find the buckets. Then every man get him a light."

"Here some buckets over here," Scofield said.

"Then all we got to find is where he keeps the oil."

"Oil?" I said.

"Coal oil, man. And hey, y'all," he called, "don't nobody be smoking in here."

I stood beside Scofield listening to the noise as he took a stack of zinc buckets and passed them out. Now the store leaped alive with flashing lights and flickering shadows.

"Keep them lights down on the floor," Dupre called. "No use letting folks see who we are. Now when you get your buckets line up and let me fill 'em."

"Listen to ole Du lay it down—he's a bitch, ain't he, buddy? He always liked to lead things. And always leading me into trouble."

"What are we getting ready to do?" I said.

"You'll see," Dupre said. "Hey, you over there. Come on from behind that counter and take this bucket. Don't you see ain't nothing in that cash register, that if it was I'd have it myself?"

Suddenly the banging of buckets ceased. We moved into the back room. By the light of a flash I could see a row of fuel drums mounted on racks. Dupre stood before them in his new hip boots and filled each bucket with oil. We moved in slow order. Our buckets filled, we filed out into the street. I stood there in the dark feeling a rising excitement as their voices played around me. What was the meaning of it all? What should I think of it, *do* about it?

"With this stuff," Dupre said, "we better walk in the middle of the street. It's just down around the corner."

Then as we moved off a group of boys ran among us and the men started using their lights, revealing darting figures in blonde wigs, the tails of their stolen dress coats flying. Behind them in hot pursuit came a gang armed with dummy rifles taken from an Army & Navy Store. I laughed with the others, thinking: A holy holiday for Clifton.

"Put out them lights!" Dupre commanded.

Behind us came the sound of screams, laughter; ahead the footfalls of the running boys, distant fire trucks, shooting, and in the quiet intervals, the steady filtering of shattered glass. I could smell the kerosene as it sloshed from the buckets and slapped against the street. . . .

Scofield touched my arm. "Here we is," he said.

We had come to a huge tenement building.

"Where are we?" I said.

This the place where most of us live," he said. "Come on."

So that was it, the meaning of the kerosene. I couldn't believe it, couldn't believe they had the nerve. All the windows seemed empty. They'd blacked it out themselves. I saw now only by flash or flame.

"Where will you live?" I said, looking up, up.

"You call *this* living?" Scofield said. "It's the only way to git rid of it, man . . ."

I looked for hesitation in their vague forms. They stood looking at the building rising above us, the liquid dark of the oil simmering dully in the stray flecks of light that struck their pails, bent forward, their shoulders bowed. None said "no," by word or stance. And in the dark windows and on the roofs above I could now discern the forms of women and children.

Dupre moved toward the building.

"Now look ahere, y'all," he said, his triple-hatted head showing grotesquely atop the stoop. "I wants all the women and chillun and the old and the sick folks brought out. And when you takes your buckets up the stairs I wants you to go clean to the top. I mean the *top!* And when you git there I want you to start using your flash-lights in every room to make sure nobody gits left behind, then when you git 'em out start splashing coal oil. Then when you git it splashed I'm going to holler, and when I holler three times I want you to light them matches and git. After that it's every tub on its own black bottom!"

It didn't occur to me to interfere, or to question . . . They had a plan. Already I could see the women and children coming down the steps. A child was crying. And suddenly everyone paused, turning, looking off into the dark. Somewhere nearby an incongruous sound shook the dark, an air hammer pounding like a machine gun. They paused with the sensitivity of grazing deer, then returned to their work, the women and children once more moving.

"That's right, y'all. You ladies move on up the street to the folks you going to stay with," Dupre said. "And keep holt them kids!"

Someone pounded my back and I swung around, seeing a woman push past me and climb up to catch Dupre's arm, their two figures seeming to blend as her voice arose, thin, vibrant and desperate.

"Please, Dupre," she said, *"please.* You know my time's almost here . . . you *know* it is. If you do it now, where am I going to go?"

Dupre pulled away and rose to a higher step. He looked down at her, shaking his thrice-hatted head. "Now git on out the way, Lottie," he said patiently. "Why you have to start this now? We done been all over it and you know I ain't go'n change. And lissen here, the resta y'all," he said, reaching into the top of his hip boot and producing a nickel-plated revolver and waving it around, "don't think they's going to be any *mind*-changing either. And I don't aim for no arguments neither."

"You goddam right, Dupre. We wid you!"

"My kid died from the t-bees in that deathtrap, but I bet a man ain't no more go'n be *born* in there," he said. "So now, Lottie, you go on up the street and let us mens git going." . . .

IV THE IMPACT OF THE GHETTO

Daniel P. Moynihan
THE NEGRO FAMILY

The Negro Family: The Case for National Action, *written as a private report by Daniel P. Moynihan for the purpose of arousing discussion within the government, became a public document touching off heated controversy throughout the nation. When the controversy over this report is combined with other events in 1965 and 1966, a new era begins in the history of race relations in the United States. Daniel P. Moynihan, Assistant Secretary of Labor in 1965, believed that a point had been reached in the civil rights movement. The government had done virtually all that it could in removing barriers to black liberty, but had done little in bringing about equality. He felt that it was impossible for a great majority of blacks to take advantage of the new opportunities. In the report Moynihan expresses deep concern over the continued deterioration of the black family at a time when there was prosperity and nearly full employment. The socioeconomic system of the past and present created, according to Moynihan, "the tangle of pathology" in the black community. Relying heavily upon the work of E. Franklin Frazier and Kenneth B. Clark, he argues that a vicious circle operates in the ghetto. Unemployed black men fail as husbands and fathers, forcing families to break up and women to work, allowing the children to fall into the patterns established by the parents. He calls for a national effort to break the pathology of the black family structure. However, by focusing only on family pathology, Moynihan aroused the ire of not only civil rights spokesmen but also many within the government as well.*

At the heart of the deterioration of the fabric of Negro society is the deterioration of the Negro family.

It is the fundamental source of the weakness of the Negro community at the present time.

There is probably no single fact of Negro American life so little understood by whites. The Negro situation is commonly perceived by whites in terms of the visible manifestations of discrimination and poverty, in part because Negro protest is directed against such obstacles, and in part, no doubt, because these are facts which involve the actions and attitudes of the white community as well. It is more difficult, however, for whites to perceive the effect that three centuries of exploitation have had on the fabric of Negro society itself.

From Office of Policy Planning and Research, United States Department of Labor, *The Negro Family: The Case for National Action* (Washington, D.C., 1965).

Here the consequences of the historic injustices done to Negro Americans are silent and hidden from view. But here is where the true injury has occurred: unless this damage is repaired, all the effort to end discrimination and poverty and injustice will come to little.

The role of the family in shaping character and ability is so pervasive as to be easily overlooked. The family is the basic social unit of American life; it is the basic socializing unit. By and large, adult conduct in society is learned as a child.

A fundamental insight of psychoanalytic theory, for example, is that the child learns a way of looking at life in his early years through which all later experience is viewed and which profoundly shapes his adult conduct.

It may be hazarded that the reason family structure does not loom larger in public discussion of social issues is that people tend to assume that the nature of family life is about the same throughout American society. The mass media and the development of suburbia have created an image of the American family as a highly standardized phenomenon. It is therefore easy to assume that whatever it is that makes for differences among individuals or groups of individuals, it is not a different family structure.

There is much truth to this; as with any other nation, Americans are producing a recognizable family system. But that process is not completed by any means. There are still, for example, important differences in family patterns surviving from the age of the great European migration to the United States, and these variations account for notable differences in the progress and assimilation of various ethnic and religious groups. A number of immigrant groups were characterized by unusually strong family bonds; these groups have characteristically progressed more rapidly than others.

But there is one truly great discontinuity in family structure in the United States at the present time: that between the white world in general and that of the Negro American.

The white family has achieved a high degree of stability and is maintaining that stability. . . .

There is considerable evidence that the Negro community is in fact dividing between a stable middle-class group that is steadily growing stronger and more successful, and an increasingly disorganized and disadvantaged lower-class group. There are indications, for example, that the middle-class Negro family puts a higher premium on family stability and the conserving of family resources than does the white middle-class family. The discussion of this paper is not, obviously, directed to the first group excepting as it is affected by the experiences of the second—an important exception.

There are two points to be noted in this context.

First, the emergence and increasing visibility of a Negro middle-class may beguile the nation into supposing that the circumstances of the remainder of the Negro community are equally prosperous, whereas just the opposite is true at present, and is likely to continue so.

Second, the lumping of all Negroes together in one statistical measurement very probably conceals the extent of the disorganization among the lower-class group. If conditions are improving for one and deteriorating for the other, the resultant statistical averages might show no change. Further, the statistics on the Negro family and most other subjects treated in this paper refer only to a specific point in time. They are a vertical measure of the situation at a given moment. They do not measure the experience of individuals over time. Thus the average monthly unemployment rate for Negro males for 1964 is recorded as 9 per cent. But *during* 1964, some 29 per cent of Negro males were unemployed at one time or another. Similarly, for example, if 36 per cent of Negro children are living in broken homes *at any specific moment*, it is likely that a far higher proportion of Negro children find themselves in that situation *at one time or another* in their lives.

Nearly a quarter of Negro women living in cities who have ever married are divorced, separated, or are living apart from their husbands.

The rates are highest in the urban Northeast where 26 per cent of Negro women ever married are either divorced, separated, or have their husbands absent.

On the urban frontier, the proportion of husbands absent is even higher. In New York City in 1960, it was 30.2 per cent, *not* including divorces.

Both white and Negro illegitimacy rates have been increasing, although from dramatically different bases. The white rate was 2 per cent in 1940; it was 3.07 per cent in 1963. In that period, the Negro rate went from 16.8 per cent to 23.6 per cent.

The number of illegitimate children per 1,000 live births increased by 11 among whites in the period 1940–63, but by 68 among non-whites. There are, of course, limits to the dependability of these statistics. There are almost certainly a considerable number of Negro children who, although technically illegitimate, are in fact the offspring of stable unions. On the other hand, it may be assumed that many births that are in fact illegitimate are recorded otherwise. Probably the two opposite effects cancel each other out.

On the urban frontier, the nonwhite illegitimacy rates are usually higher than the national average, and the increase of late has been drastic.

In the District of Columbia, the illegitimacy rate for nonwhites grew from 21.8 per cent in 1950, to 29.5 per cent in 1964.

A similar picture of disintegrating Negro marriages emerges from the divorce statistics. Divorces have increased of late for both whites and nonwhites, but at a much greater rate for the latter. In 1940 both groups had a divorce rate of 2.2 per cent. By 1964 the white rate had risen to 3.6 per cent, but the nonwhite rate had reached 5.1 per cent—40 per cent greater than the formerly equal white rate.

As a direct result of this high rate of divorce, separation, and desertion, a very large per cent of Negro families are headed by females. While the percentage of such families among whites has been dropping since 1940, it has been rising among Negroes.

The per cent of nonwhite families headed by a female is more than double the per cent for whites. Fatherless nonwhite families increased by a sixth between 1950 and 1960, but held constant for white families.

It has been estimated that only a minority of Negro children reach the age of 18 having lived all their lives with both their parents.

Once again, this measure of family disorganization is found to be diminishing among white families and increasing among Negro families.

The majority of Negro children receive public assistance under the AFDC program at one point or another in their childhood.

At present, 14 per cent of Negro children are receiving AFDC assistance, as against 2 per cent of white children. Eight per cent of white children receive such assistance at some time, as against 56 per cent of nonwhites, according to an extrapolation based on HEW data. (Let it be noted, however, that out of a total of 1.8 million nonwhite illegitimate children in the nation in 1961, 1.3 million were *not* receiving aid under the AFDC program, although a substantial number have, or will, receive aid at some time in their lives.)

Again, the situation may be said to be worsening. The AFDC program, deriving from the long-established Mothers' Aid programs, was established in 1935 principally to care for widows and orphans, although the legislation covered all children in homes deprived of parental support because one or both of their parents are absent or incapacitated.

In the beginning, the number of AFDC families in which the father was absent because of desertion was less than a third of the total. Today it is two-thirds. HEW estimates "that between two-thirds and three-fourths of the 50 per cent increase from 1948 to 1955 in the number of absent-father families receiving ADC may be explained by an increase in broken homes in the population."

A 1960 study of Aid to Dependent Children in Cook County, Ill. stated:

> The "typical" ADC mother in Cook County was married and had children by her husband, who deserted; his whereabouts are unknown, and he does not contribute to the support of his children. She is not free to re-marry and has had an illegitimate child since her husband left. (Almost 90 per cent of the ADC families are Negro.)

The steady expansion of this welfare program, as of public assistance programs in general, can be taken as a measure of the steady disintegration of the Negro family structure over the past generation in the United States. . . .

The most perplexing question about American slavery, which has never been altogether explained, and which indeed most Americans hardly know exists, has been stated by Nathan Glazer as follows: "Why was American slavery the most awful the world has ever known?" The only thing that can be said with certainty is that this is true: it was.

American slavery was profoundly different from, and in its lasting effects on individuals and their children, indescribably worse than, any recorded servitude, ancient or modern. The peculiar nature of American slavery was noted by Alexis de Tocqueville and others, but it was not until 1948 that Frank Tannenbaum, a South American specialist, pointed to the striking differences between Brazilian and American slavery. The feudal, Catholic society of Brazil had a legal and religious tradition which accorded the slave a place as a human being in the hierarchy of society—a luckless, miserable place, to be sure, but a place withal. In contrast, there was nothing in the tradition of English law or Protestant theology which could accommodate to the fact of human bondage—the slaves were therefore reduced to the status of chattels—often, no doubt, well cared for, even privileged chattels, but chattels nevertheless.

With the emancipation of the slaves, the Negro American family began to form in the United States on a widespread scale. But it did so in an atmosphere markedly different from that which has produced the white American family.

The Negro was given liberty, but not equality. Life remained hazardous and marginal. Of the greatest importance, the Negro male, particularly in the South, became an object of intense hostility, an attitude unquestionably based in some measure on fear.

When Jim Crow made its appearance toward the end of the 19th century, it may be speculated that it was the Negro male who was most humiliated thereby; the male was more likely to use public facilities, which rapidly became segregated once the process began, and just as important, segregation, and the submissiveness it exacts, is surely more destructive to the male than to the female personality. Keeping the Negro "in his place" can be translated as keeping the Negro male in his place: the female was not a threat to anyone.

Unquestionably, these events worked against the emergence of a strong father figure. The very essence of the male animal, from the bantam rooster to the four-star general, is to strut. Indeed, in 19th century America, a particular type of exaggerated male boastfulness became almost a national style. Not for the Negro male. The "sassy nigger" was lynched.

Country life and city life are profoundly different. The gradual shift of American society from a rural to an urban basis over the past century and a half has caused abundant strains, many of which are still much in evidence. When this shift occurs suddenly, drastically, in one or two generations, the effect is immensely disruptive of traditional social patterns.

It was this abrupt transition that produced the wild Irish slums of the 19th Century Northeast. Drunkenness, crime, corruption, discrimination, family disorganization, juvenile delinquency were the routine of that era. In our own time, the same sudden transition has produced the Negro slum—different from, but hardly better than its predecessors, and fundamentally the result of the same process.

The promise of the city has so far been denied the majority of the Negro migrants, and most particularly the Negro family.

In 1939, E. Franklin Frazier described its plight movingly in that part of *The Negro Family* entitled "In the City of Destruction:"

> *The impact of hundreds of thousands of rural southern Negroes upon northern metropolitan communities presents a bewildering spectacle. Striking contrasts in levels of civilization and economic well-being among these newcomers to modern civilization seem to baffle any attempt to discover order and direction in their mode of life.*
>
> *In many cases, of course, the dissolution of the simple family organization has begun before the family reaches the northern city. But, if these families have managed to preserve their integrity until they reach the northern city, poverty, ignorance, and color force them to seek homes in deteriorated slum areas from which practically all institutional life has disappeared. Hence, at the same time that these simple rural families are losing their internal cohesion, they are being freed from the controlling force of public opinion and communal institutions. Family desertion among Negroes in cities appears, then, to be one of the inevitable consequences of the impact of urban life on the simple family organization and folk culture which the Negro has evolved in the rural South. The distribution of desertions in relation to the general economic and cultural organization of Negro communities that have grown up in our American cities shows in a striking manner the influence of selective factors in the process of adjustment to the urban environment.*

Frazier concluded his classic study, *The Negro Family*, with the prophecy that the "travail of civilization is not yet ended."

> *First, it appears that the family which evolved within the isolated world of the Negro folk will become increasingly disorganized. Modern means of communication will break down the isolation of the world of the black*

*folk, and, as long as the bankrupt system of southern agriculture exists,
Negro families will continue to seek a living in the towns and cities of
the country. They will crowd the slum areas of southern cities or make
their way to northern cities where their family life will become disrupted
and their poverty will force them to depend upon charity.*

In every index of family pathology—divorce, separation, and desertion, female family head, children in broken homes, and illegitimacy—the contrast between the urban and rural environment for
Negro families is unmistakable.

Harlem, into which Negroes began to move early in this century,
is the center and symbol of the urban life of the Negro American.
Conditions in Harlem are not worse, they are probably better than
in most Negro ghettos.

The dimensions of the problems of Negro Americans are com-
pounded by the present extraordinary growth in Negro population.
At the founding of the nation, and into the first decade of the 19th
century, one American in five was a Negro. The proportion declined
steadily until it was only one in ten by 1920, where it held until the
1950s, when it began to rise. Since 1950, the Negro population has
grown at a rate of 2.4 per cent per year compared with 1.7 per cent
for the total population. If this rate continues, in seven years one
American in eight will be nonwhite.

These changes are the result of a declining Negro death rate,
now approaching that of the nation generally, and a fertility rate
that grew steadily during the postwar period. By 1959, the ratio of
white to nonwhite fertility rates reached 1:1.42. Both the white and
nonwhite fertility rates have declined since 1959, but the differential
has not narrowed.

Family size increased among nonwhite families between 1950 and
1960—as much for those without fathers as for those with fathers.
Average family size changed little among white families, with a slight
increase in the size of husband-wife families balanced by a decline
in the size of families without fathers.

Negro women not only have more children, but have them earlier.
Thus in 1960, there were 1,247 children ever born per thousand ever-
married nonwhite women 15 to 19 years of age, as against only 725
among white women, a ratio of 1.7:1. The Negro fertility rate overall

is now 1.4 times the white, but what might be called the generation rate is 1.7 times the white.

This population growth must inevitably lead to an unconcealable crisis in Negro unemployment. The most conspicuous failure of the American social system in the past ten years has been its inadequacy in providing jobs for Negro youth. Thus, in January 1965, the unemployment rate for Negro teenagers stood at 29 per cent. This problem will now become steadily more serious.

During the rest of the 1960s the nonwhite civilian population 14 years of age and over will increase by 20 per cent—more than double the white rate. The nonwhite labor force will correspondingly increase 20 per cent in the next six years, double the rate of increase in the nonwhite labor force of the past decade.

As with the population as a whole, there is much evidence that children are being born most rapidly in those Negro families with the least financial resources. This is an ancient pattern, but because the needs of children are greater today it is very possible that the education and opportunity gap between the offspring of these families and those of stable middle-class unions is not closing, but is growing wider.

A cycle is at work; too many children too early make it most difficult for the parents to finish school. (In February, 1963, 38 per cent of the white girls who dropped out of school did so because of marriage or pregnancy, as against 49 per cent of nonwhite girls.) An Urban League study in New York reported that 44 per cent of girl dropouts left school because of pregnancy.

Low education levels in turn produce low income levels, which deprive children of many opportunities, and so the cycle repeats itself.

The object of this study has been to define a problem, rather than propose solutions to it.

What then is that problem? We feel the answer is clear enough. Three centuries of injustice have brought about deep-seated structural distortions in the life of the Negro American. At this point, the present tangle of pathology is capable of perpetuating itself without assistance from the white world. The cycle can be broken only if these distortions are set right.

In a word, a national effort toward the problems of Negro Americans must be directed toward the question of family structure. The object should be to strengthen the Negro family so as to enable it to raise and support its members as do other families. After that, how this group of Americans chooses to run its affairs, take advantage of its opportunities, or fail to do so, is none of the nation's business.

The fundamental importance and urgency of restoring the Negro American Family structure has been evident for some time. E. Franklin Frazier put it most succinctly in 1950:

> As the result of family disorganization a large proportion of Negro children and youth have not undergone the socialization which only the family can provide. The disorganized families have failed to provide for their emotional needs and have not provided the discipline and habits which are necessary for personality development. Because the disorganized family has failed in its function as a socializing agency, it has handicapped the children in their relations to the institutions in the community. Moreover, family disorganization has been partially responsible for a large amount of juvenile delinquency and adult crime among Negroes. Since the widespread family disorganization among Negroes has resulted from the failure of the father to play the role in family life required by American society, the mitigation of this problem must await those changes in the Negro and American society which will enable the Negro father to play the role required of him.

Nothing was done in response to Frazier's argument. Matters were left to take care of themselves, and as matters will, grew worse not better. The problem is now more serious, the obstacles greater. There is, however, a profound change for the better in one respect. The President has committed the nation to an all out effort to eliminate poverty wherever it exists, among whites or Negroes, and a militant, organized, and responsible Negro movement exists to join in that effort.

Elizabeth Herzog

IS THERE A "BREAKDOWN" OF THE NEGRO FAMILY?

One of the critics within the government of the Moynihan Report was Eliza-
beth Herzog, bureau chief in the Department of Health, Education and Wel-
fare. In the following article, Elizabeth Herzog questions whether the alarmist
tone of the Moynihan Report is justified and to what degree the statistics
within the report reflect racial or economic characteristics. A major point
emphasized by Moynihan is that the number of female-headed black families
is increasing at an alarming rate during a period of prosperity. Herzog points
out that, in fact, the percentage increase is minimal. A possible reason why
she and other government critics attacked the report was because they
wanted to keep the War on Poverty out of the civil rights arena. By making
the problems which affected black America economic rather than cultural
or pathological they had hoped to reduce the controversy over government
programs.

Much has been said of late—and often with great heat—about
the Negro family. Despite prevailing consensus on a number of
points, controversy has been generated with regard to other points
because one man's fact is another man's fiction. Some points of
consensus deserve mention before points of controversy. First, it
is generally agreed that a harmonious two-parent home is better
for children than a one-parent home—and better for parents, too,
in this society. It is agreed also that fatherless homes are far more
frequent among Negroes than among whites and that in both groups
their frequency rises as income falls.

Another point of firm consensus is that strong action is needed
to remedy adverse conditions that have existed far too long, especially for low-income Negroes; and that these conditions bear
especially on the low-income Negro man, whose disadvantaged
situation takes heavy toll of himself, his children, their mother, and
the family unit as a whole. All of these statements have long been
accepted by serious students of Negro family life.[1]

Reprinted with permission of the National Association of Social Workers and the
author, from *Social Work*, Vol. 2, No. 1 (January 1966) pp. 3–10.
[1] St. Clair Drake and Horace R. Cayton, *Black Metropolis* (New York: Harcourt,
Brace, and Co., 1945); E. Franklin Frazier, *The Negro Family in the United States*

The controversy centers mainly on the following points: (1) whether "the" Negro family is "crumbling" at a disastrous rate, (2) whether the amount of breakdown that exists is primarily due to poverty, or to cultural inheritance, or to a cycle of self-perpetuating pathology, (3) whether the remedy is to be sought primarily through improving the economic, social, and legal status of Negroes or primarily through conducting a remedial campaign aimed directly at the Negro family.

The Moynihan Report

Impetus has been given to these and related questions by the much-discussed "Moynihan report."[2] Released to the general public in the late fall of 1965, this publication presents census figures and findings from special studies to document the grim effects of poverty and discrimination and their impact on Negro families. It brings together all-too-familiar evidence that the frequency of broken marriage, female-headed families, births out of wedlock, and dependence on public assistance are much higher among Negroes than among whites. In doing so, it recognizes that these problems are most acute among the very poor and least acute at the middle- and upper-income levels. It points out also that they are more acute in cities than in rural areas and thus are intensified by continuing urbanization.

The report further documents the higher unemployment rates and lower wage rates among Negroes than among whites. It states, as others have done, the 2 to 1 white-Negro unemployment ratio that has persisted for years, the lower wages available to Negroes, and the fact that the median nonwhite family income is little more than half the median for white families. To this discrepancy is added the fact that the families of the poor tend to be larger than middle-class families. "Families of six or more children have median

(Chicago: University of Chicago Press, 1939); Hylan Lewis, "The Changing Negro Family," in Eli Ginzberg, ed., *The Nation's Children, Vol. 1: The Family and Social Change* (New York: Columbia University Press, 1960); Thomas F. Pettigrew, *A Profile of the Negro American* (Princeton, N.J.: D. Van Nostrand Co., 1964).
[2] *The Negro Family: The Case for National Action* (Washington, D.C.: U.S. Department of Labor, Office of Planning and Research, 1965).

incomes 24 per cent below families with three."[3] Other sources tell how heavily this fertility differential bears on Negro families: in 1963, according to the Social Security Administration Index, 60 per cent of non-white children under 18 lived in poverty as compared with 16 per cent of white children.[4]

The effect on marital and family stability of the man's economic instability is also discussed. The sad cycle has become familiar in the professional literature: the man who cannot command a stable job at adequate wages cannot be an adequate family provider; the man who cannot provide for his family is likely to lose status and respect in his own eyes and in the eyes of others—including his family. His inability to provide drains him of the will to struggle with continuing and insuperable family responsibilities. It is an incentive to desertion, especially if his family can receive public assistance only when he is gone.

A good deal of the Moynihan report is devoted to interpretation of the documented figures and, quite naturally, it is on the interpretation that opinions diverge.[5] It is not the purpose of this paper to summarize fully, to concur with, or to take issues with the report as such, but rather to consider some propositions that were in circulation before it was published and to which it has given increased currency. With regard to the report itself, its factual summary has shocked some Americans into new recognition of old and unpalatable facts about the toll exacted by poverty coupled with discrimination; and its interpretive sections have challenged us to an assessment of evidence—two substantial services. Some of the propositions attributed to it may be misinterpretations of the

---

[3] *Ibid.,* p. 24.

[4] Mollie Orshansky, "Who's Who Among the Poor: A Demographic View of Poverty," *Social Security Bulletin,* Vol. 28, No. 7 (July 1965), pp. 3–32.

[5] Midway between statistical report and interpretation is discussion of a "startling increase in welfare dependency," described as occurring at a time when employment was increasing. *See* U.S. Department of Labor, *The Negro Family: The Case for National Action,* op. cit., p. 12. It would require extensive and sophisticated analysis to determine the extent to which this upswing in AFDC recipients related to changes in families, or to liberalization of AFDC policies following new legislation, or to changes in population distribution. Similarly, differentials in rates of juvenile delinquency would need to be controlled for income and analyzed in light of differential rates of apprehension and treatment of presumed offenders, white or nonwhite.

author's intended meaning. In any case, they have taken on a life of their own and are met frequently in other current writings. Accordingly, they will be considered here on their own merits, without reference to any particular document.

Fatherless Families

One recurrent proposition concerns the "rapid deterioration" of the Negro family, often referred to as "crumbling" and presumably near dissolution. The incidence of fatherless families is used as the primary index of family breakdown. Although questions can be—and have been—raised about this index, such questions do not dominate the mainstream of the argument and will be disregarded here. But if one accepts the proportion of fatherless homes as a primary index of family breakdown, does it then follow, on the basis of the evidence, that the Negro family is rapidly deteriorating?

It is important to differentiate between sudden acceleration of family crisis and relatively sudden perception of a long-chronic situation, since the diagnosis of a social condition influences the prescription for relieving it and the context in which the prescription is filled.

Actually, census figures do not justify any such alarmist interpretation. It seems worthwhile to review these figures, not because there is no urgent need for remedial action—the need is urgent, especially in the area of jobs for low-income Negro men. Rather it is important to keep the problem in perspective and to avoid feeding prejudices that can all too readily seize upon statistical misconceptions as reason to delay rather than to speed such action.

As already noted, census figures do show much higher rates of fatherless families for Negroes than for whites. The 1964 figures show almost 9 per cent of white families headed by a woman as compared with 23 per cent of nonwhite families; a difference of this order has persisted for years.[6] The figures do not, however, document a rapid increase in those rates during recent years. On the contrary—and this is a point curiously slighted by commentators on both sides of the argument—they show a gradual increase from

---

[6] These figures are available for white and nonwhite rather than for white and Negro families. However, most of the nonwhite (about 92 per cent) are Negroes.

1949 (19 per cent) to 1959 (24 per cent). Moreover, from 1960 to 1964 the proportion of female-headed families among Negroes showed no net rise at all, standing at 23 per cent in 1964. The total rise from 1949 to 1964 was about 5 percentage points, that is, about one-third of a percentage point a year. In 1940, the proportion was 18 per cent.[7] Thus, an accurate description would be that during the past twenty-five years there has been a gradual rise, preceded and followed by a plateau, but not an acute increase in the overall proportion of broken homes among Negroes. . . .

Illegitimacy

Another generalization also related to family breakdown is met so often that by now it threatens to attain the status of "fact," namely, that there has been an "alarming rise" in illegitimacy.

It is true that the number of births out of wedlock has soared. In 1964 the number was 276,000 as compared with 176,000 in 1954.[8] This is a tremendous number, and the more distressing since there has been no services explosion to keep pace with the population explosion. However, in terms of people's behavior, the only relevant index of increase in illegitimacy is *rate,* that is, the number of births out of wedlock per 1,000 unmarried women of child-bearing age.

The rise in rate (as differentiated from numbers) was relatively steady over several decades. This rise represents a long-term trend and not a sudden upsurge. Moreover, in the last seven years reported (1957–1964) the rate has oscillated within about two points,

[7] Percentages have been rounded. The exact rise was from 18.8 per cent to 23.6 per cent, or 4.4 percentage points. The 1940 figure was 17.8 per cent, as recomputed according to the definition of "family" introduced in 1947. Bureau of the Census, *Current Population Reports.* Series P-20, Nos. 125, 116, 106, 100, 88, 83, 75, 67, 53, 44, 33, and 26 (Washington, D.C.: U.S. Department of Commerce); Bureau of Labor Statistics, *The Negroes in the United States: Their Economic and Social Situation* (Washington, D.C.: U.S. Department of Labor, 1965); Bureau of the Census, *16th Census of the U.S. 1940. Population—Families—Types of Families* (Washington, D.C.: U.S. Department of Commerce, 1940).

[8] *Monthly Vital Statistics Reports, Advance Report, Final Natality Statistics, 1964* (Washington, D.C.: U.S. Department of Health, Education, and Welfare, National Center for Health Statistics, Public Health Service. October 22, 1965); *Vital Statistics of the United States, 1963. Volume 1—Natality* (Washington, D.C.: National Center for Health Statistics, Public Health Service, Department of Health, Education, and Welfare, 1964).

Families Headed by a Woman as Per Cent of All Families by Color: Selected Periods, 1949–1964

Year	*Families Headed by a Woman As Per Cent of Total*	
	White	*Nonwhite*
1964	8.8	23.4
1963	8.6	23.3
1962	8.6	23.2
1961	8.9	21.6
1960	8.7	22.4
1959	8.4	23.6
1958	8.6	22.4
1957	8.9	21.9
1956	8.8	20.5
1955	9.0	20.7
1954	8.3	19.2
1953	8.4	18.1
1952	9.2	17.9
1950	8.4	19.1
1949	8.8	18.8

Source: U.S. Department of Commerce, Bureau of the Census: Current Population Reports, P-20, No. 125, 116, 106, 100, 88, 83, 75, 67, 53, 44, 33, and 26. Figures for 1963 and 1964 are drawn from Bureau of Labor Statistics, *The Negroes in the United States: Their Economic and Social Situation* (Washington, D.C., U.S. Department of Labor) Table IV, a, 1.

at about the same level, rising or falling one point or less annually, but in effect representing a seven-year plateau. Since all national illegitimacy figures are based on estimates, with a number of states not reporting, very slight changes should not be regarded as significant. Thus, the current picture is a large rise in *numbers* and a levelling off in the *rate* of nonwedlock births.[9] Rates for teenagers have increased less than for other groups, and for those under fifteen the rate has not increased since 1947.[10] (The ratio— the proportion of live births that are out of wedlock—has risen

[9] Elizabeth Herzog, "The Chronic Revolution: Births Out of Wedlock." Paper presented at meeting of American Orthopsychiatric Association, March 1965. To be published in a forthcoming issue of *Journal of Clinical Pediatrics*.
[10] Rates are not available by color except for a few years.

for both whites and nonwhites. However, *ratio* is far less meaningful than *rate* as an index of change.)

The recent relative stability of rate does not diminish the problems caused by nonwedlock births but it should affect the conclusions drawn from the statistics, the measures taken to act on those conclusions, and the attitudes of those who ponder the meaning of the figures.

Over half the children born out of wedlock are nonwhite, although only 12 per cent of the population are nonwhite. The reasons for this difference have been much discussed and need only be mentioned here. They include (1) less use of contraception, (2) less use of abortion, (3) differences in reporting, (4) reluctance to lose a public assistance grant by admitting to a man in the house, (5) the expense of divorce and legal separation. It seems probable that, even if discount could be made for these and other factors, a difference would remain. It would be a much smaller difference, however, and conceivably could still relate more to income than to color.[11]

If further evidence were needed on this virtually unchallenged relation between income and illegitimacy rates, figures on rates in high- and low-income tracts should be sufficient. Pakter and associates, for example, found that the proportion of births out-of-wedlock in relation to total nonwhite births varied from a high of 38 per cent in the Central Harlem district to a comparative low of 9 per cent in the Pelham Bay District.[12]

Attitudes toward illegitimacy and toward marriage are clearly linked with the economic position of the Negro male. A male head of house who is not a breadwinner and provider is a hazard to the happiness of the marriage, and his loss of economic status is so great a hazard to his intrafamily status that he may decamp, either to protect his own ego or to make his family eligible for support from AFDC. Recent changes in the AFDC program are aimed against the latter reason for family desertion.

[11] Elizabeth Herzog, "Unmarried Mothers: Some Questions to Be Answered and Some Answers to Be Questioned," *Child Welfare*, Vol. 41, No. 8 (October 1962), pp. 339–350.
[12] Jean Pakter, Henry J. Rosner, Harold Jacobziner, and Frieda Greenstein, "Out-of-Wedlock Births in New York City. I—Sociologic Aspects," *American Journal of Public Health*, Vol. 51, No. 5 (May 1961), pp. 683–696.

Slavery Is Not the Explanation

Among the most frequent and most challenged generalizations relating to low-income Negro families is the assumption that their
present characteristics are influenced more by the legacy of slavery
than by postslavery discriminations and deprivations. The challenge
rests chiefly on (1) the similarity between very poor Negro families
and very poor white families, and (2) the fact that slavery ended
a hundred years ago while the postslavery situation is contemporary
and appalling. Adequately controlled comparisons within different
income levels show that the differences associated with income
outweigh those associated with color. Family structure, for example,
differs more between different income levels than between Negro
and white families. The same is true of differences between Negro
and white children in educational achievement, and—when income
is controlled—the relative position of men with respect to women,
economically and educationally, is the same for whites as for non-
whites.[13]

Descriptions of white families at the very low income levels
read very much like current descriptions of poor Negro families,
with high incidence of broken homes, "mother dominance," births
out of wedlock, educational deficit, crowded living, three-generation
households, and failure to observe the norms of middle-class behavior.[14] Such families are described by Hollingshead and Redlich:

*Doctors, nurses, and public officials who know these families best esti-
mate from one-fifth to one-fourth of all births are illegitimate.*

*Death, desertion, separation, or divorce has broken more than half the
families (56%). The burden of child care, as well as support, falls on
the mother more often than on the father when the family is broken. The
mother-child relation is the strongest and most enduring family tie. Here
we find a conglomerate of broken homes where two or three generations
live together, where boarders and roomers, in-laws and common-law liai-*

[13] Myron J. Lefcowitz, "Poverty and Negro-White Family Structures." Unpub-
lished background paper for White House Conference on Civil Rights, Washing-
ton, D.C., November 1965.
[14] Walter B. Miller, "Implications of Urban Lower-Class Culture for Social Work,"
Social Service Review, Vol. 33, No. 3 (September 1959), pp. 219–236; W. Lloyd
Warner and Paul S. Lunt, *The Social Life of a Modern Community* (New Haven:
Yale University Press, 1941); James West, *Plainville, USA* (New York: Columbia
University Press, 1945).

sons share living quarters. Laws may be broken and the moral standards of the higher classes flouted before the children's eyes day after day.[15]

These are descriptions of white families in the North, with no heritage of slavery to explain their way of life. It seems unlikely that the slavery-specific thesis is needed to explain the occurrence among Negroes of patterns so similar to those produced in other groups merely by poverty, and so often described in other contexts as "the culture of poverty."[16]

It is difficult to be sure how much—if any—difference would remain in proportions of female-headed families if really sensitive comparisons were made between Negroes and whites on the same income level. Available income breakdowns employ rather broad groupings, and Negroes tend to be overrepresented at the lower layers of each grouping. It seems reasonable to assume that some differences between white and nonwhite would remain even with a more sensitive income classification. Yet it does not necessarily follow that they might be ascribed primarily to the legacy of slavery rather than to the hundred years since slavery. It seems more likely that differences between low-income white and Negro families, beyond that explained by income alone, may be attributed primarily to postslavery factors of deprivation and discrimination affecting every facet of life: occupation, education, income, housing, nutrition, health and mortality, social status, self-respect—the documented list is long and the documenting references myriad.[17]

The habit of analyzing data by color rather than by income encourages the tendency to attribute to race-related factors differences that may in fact be due to income level. Studies of prenatal care, for example, indicate that in effect one is comparing the prosperous with the poor in all three of the following comparisons: white mothers with nonwhite mothers; married mothers with un-

[15] August B. Hollingshead, *Elmtown's Youth.* (New York: John Wiley & Sons, 1949), pp. 116, 117; Hollingshead and Fredrick C. Redlich, *Social Class and Mental Illness: A Community Study* (New York: John Wiley & Sons, 1958), p. 125.
[16] Oscar Lewis, *The Children of Sanchez: Autobiography of a Mexican Family.* (New York: Random House, 1961).
[17] Dorothy K. Newman, "Economic Status of the Negro." Unpublished background paper for White House Conference on Civil Rights, Washington, D.C., November 1965; Alvin L. Schorr, *Slums and Social Insecurity,* Research Report No. 1 (Washington, D.C.: U.S. Department of Health, Education, and Welfare, Social Security Administration, 1963).

married mothers; all mothers who do with all mothers who do not obtain prenatal care.[18]

All the points mentioned here and some not mentioned are important. However, the emphasis on rapid deterioration is so central to current discussion of the low-income Negro family and to means proposed for alleviating its current problems that it deserves major emphasis—along with the slavery-specific thesis to which it is so often linked.

There has been little disposition to challenge the ample evidence that family structure and functioning in our society are strongly linked with social and economic status. The questions raised, as Robert Coles put it, have to do with which is the cart and which is the horse.[19] The alleged rapid acceleration of family breakdown has been cited as evidence that among low-income Negroes the family is the horse. Therefore it is important to recognize that according to the chief index used by proponents of this view no rapid acceleration of family breakdown is evident.

If there has been no substantial change in family structure during the past two decades, then there are no grounds for claiming that a new "tangle of pathology" has set up a degenerative process from within, over and above response to the long continued impact of social and economic forces from without; and that this process is specific to a Negro "culture" inherited from days of slavery.

Two Views—and Two Remedies

Both sides of the controversy agree that there is urgent need for strong action to increase the proportion of sound, harmonious two-parent homes among low-income Negroes. They disagree on whether that action should be focused primarily on intra-family or extra-family problems. The acute-crisis view suggests that primary attention be given to the family as such. The other view suggests

[18] Elizabeth Herzog and Rose Bernstein, *Health Services for Unmarried Mothers,* Children's Bureau Publication No. 425 (Washington, D.C.: U.S. Department of Health, Education, and Welfare, Welfare Administration, 1964).
[19] Robert Coles, *"There's Sinew in the Negro Family."* Background paper for White House Conference on Civil Rights, Washington, D.C., November 1965. Reprinted from *The Washington Post,* October 10, 1965, p. E. 1.

that the best way to strengthen low-income families as families is to give primary attention to building up the economic and social status of Negro men.

According to this view, a number of noneconomic supports can and should be given to low-income Negro families, pending the time when fewer of them are fatherless. Such helps should include, among other things, (1) aids for the overburdened mother in her multiple role as homemaker, child-rearer, and breadwinner; and (2) effective male models introduced into the lives of children—girls as well as boys. A number of new ways for providing both kinds of support have been proposed. In the long run, however, according to this view, what these families need most is jobs for Negro men—jobs with status, with stability, with future, and with fair wages. No one claims that this can be achieved easily, quickly, or cheaply; but many believe it can and must be done.

What is new for the white majority is not that it is suddenly faced with an explosive breakdown of "the" Negro family. What is new is the recognition of a long-standing situation, plus the determination to do something about it. If we are able to achieve that recognition and determination, however belatedly, then surely we must be able to act on this basis rather than to galvanize ourselves into action by believing that suddenly the Negro family is a bomb or a mine which will explode in our faces if it is not quickly defused. Surely we are able to act, not because of panic but because action is long overdue, and inaction flies in the face of decency.

What is new for the Negro minority is not a sudden acceleration of family breakdown. What is new is an injection of hope that attacks apathy and fatalism and sparks insistence on full justice. It is not increased family breakdown that activates outbreaks such as occurred in Harlem, Watts, and elsewhere. It is the recognition that the families of the "dark ghetto" no longer need to continue to accept the ghetto and what it does to them.

It must, of course, be recognized that "the" Negro family is itself a fiction. Different family forms prevail at different class and income levels throughout our society. In addition, at any given level a wide variety of families are found, each with its individual characteristics—some of which are and some of which are not class linked. When the great diversity among low-income families is ignored, there is danger that the deplored characteristics of some will be imputed to all.[20] At the same time, most writers—including the present one—find it almost impossible to avoid falling into the oversimplified form of reference to "the" Negro family that constantly risks oversimplified thinking.

It is necessary also to caution one's self and others that, while problems must be discussed and attacked, strengths must not be forgotten. Problem-focused discussions, however necessary and constructive, also invite distortion. Not all fathers are absent fathers among the poor—in fact, about two-thirds of them are present among low-income Negro families. And, as Erik Erikson reminds us, there are impressive strengths in many Negro mothers.[21] Robert Coles, after living among low-income Negroes for months, wrote:

> *I was constantly surprised at the endurance shown by children we would all call poor or, in the current fashion, "culturally disadvantaged.". . . What enabled such children from such families to survive, emotionally and educationally, ordeals I feel sure many white middle-class boys and girls would find impossible? What has been the source of strength shown by the sit-in students, many of whom do not come from comfortable homes but, quite the contrary, from rural cabins or slum tenements?*[22]

One may go on to speculate: What are the sources of strength and self-discipline that make possible a Montgomery bus boycott or a March on Washington, conducted without violence? We do well to ponder such questions, for we shall have to mobilize the strengths of families in poverty as well as the wisdom of others who ponder their problems, if we are at last "to fulfill these rights."

[20] Hylan Lewis, *Culture, "Class and the Behavior of Low Income Families."* Unpublished background paper for White House Conference on Civil Rights, Washington, D.C., November 1965; Elizabeth Herzog, "Some Assumptions About the Poor," *Social Service Review*, Vol. 37, No. 4 (December 1963), pp. 389–402.
[21] Erik H. Erikson, "The Concept of Identity in Race Relations: Notes and Queries." To be published in December 1965 issue of *Daedalus*.
[22] Robert Coles, *op. cit.*, p. E 1 (*The Washington Post*).

Ulf Hannerz

ANOTHER LOOK AT LOWER-CLASS BLACK CULTURE

Ulf Hannerz, lecturer in social anthropology at the University of Stockholm, spent two years in a black neighborhood in the Washington ghetto. From this experience came his book, Soulside: Inquiries into Ghetto Culture and Community, *published in 1969, and a number of essays. The following selection is taken from one of his essays, published in* Soul, *an anthology edited by Lee Rainwater. In this selection Hannerz attempts to answer some of the major questions dealing with the impact of the ghetto. These questions include: is black culture sick or healthy, is it determined by internal or external pressures, and is it a lower-class culture or a separate culture in the process of being defined? He also synthesizes much of the earlier work done on the black family and lower-class black culture.*

Some 5.7 million people were simply not counted in the 1960 census, and most of them, it now appears, were Negro men living in northern cities. This statistical oversight, if that is what it was, is not unique to the government's census takers. Ever since the beginnings of the scholarly study of black people in the Americas, there has been an interesting fascination with the differences between the family life of Negroes and that of their white counterparts, the chief difference being seen as the dominant, not to say dominating, role of women in black families.

From E. Franklin Frazier's pioneering 1932 study of *The Negro Family in Chicago* through Melville Herskovits' *The Myth of the Negro Past* in 1941 to the so-called Moynihan Report of 1965, social scientists have been repeatedly rediscovering, analyzing and worrying over the crucial role of the mother (or grandmother) in the family structure of blacks in the New World. Herskovits saw the centrality of the mother as an African vestige, typical of the polygynous marriage in which every woman, with her offspring, formed a separate unit. Frazier is generally regarded as the first to ascribe to the institution of slavery itself the strongest influence in undermining the stability of marriage, an influence that was later

From Ulf Hannerz, "What Ghetto Males Are Like: Another Look," in *Afro-American Anthropology*, Norman E. Whitten, Jr. and John F. Szwed, editors. Adapted with the permission of The Macmillan Company. Copyright © 1970 by The Free Press, A Division of The Macmillan Company.

reinforced when blacks encountered what Frazier perceived as the peculiarly urban evils of anonymity, disorganization and the lack of social support and controls. Moynihan, like Frazier, sees the matriarchal family as being practically without strengths, at least in the context of the larger American society, but his Report emphasizes the ways in which employer discrimination and, more recently, welfare policies have contributed to the breaking up (or foreclosure) of the male-dominated family unit among blacks.

In all of these studies, however, the black *man*—as son, lover, husband, father, grandfather—is a distant and shadowy figure "out there somewhere" . . . if only because his major characteristic as far as the household is concerned is his marginality or absence.

I do not mean to suggest that the black man is undiscovered territory. Obviously he is not. His popular image was fixed for one (long) era in *Uncle Tom's Cabin* and prophetically fashioned for our own time in Norman Mailer's essay "The White Negro." Here is Mailer's Hipster, modeled on the Negro: "Sharing a collective disbelief in the words of men who had too much money and controlled too many things, they knew almost as powerful a disbelief in the socially monolithic ideas of the single mate, the solid family and the respectable love life." . . .

This essay is an attempt to outline the social processes within the ghetto communities of the northern United States whereby the identity of street-corner males is established and maintained. To set the stage and state the issues involved in this essay, I'd like to look at the views of two other observers of the ghetto male. One is Charles Keil, whose *Urban Blues* (1966) is a study of the bluesman as a "culture hero." According to Keil, the urban blues singer, with his emphasis on sexuality, "trouble" and flashy clothes, manifests a cultural model of maleness that is highly valued by ghetto dwellers and relatively independent of the mainstream cultural tradition. Keil criticizes a number of authors who, without cavilling at this description of the male role, tend to see it as rooted in the individual's anxiety about his masculinity. This, Keil finds, is unacceptably ethnocentric:

> *Any sound analysis of Negro masculinity should first deal with the statements and responses of Negro women, the conscious motives of the men*

themselves and the Negro cultural tradition. Applied in this setting, psychological theory may then be able to provide important new insights in place of basic and unfortunate distortions.

Keil, then, comes out clearly for a cultural interpretation of the male role we are interested in here. But Elliot Liebow in *Tally's Corner* (1967), a study resulting from the author's participation in a research project that definitely considered ghetto life more in terms of social problems than as a culture, reaches conclusions which, in some of their most succinct formulations, quite clearly contradict Keil's:

Similarities between the lower-class Negro father and son . . . do not result from "cultural transmission" but from the fact that the son goes out and independently experiences the same failures, in the same areas, and for much the same reasons as his father.

Thus father and son are "independently produced look-alikes." With this goes the view that the emphasis on sexual ability, drinking and so forth is a set of compensatory self-deceptions which can only unsuccessfully veil the street-corner male's awareness of his failure.

Keil and Liebow, as reviewed here, may be taken as representatives of two significantly different opinions on why black people in the ghettos, and in particular the males, behave differently than other Americans. One emphasizes a cultural determinism internal to the ghetto, the other an economic determinism in the relationship between the ghetto and the wider society. It is easy to see how the two views relate to one's perspective on the determinants of the domestic structure of ghetto dwellers. And it is also easy to see how these perspectives have considerable bearing on public policy, especially if it is believed that the ghetto family structure somehow prevents full participation by its members in the larger American society and economy. If it is held, for example, that broad social and economic factors, and particularly poverty, make ghetto families the way they are—and this seems to be the majority opinion among social scientists concerned with this area—then public policy should concentrate on mitigating or removing those elements that distort the lives of black people. But if the style of life in the ghetto is culturally determined and more or less independent of other "outside" factors, then public policy will have to take a different course, or drop the problem altogether *qua* problem.

Admittedly, the present opportunity structure places serious obstacles in the way of many ghetto dwellers, making a mainstream life-style difficult to accomplish. And if research is to influence public policy, it is particularly important to point to the wider structural influences that *can* be changed in order to give equal opportunity to ghetto dwellers. Yet some of the studies emphasizing such macro-structural determinants have resulted in somewhat crude conceptualizations that are hardly warranted by the facts and which in the light of anthropological theory appear very oversimplified.

First of all, let us dispose of some of the apparent opposition between the two points of view represented by Keil and Liebow. There is not necessarily any direct conflict between ecological-economic and cultural explanations; the tendency to create such a conflict in much of the current literature on poverty involves a false dichotomy. In anthropology, it is a commonplace that culture is usually both inherited and influenced by the community's relationship to its environment. Economic determination and cultural determinism can go hand in hand in a stable environment. Since the ecological niche of ghetto dwellers has long remained relatively unchanged, there seems to be no reason why their adaptation should not have become in some ways cultural. It is possible, of course, that the first stage in the evolution of the specifically ghetto life-style consisted of a multiplicity of identical but largely independent adaptations from the existing cultural background—mainstream or otherwise—to the given opportunity structure, as Liebow suggests. But the second stage of adaptation—involves a perception of the first-stage adaptation as a normal condition, a state of affairs which from then on can be expected. What was at first independent-adaptation becomes transformed into a ghetto heritage of assumptions about the nature of man and society.

Yet Liebow implies that father and son are independently produced as streetcorner men, and that transmission of a ghetto-specific culture has a negligible influence. To those adhering to this belief, strong evidence in its favor is seen in the fact that ghetto dwellers—both men and women—often express conventional sentiments about sex and other matters. Most ghetto dwellers would certainly agree, at times at least, that education is a good thing, that gambling and drinking are bad, if not sinful, and that a man and a woman should be true to each other. Finding such opinions, and heeding Keil's admonition to listen to the statements and responses of the black people themselves, one may be led to doubt that there is much of a specific ghetto culture. But then, after having observed behavior among these same people that often and clearly contradicts their stated values, one has to ask two questions: Is there any reason to believe that ghetto-specific behavior is cultural? And, if it *is* cultural, what is the nature of the coexistence of mainstream culture and ghetto-specific culture in the black ghetto?

To answer the first question, one might look at the kinds of communications that are passed around in the ghetto relating to notions of maleness. One set of relationships in which such communications occur frequently is the family; another is the male peer group.

Much has been made of the notion that young boys in the ghetto, growing up in matrifocal households, are somehow deficient in or uncertain about their masculinity, because their fathers are absent or peripheral in household affairs. It is said that they lack the role models necessary for learning male behavior; there is a lack of the kind of information about the nature of masculinity which a father would transmit unintentionally merely by going about his life at home. The boys therefore supposedly experience a great deal of sex-role anxiety as a result of this cultural vacuum. It is possible that such a view contains more than a grain of truth in the case of some quite isolated female-headed households. Generally speaking, however, there may be less to it than meets the eye. First of all, a female-headed household without an adult male in residence but where young children are growing up—and where, therefore, it is likely that the mother is still rather young—is seldom one where adult males are totally absent. More or less steady boyfriends (sometimes including the separated father)

go in and out. Even if these men do not assume a central household role, the boys can obviously use them as source material for
the identification of male behavior. To be sure, the model is not
a conventional middle-class one, but it still shows what males are
like.

Furthermore, men are not the only ones who teach boys about
masculinity. Although role-modeling is probably essential, other social processes can contribute to identity formation. Mothers, grandmothers, aunts and sisters who have observed men at close range
have formed expectations about the typical behavior of men which
they express and which influence the boys in the household. The
boys will come to share in the women's imagery of men, and often
they will find that men who are not regarded as good household
partners (that is, "good" in the conventional sense) are still held to
be attractive company. Thus the view is easily imparted that the
hard men, good talkers, clothes-horses and all, are not altogether
unsuccessful as men. The women also act more directly toward the
boys in these terms—they have expectations of what men will do,
and whether they wish the boys to live up (or down) to the expectations, they instruct them in the model. Boys are advised not to "mess
with" girls, but at the same time it is emphasized that messing
around is the natural thing they will otherwise go out and do—and
when the boys start their early adventures with the other sex, the
older women may scold them but at the same time point out, not
without satisfaction, that "boys will be boys." This kind of maternal
(or at least adult female) instruction of young males is obviously a
kind of altercasting, or more exactly, socialization to an alter role—
that is, women cast boys in the role complementary to their own
according to their experience of man-woman relationships. One single mother of three boys and two girls put it this way:

> *You know, you just got to act a little bit tougher with boys than with*
> *girls, cause they just ain't the same. Girls do what you tell them to do*
> *and don't get into no trouble, but you just can't be sure about the boys.*
> *I mean, you think they're OK and next thing you find out they're playing*
> *hookey and drinking wine and maybe stealing things from cars and what*
> *not. There's just something bad about boys here, you know. But what*
> *can you say when many of them are just like their daddies? That's the*

man in them coming out. You can't really fight it, you know that's the way it is. They know, too, but you just got to be tougher.

This is in some ways an antagonistic socialization, but it is built upon an expectation that it would be unnatural for men not to turn out to be in some ways bad—that is fighters, drinkers, lady killers and so forth. There is one thing worse than a no-good man—the sissy, who is his opposite. A boy who seems weak is often reprimanded and ridiculed not only by his peers but also by adults, including his mother and older sisters. The combination of role-modeling by peripheral fathers or temporary boyfriends with altercasting by adult women certainly provides for a measure of male role socialization within the family.

And yet, when I said that the view of the lack of models in the family was too narrow, I was not referring to the observers' lack of insight into many matrifocal ghetto families as much as I was to the emphasis they placed on the family as *the* information storage unit of a community's culture. I believe it is an ethnocentrism on the part of middle-class commentators to take it for granted that if information about sex roles is not transmitted from father to son within the family, it is not transmitted from generation to generation at all. In American sociology, no less than in the popular mind, there is what Ray Birdwhistell has termed a "sentimental model" of family life, according to which the family is an inward-turning isolated unit, meeting most of the needs of its members, and certainly their needs for sociability and affection. The "sentimental model" is hardly ever realistic even as far as middle-class American families are concerned, and it has even less relevance for black ghetto life. Ghetto children live and learn out on the streets just about as much as within the confines of the home. Even if mothers, aunts and sisters do not have street-corner men as partners, there is an ample supply of them on the front stoop or down at the corner. Many of these men have such a regular attendance record as to become quite familiar to children and are frequently very friendly with them. Again, therefore, there is no lack of adult men to show a young boy what men are like. It seems rather unlikely that one can deny all role-modeling effect of these men on their young neighbors. They may be missing in the United States census records, but they are not missing in the ghetto community.

Much of the information gained about sex roles outside the family comes not from adult to child, however, but from persons in the same age-grade or only slightly higher. The idea of culture being stored in lower age-grades must be taken seriously. Many ghetto children start participating in the peer groups of the neighborhood at an early age, often under the watchful eye of an elder brother or sister. In this way they are initiated into the culture of the peer group by interacting with children—predominantly of the same sex—who are only a little older than they are. And in the peer-group culture of the boys, the male sex role is a fairly constant topic of concern. Some observers have felt that this is another consequence of the alleged sex role anxiety of ghetto boys. This may be true, of course, at least in that it may have had an important part in the development of male peer-group life as a dominant element of ghetto social structure. Today, however, such a simple psychosocial explanation will not do. Most ghetto boys can hardly avoid associating with other boys, and once they are in the group, they are efficiently socialized into a high degree of concern with their sex role. Much of the joking, the verbal contests and the more or less obscene songs among small ghetto boys, serve to alienate them from dependence on mother figures and train them to the exploitative, somewhat antagonistic attitude toward women which is typical of streetcorner men. . . .

It is hard to avoid the conclusion, then, that there is a cultural element involved in the sex roles of streetcorner males, because expectations about sex are manifestly shared and transmitted rather than individually evolved. (If the latter had been the case, of course, it would have been less accurate to speak of these as roles, since roles are by definition cultural.) This takes us to the second question stated above, about the coexistence of conventional and ghetto-specific cultures. Streetcorner men certainly are aware of the male ideal of mainstream America—providing well for one's family, remaining faithful to one's spouse, staying out of trouble, etc.—and now and then everyone of them states it as his own ideal. What we find here, then, may be seen as a bicultural situation. Mainstream culture and ghetto-specific culture provide different models for living, models familiar to everyone in the ghetto. Actual behavior may lean more toward one model or more toward the other, or it may be some kind of mixture, at one point or over time. The ghetto-specific culture, including the streetcorner male role, is adapted to the situation and the experience of the ghetto dweller; it tends to involve relatively little idealization but offers shared expectations concerning self, others and the environment. The mainstream culture, from the ghetto dweller's point of view, often involves idealization, but there is less real expectation that life will actually follow the paths suggested by those ideals. This is not to say that the ghetto-specific culture offers no values of its own at all, or that nothing of mainstream culture ever appears realistic in the ghetto; but in those areas of life where the two cultures exist side by side as alternative guides to action (for naturally, the ghetto-specific culture, as distinct from mainstream culture, is not a "complete" culture covering all areas of life), the ghetto-specific culture is often taken to forecast what one can actually expect from life, while the mainstream norms are held up as perhaps ultimately more valid but less attainable under the given situational constraints. "Sure it would be good to have a good job and a good home and your kids in college and all that, but you got to be yourself and do what you know." Of course, this often makes the ghetto-specific cultural expectations into self-fulfilling prophecies, as ghetto dwellers try to attain what they believe they can attain; but, to be sure, self-fulfilling prophecies and realistic assessments may well coincide.

On the whole, one may say that both mainstream culture and ghetto-specific culture are transmitted within many ghetto families. I have noted how socialization into the ghetto male role within the household is largely an informal process, in which young boys may pick up bits and pieces of information about masculinity from the women in the house as well as from males who may make their entrances and exits. On the other hand, when adult women—usually mothers or grandmothers—really "tell the boys how to behave," they often try to instill in them mainstream, not to say puritanical norms—drinking is bad, sex is dirty and so forth. The male peer groups, as we have seen, are the strongholds of streetcorner maleness, although there are times when men cuss each other out for being "no good." Finally, of course, mainstream culture is transmitted in contacts with the outside world, such as in school or through the mass

media. It should be added, though, that the latter may be used
selectively to strengthen some elements of the streetcorner male
role; ghetto men are drawn to Westerns, war movies and crime
stories both in the movie house and on their TV sets. . . .

. . . Thus we can see how the life careers of some ghetto men
take them through many and partly unpredictable shifts and drifts
between mainstream and ghetto-specific cultures, while others remain quite stable in one allegiance or another.

The sociocultural situation in the black ghetto is clearly complicated. The community shows a great heterogeneity of life-styles;
individuals become committed in some degree to different ways of
being by the impersonally-enforced structural arrangements to which
they are subjected, but unpredictable contingencies have an influence, and their personal attachments to life-styles also vary. The
socioeconomic conditions impose limits on the kinds of life ghetto
dwellers may have, but these kinds of life are culturally transmitted
and shared as many individuals in the present, and many in the
past, live or have lived under the same premises. When the latter is
the case, it is hardly possible to invent new adaptations again and
again, as men are always observing each other and interacting with
each other. The implication of some of Frazier's writings, that ghetto
dwellers create their way of life in a cultural limbo—an idea which
has had more modern expressions—appears as unacceptable in this
case as in any other situation where people live together, and in
particular where generations live together. The behavior of the streetcorner male is a natural pattern of masculinity with which ghetto
dwellers grow up and which to some extent they grow into. To see
it only as a complex of unsuccessful attempts at hiding failures by
self-deception seems, for many of the men involved, to be too much
psychologizing and too little sociology. But this does not mean that
the attachment to the ghetto-specific culture is very strong among its
bearers.

The question whether streetcorner males have mainstream culture
or a specific ghetto culture, then, is best answered by saying that
they have both, in different ways. There can be little doubt that this
is the understanding most in line with that contemporary trend in
anthropological thought which emphasizes the sharing of cultural
imagery, of expectations and definitions of reality, as the medium

whereby individuals in a community interact. It is noteworthy that many of the commentators who have been most skeptical of the idea of a ghetto-specific culture, or more generally a "culture of poverty," have been those who have taken a more narrow view of culture as a set of values about which an older generation consciously instructs the younger ones in the community.

Obviously, the answer to whether there is a ghetto-specific culture or not will depend to some extent on what we shall mean by culture. Perhaps this is too important a question to be affected by a mere terminological quibble, and perhaps social policy, in some areas, may well proceed unaffected by the questions raised by a ghetto-specific culture. On the other hand, in an anthropological study of community life, the wider view of cultural sharing and transmission which has been used here will have to play a part in our picture of the ghetto, including that of what ghetto males are like.

V GHETTO REVOLT

Stokely Carmichael and Charles V. Hamilton
WHITE POWER: THE COLONIAL SITUATION

James Meredith, who had integrated the University of Mississippi in 1962, began his one man "march against fear" through Mississippi in June 1966. During his march he was shot and wounded. Thousands came to Mississippi to carry on with Meredith's march. Stokely Carmichael, the newly elected chairman of the Student Nonviolent Coordinating Committee (SNCC), emerged as the major figure of this demonstration. "Black Power," Carmichael's slogan, soon replaced "We Shall Overcome" as the motto of the civil rights movement. Carmichael, born in Trinidad in 1942, came to the United States in 1953. During his college years at Howard University he was active in student movements. This social involvement carried him into the civil rights movement and he became a fieldworker for SNCC. By 1966 Carmichael, frustrated and disgusted with the failure of integration to bring full equality to black people, became the popularizer of Black Power. Black Power has many different meanings, but central to it is the belief that black Americans should direct their own destinies. A major obstacle to achieving self-determination, many blacks believe, is the colonialism practiced by white America. In 1967 Carmichael became coauthor with Charles V. Hamilton, a respected black political scientist, of Black Power: The Politics of Liberation in America. *They believed their book presented "a political framework and ideology which represents the last reasonable opportunity for this society to work out its racial problems short of prolonged destructive guerrilla warfare." The selection included below is taken from their opening chapter. It introduces the reader to the colonial thesis, that is, black ghettos are colonies of white America.*

As Charles Silberman wrote in *Crisis in Black and White:*

> *What we are discovering, in short, is that the United States—all of it, North as well as South, West as well as East—is a racist society in a sense and to a degree that we have refused so far to admit, much less face. . . . The tragedy of race relations in the United States is that there is no American Dilemma. White Americans are not torn and tortured by the conflict between their devotion to the American creed and their actual behavior. They are upset by the current state of race relations, to be sure. But what troubles them is not that justice is being denied but that their peace is being shattered and their business interrupted [pp. 9–10].*

To put it another way, there is no "American dilemma" because black people in this country form a colony, and it is not in the interest of the colonial power to liberate them. Black people are legal citizens of the United States with, for the most part, the same *legal* rights as other citizens. Yet they stand as colonial subjects in relation to the white society. Thus institutional racism has another name: colonialism.

Obviously, the analogy is not perfect. One normally associates a colony with a land and people subjected to, and physically separated from, the "Mother Country." This is not always the case, however; in South Africa and Rhodesia, black and white inhabit the same land—with blacks subordinated to whites just as in the English, French, Italian, Portuguese and Spanish colonies. It is the objective relationship which counts, not rhetoric (such as constitutions *articulating* equal rights) or geography.

The analogy is not perfect in another respect. Under classic colonialism, the colony is a source of cheaply produced raw materials (usually agricultural or mineral) which the "Mother Country" then processes into finished goods and sells at high profit—sometimes back to the colony itself. The black communities of the United States do not export anything except human labor. But is the differentiation more than a technicality? Essentially, the African colony is selling its labor; the product itself does not belong to the "subjects" because the land is not theirs. At the same time, let us look at the black people of the South: cultivating cotton at $3.00 for a ten-hour day and from that buying cotton dresses (and food and other goods) from white manufacturers. Economists might wish to argue this point endlessly; the objective relationship stands. Black people in the United States have a colonial relationship to the larger society, a relationship characterized by institutional racism. That colonial status operates in three areas—political, economic, social—which we shall discuss one by one.

Colonial subjects have their political decisions made for them by the colonial masters, and those decisions are handed down directly or through a process of "indirect rule." Politically, decisions which affect black lives have always been made by white people— the "white power structure." There is some dislike for this phrase because it tends to ignore or oversimplify the fact that there are many centers of power, many different forces making decisions.

Those who raise that objection point to the pluralistic character of the body politic. They frequently overlook the fact that American pluralism quickly becomes a monolithic structure on issues of race. When faced with demands from black people, the multi-faction whites unite and present a common front. This is especially true when the black group increases in number: ". . . a large Negro population is politically both an asset and a liability. A large Negro populace may not only expect to influence the commitments and behavior of a governor, but it also may expect to arouse the fears of many whites. The larger the Negro population, the greater the perceived threat (in the eyes of whites) and thus the greater the resistance to broad civil rights laws." . . .

The black community perceives the "white power structure" in very concrete terms. The man in the ghetto sees his white landlord come only to collect exorbitant rents and fail to make necessary repairs, while both know that the white-dominated city building inspection department will wink at violations or impose only slight fines. The man in the ghetto sees the white policeman on the corner brutally manhandle a black drunkard in a doorway, and at the same time accept a pay-off from one of the agents of the white-controlled rackets. He sees the streets in the ghetto lined with uncollected garbage, and he knows that the powers which could send trucks in to collect that garbage are white. When they don't, he knows the reason: the low political esteem in which the black community is held. He looks at the absence of a meaningful curriculum in the ghetto schools—for example, the history books that woefully overlook the historical achievements of black people—and he knows that the school board is controlled by whites. He is not about to listen to intellectual discourses on the pluralistic and fragmented nature of political power. He is faced with a "white power structure" as monolithic as Europe's colonial offices have been to African and Asian colonies.

There is another aspect of colonial politics frequently found in colonial Africa and in the United States: the process of indirect rule. . . . In other words, the white power structure rules the black community through local blacks who are responsive to the white leaders, the downtown, white machine, not to the black populace. These black politicians do not exercise effective power. They cannot be relied upon to make forceful demands in behalf of their black constituents, and they become no more than puppets. They put loyalty to a political party before loyalty to their constituents and thus nullify any bargaining power the black community might develop. Colonial politics causes the subject to muffle his voice while participating in the councils of the white power structure. The black man forfeits his opportunity to speak forcefully and clearly for his race, and he justifies this in terms of expediency. Thus, when one talks of a "Negro Establishment" in most places in this country, one is talking of an Establishment resting on a white power base; of hand-picked blacks whom that base projects as showpieces out front. These black "leaders" are, then, only as powerful as their white kingmakers will permit them to be. This is no less true of the North than the South. . . .

In time, one notes that a gap develops between the leadership and the followers. The masses, correctly, no longer view the leaders as their legitimate representatives. They come to see them more for what they are, emissaries sent by the white society. Identity between the two is lost. . . .

This process of cooptation and a subsequent widening of the gap between the black elites and the masses is common under colonial rule. There has developed in this country an entire class of "captive leaders" in the black communities. These are black people with certain technical and administrative skills who could provide useful leadership roles in the black communities but do not because they have become beholden to the white power structure. These are black school teachers, county agents, junior executives in management positions with companies, etc. . . .

Those who would assume the responsibility of representing black people in this country must be able to throw off the notion that they can effectively do so and still maintain a maximum amount of security. Jobs will have to be sacrificed, positions of prestige and status given up, favors forfeited. It may well be—and we think it is—that leadership and security are basically incompatible. When one forcefully challenges the racist system, one cannot, at the same time, expect that system to reward him or even treat him comfortably. Political leadership which pacifies and stifles its voice and then rationalizes this on grounds of gaining "something for my people" is, at bottom, gaining only meaningless, token rewards that an affluent society is perfectly willing to give.

A final aspect of political colonialism is the manipulation of political boundaries and the devising of restrictive electoral systems. The point is frequently made that black people are only ten per cent of the population—no less a personage than President Johnson has seen fit to remind us of this ratio. It is seldom pointed out that this minority is geographically located so as to create potential majority blocs—that strategic location being an ironic side-effect of segregation. But black people have never been able to utilize fully their numerical voting strength. Where we could vote, the white political machines have gerrymandered black neighborhoods so that the true voting strength is not reflected in political representation. . . .

The economic relationship of America's black communities to the larger society also reflects their colonial status. The political power exercised over those communities goes hand in glove with the economic deprivation experienced by the black citizens.

Historically, colonies have existed for the sole purpose of enriching, in one form or another, the "colonizer"; the consequence is to maintain the economic dependency of the "colonized." All too frequently we hear of the missionary motive behind colonization: to "civilize," to "Christianize" the underdeveloped, backward peoples. . . . One is immediately reminded of the bitter maxim voiced by many black Africans today: the missionaries came for our goods, not for our good. Indeed, the missionaries turned the Africans' eyes toward heaven, and then robbed them blind in the process. The colonies were sources from which raw materials were taken and markets to which finished products were sold. Manufacture and production were prohibited if this meant—as it usually did—competition with the "mother country." Rich in natural resources, Africa did not reap the benefit of these resources herself. In the Gold Coast (now Ghana), where the cocoa crop was the largest in the world, there was not one chocolate factory.

This same economic status has been perpetrated on the black community in this country. Exploiters come into the ghetto from outside, bleed it dry, and leave it economically dependent on the larger society. As with the missionaries, these exploiters frequently come as the "friend of the Negro," pretending to offer worthwhile goods and services, when their basic motivation is personal profit and their basic impact is the maintenance of racism. Many of the social welfare agencies—public and private—frequently pretend to offer "uplift" services; in reality, they end up creating a system which dehumanizes the individual and perpetuates his dependency. Conscious or unconscious, the paternalistic attitude of many of these agencies is no different from that of many missionaries going into Africa.

Professor Kenneth Clark described the economic colonization of the *Dark Ghetto* as follows:

> The ghetto feeds upon itself; it does not produce goods or contribute to the prosperity of the city. It has few large businesses. . . . Even though the white community has tried to keep the Negro confined in ghetto pockets, the white businessman has not stayed out of the ghetto. A ghetto, too, offers opportunities for profit, and in a competitive society profit is to be made where it can.
>
> In Harlem there is only one large department store and that is owned by whites. Negroes own a savings and loan association; and one Negro-owned bank has recently been organized. The other banks are branches of white-owned downtown banks. Property—apartment houses, stores, businesses, bars, concessions, and theaters—are for the most part owned by persons who live ouside the community and take their profits home. . . .
>
> When tumult arose in ghetto streets in the summer of 1964, most of the stores broken into and looted belonged to white men. Many of these owners responded to the destruction with bewilderment and anger, for they felt that they had been serving a community that needed them. They did not realize that the residents were not grateful for this service but bitter, as natives often feel toward the functionaries of a colonial power who in the very act of service, keep the hated structure of oppression intact [pp. 27–28].

It is a stark reality that the black communities are becoming more and more economically depressed. In June, 1966, the Bureau of Labor Statistics reported on the deteriorating condition of black people in this country. In 1948, the jobless rate of non-white males between the ages of fourteen and nineteen was 7.6 per cent. In 1965, the percentage of unemployment in this age group was 22.6 per cent. The corresponding figures for unemployed white male teen-agers were 8.3 per cent in 1948, and 11.8 per cent in 1965.

In the ten-year period from 1955 to 1965, total employment for youth between the ages of fourteen and nineteen increased from 2,642,000 to 3,612,000. Non-white youth got only 36,000 of those 970,000 new jobs. As for adults, the ratio of non-white to white adult unemployment has remained double: in June, 1966, 4.1 per cent for whites and 8.3 per cent for non-whites.

Lest someone talk about educational preparation, let it quickly be added here that *unemployment rates in 1965 were higher for non-white high school graduates than for white high school dropouts.* Furthermore, the median income of a non-white male college graduate in 1960 was $5,020—actually $110 less than the earnings of white males with only one to three years of high school. Dr. Andrew F. Brimmer, the Negro former Assistant Secretary for Economic Affairs in the Department of Commerce, further highlights this situation in speaking of expected lifetime earnings:

> *Perhaps the most striking feature . . . is the fact that a non-white man must have between one and three years of college before he can expect to earn as much as a white man with less than eight years of schooling, over the course of their respective working lives.* Moreover, even after completing college and spending at least one year in graduate school, a non-white man can expect to do about as well as a white person who only completed high school.

A white man with four years of high school education can expect to earn about $253,000 in his lifetime. A black man with five years or more of college can expect to earn $246,000 in his lifetime. Dr. Brimmer is presently a member of the Federal Reserve Board, and many people will point to his new position as an indication of "the progress of Negroes." . . .

Again, as in the African colonies, the black community is sapped senseless of what economic resources it does have. Through the exploitative system of credit, people pay "a dollar down, a dollar a week" literally for years. Interest rates are astronomical, and the merchandise—of relatively poor quality in the first place—is long since worn out before the final payment. Professor David Caplovitz of Columbia University has commented in his book, *The Poor Pay More,* "The high markup on low-quality goods is thus a major device used by merchants to protect themselves against the risks of their credit business" (p. 18). Many of the ghetto citizens, because of unsteady employment and low incomes, cannot obtain credit from more legitimate businesses; thus they must do without important items or end up being exploited. They are lured into the stores by attractive advertising displays hawking, for example, three rooms of furniture for "only $199." Once inside, the unsuspecting customer is persuaded to buy lesser furniture at a more expensive price, or he is told that the advertised items are temporarily out of stock and is shown other goods. More frequently than not, of course, all the items are overpriced. . . .

This is why the society does nothing meaningful about institutional racism: because the black community has been the creation of, and dominated by, a combination of oppressive forces and special interests in the white community. The groups which have access to the necessary resources and the ability to effect change benefit politically and economically from the continued subordinate status of the black community. This is not to say that every single white American consciously oppresses black people. He does not need to. Institutional racism has been maintained deliberately by the power structure and through indifference, inertia and lack of courage on the part of white masses as well as petty officials. Whenever black demands for change become loud and strong, indifference is replaced by active opposition based on fear and self-interest. The line between purposeful suppression and indifference blurs. One way or another, most whites participate in economic colonialism.

Indeed, the colonial white power structure has been a most formidable foe. It has perpetuated a vicious circle—the poverty cycle—in which the black communities are denied good jobs, and therefore stuck with a low income and therefore unable to obtain a good education with which to obtain good jobs. . . . They cannot qualify for credit at most reputable places; they then resort to unethical merchants who take advantage of them by charging higher prices for inferior goods. They end up having less funds to buy in bulk, thus unable to reduce overall costs. They remain trapped.

In the face of such realities, it becomes ludicrous to condemn black people for "not showing more initiative." Black people are not in a depressed condition because of some defect in their character. The colonial power structure clamped a boot of oppression on the neck of the black people and then, ironically, said "they are not ready for freedom." Left solely to the good will of the oppressor, the oppressed would never be ready.

And no one accepts blame. And there is no "white power structure" doing it to them. And they are in that condition "because they are lazy and don't want to work." And this is not colonialism. And this is the land of opportunity, and the home of the free. And people should not become alienated.

But people *do* become alienated. . . .

The social and psychological effects on black people of all their degrading experiences are also very clear. From the time black people were introduced into this country, their condition has fostered human indignity and the denial of respect. Born into this society today, black people begin to doubt themselves, their worth as human beings. Self-respect becomes almost impossible. Kenneth Clark describes the process in *Dark Ghetto:*

> Human beings who are forced to live under ghetto conditions and whose daily experience tells them that almost nowhere in society are they respected and granted the ordinary dignity and courtesy accorded to others will, as a matter of course, begin to doubt their own worth. Since every human being depends upon his cumulative experiences with others for clues as to how he should view and value himself, children who are consistently rejected understandably begin to question and doubt whether they, their family, and their group really deserve no more respect from the larger society than they receive. These doubts become the seeds of a pernicious self- and group-hatred, the Negro's complex and debilitating prejudice against himself.
>
> The preoccupation of many Negroes with hair straighteners, skin bleachers, and the like illustrates this tragic aspect of American racial prejudice—Negroes have come to believe in their own inferiority [pp. 63–64].

There was the same result in Africa. . . .

In a manner similar to that of the colonial powers in Africa, American society indicates avenues of escape from the ghetto for those individuals who adapt to the "mainstream." This adaptation means to disassociate oneself from the black race, its culture, community and heritage, and become immersed (dispersed is another term) in the white world. What actually happens, as Professor E. Franklin Frazier pointed out in his book, *Black Bourgeoisie,* is that the black person ceases to identify himself with black people yet is obviously unable to assimilate with whites. He becomes a "marginal man," living on the fringes of both societies in a world largely of "make believe." This black person is urged to adopt American middle-class standards and values. As with the black African who had to become a "Frenchman" in order to be accepted, so to be an American, the black man must strive to become "white." To the extent that he does, he is considered "well adjusted"—one who has "risen above the race question." These people are frequently held up by the white Establishment as living examples of the progress being made by the society in solving the race problem. Suffice it to say that precisely because they are required to denounce—overtly or covertly—their black race, *they are reinforcing racism in this country.*

In the United States, as in Africa, their "adaptation" operated to deprive the black community of its potential skills and brain power. All too frequently, these "integrated" people are used to blunt the true feelings and goals of the black masses. They are picked as "Negro leaders," and the white power structure proceeds to talk to and deal only with them. Needless to say, no fruitful, meaningful dialogue can take place under such circumstances. Those hand-picked "leaders" have no viable constituency for which they can speak and act. All this is a classic formula of colonial co-optation.

At all times, then, the social effects of colonialism are to degrade and to dehumanize the subjected black man. White America's School of Slavery and Segregation, like the School of Colonialism, has taught the subject to hate himself and to deny his own humanity. The white society maintains an attitude of superiority and the black community has too often succumbed to it, thereby permitting the whites to believe in the correctness of their position. Racist assumptions of white superiority have been so deeply engrained into the fiber of the society that they infuse the entire functioning of the national subconscious. They are taken for granted and frequently not even recognized. As Professors Lewis Killian and Charles Grigg express it in their book, *Racial Crisis in America:*

> At the present time, integration as a solution to the race problem demands that the Negro foreswear his identity as a Negro. But for a lasting solution, the meaning of "American" must lose its implicit racial modifier, "white." Even without biological amalgamation, integration requires a sincere acceptance by all Americans that it is just as good to be a black American as to be a white American. Here is the crux of the problem of race relations—the redefinition of the sense of group position so that the status advantage of the white man is no longer an advantage, so that an American may acknowledge his Negro ancestry without apologizing for it. . . . They [black people] live in a society in which to be unconditionally "American" is to be white, and to be black is a misfortune [pp. 108–9].

The time is long overdue for the black community to redefine itself, set forth new values and goals, and organize around them.

The editor wishes to thank the following for permission to use excerpts included in Carmichael and Hamilton's "White Power: The Colonial Situation": Random House for Charles Silberman, *Crisis in Black and White* (copyright 1964 by Random House, Inc.); Prentice-Hall for Lewis Killian and Charles Grigg, *Racial Crisis in America: Leadership in Conflict* (copyright 1964 by Prentice-Hall, Inc.); and Harper and Row for Kenneth B. Clark, *Dark Ghetto* (copyright 1965 by Harper and Row).

Christopher Lasch

BLACK POWER: CULTURAL
NATIONALISM IN POLITICS

*The colonial analogy was first explored seriously by Kenneth B. Clark in
Dark Ghetto (1965) and later popularized by Carmichael and Hamilton in
Black Power (1967). The colonial analogy, especially as it is used in the
latter book, sees the ghetto not only as a colony but also as having a culture
distinct from white America. This cultural nationalism emphasizes the African inheritance and is critical of American liberalism and white scholarship.
Controversies over the Moynihan Report and* The Confessions of Nat Turner
*have divided black and white intellectuals. In turn many white intellectuals
are extremely critical of the Black Power ideology. One of these critics is
Christopher Lasch, the historian of the American Left. In the following selection, taken from Lasch's work* The Agony of the American Left, *he is very
critical of the exponents of Black Power, especially Carmichael and Hamilton.*

Because Black Power has many sources, it abounds in contradic-
tions. On the one hand Black Power derives from a tradition of
Negro separatism, self-discipline, and self-help, advocating traditional "nationalist" measures ranging from cooperative businesses
to proposals for complete separation. On the other hand, some
of the spokesmen for Black Power contemplate guerrilla warfare
against American "colonialism." In general, CORE [Congress of
Racial Equality] is closer to the first position, SNCC [Student Nonviolent Coordinating Committee] to the second. But the ambiguity
of Black Power derives from the fact that both positions frequently
coexist—as in *Black Power,* the book by Stokely Carmichael and
Charles V. Hamilton which was intended, apparently, to be the
manifesto of the new movement but which has evoked very little
enthusiasm either among advocates of Black Power or among
radicals in general.

This book is disappointing, first of all because it makes so few
concrete proposals for action, and these seem hardly revolutionary
in nature: black control of black schools, black-owned businesses,

From Christopher Lasch, *The Agony of the American Left.* Copyright 1966, 1967, 1968
by Christopher Lasch. Reprinted by permission of Alfred A. Knopf, Inc.

and the like. Carmichael and Hamilton talk vaguely of a "major reorientation of the society" and of "the necessarily total revamping of the society" (expressions they use interchangeably) as the "central goal" of Black Power, and they urge black people not to enter coalitions with groups not similarly committed to sweeping change. But they never explain why their program demands such changes, or indeed why it would be likely to bring them about.

In order to deal with this question, one would have to discuss the relation of the ghetto to the rest of American society. To what extent does American society *depend* on the ghetto? It is undoubtedly true, as the advocates of Black Power maintain, that there is no immediate prospect that the ghettos will disappear. But it is still not clear whether the ghettos in their present state of inferiority and dependence are in some sense necessary for the functioning of American society—that is, whether powerful interests have a stake in perpetuating them—or whether they persist because American society can get along so well without black people that there is no motive either to integrate them by getting rid of the ghettos or to allow the ghettos to govern themselves. In other words, what interests have a stake in maintaining the present state of affairs? Does the welfare of General Motors depend on keeping the ghetto in a state of dependence? Would self-determination for the ghetto threaten General Motors? Carmichael and Hamilton urge black people to force white merchants out of the ghetto and to replace them with black businesses, but it is not clear why this program, aimed at businesses which themselves occupy a marginal place in American corporate capitalism, would demand or lead to a "total revamping of the society."

On this point the critics of Black Power raise what appears to be a telling objection, which can be met only by clarifying the Black Power position beyond anything Carmichael and Hamilton have done. Paul Feldman writes: "A separatist black economy—unless it were to be no more than a carbon copy of the poverty that already prevails—would need black steel, black automobiles, black refrigerators. And for that, Negroes would have to take control of General Motors and U.S. Steel: hardly an immediate prospect, and utter fantasy as long as Carmichael proposes to 'go it alone.' "

But a related criticism of Black Power, that it merely proposes to substitute for white storekeepers black storekeepers who would then continue to exploit the ghetto in the same ways, seems to me to miss the point, since advocates of Black Power propose to replace white businesses with black *cooperatives.* In this respect Black Power does challenge capitalism, at least in principle; but the question remains whether a program aimed at small businessmen effectively confronts capitalism at any very sensitive point.

Still, small businessmen, whatever their importance outside, are a sensitive issue in the ghetto and getting rid of them might do wonders for Negro morale. Not only that, but Negro cooperatives would help to reduce the flow of capital out of the ghetto, contributing thereby, if only modestly, to the accumulation of capital as well as providing employment. A "separatist black economy" is not really what Black Power seems to point to, any more than it points to exploitive Negro shopkeepers in place of white ones. "In the end," Feldman writes, "the militant-sounding proposals for a build-it-yourself black economy (a black economy, alas, without capital) remind one of . . . precisely those white moderates who preach self-help to the Negroes." But Black Power envisions (or seems to envision) *collective* self-help, which is not the same thing as individualist petty capitalism on the one hand, or, on the other hand, a separate black economy. . . .

Black Power contains many other examples of sloppy analysis and the failure to pursue any line of reasoning through to its consequences. Basic questions are left in doubt. Is the Negro issue a class issue, a race issue, or a "national" (ethnic) issue? Treating it as a class issue—as the authors appear to do when they write that the "only coalition which seems acceptable to us," in the long run, is "a coalition of poor blacks and poor whites"—further weakens the ethnic analogy and blurs the concept of black people as a "nation"—the essential premise, one would think, of "Black Power."

Paul Feldman seems to me on the wrong track when he accuses SNCC of resorting to "what is primarily a racial rather than an economic approach." On the contrary, the advocates of Black Power tend, if anything, toward a misplaced class analysis, derived from popularized Marxism or from Castroism, which considers the American Negro as an exploited proletarian. Thus Carmichael and Hamilton try to sustain their analogy of the Negroes as a "colonial" people by arguing that the Negro communities "export" cheap labor. This may be true of the South, where Negroes do represent cheap labor (although mechanization is changing the situation even in the South) and where racism, accordingly, is functionally necessary as a way of maintaining class exploitation. Here the Negroes might be mobilized behind a program of class action designed to change society in fundamental ways. In the North, however, the essential feature of the Negro's situation is precisely his dispensability, which is increasingly evident in the growing unemployment of Negro men, particularly young men. As Bayard Rustin has pointed out, ghetto Negroes do not constitute an exploited proletariat. They should be regarded not as a working class but as a lower class or *lumpenproletariat*. "The distinction," he writes, "is important. The working class is employed. It has a relation to the production of goods and services; much of it is organized in unions. It enjoys a measure of cohesion, discipline and stability lacking in the lower class. The latter is unemployed or marginally employed. It is relatively unorganized, incohesive, unstable. It contains the petty criminal and antisocial elements. Above all, unlike the working class, it lacks the sense of a stake in society. When the slum proletariat is black, its alienation is even greater."

It is precisely these conditions, however, that make Black Power more relevant to the ghetto than "civil rights," if Black Power is understood as a form of ethnic solidarity which addresses itself to the instability and to the "antisocial" elements of ghetto life, and tries to organize and "socialize" those elements around a program of collective self-help. The potential usefulness of black nationalism, in other words, lies in its ability to organize groups which neither the church, the unions, the political parties, nor the social workers have been able to organize. Rustin's analysis, while it effectively refutes the idea that the Negro lower class can become a revolutionary political force in any conventional sense, does not necessarily lead one to reject Black Power altogether, as he does, or to endorse "coalitions." Actually it can be used as an argument *against* coalitions, on the grounds that a marginal lower class has no interests in common with, say, the labor movement. If the Negroes are a lower class as opposed to a working class, it is hard to see, theoretically, why the labor movement is "foremost among [the Negroes'] political allies," as Paul Feldman believes. Theory aside, experience does not bear out this contention.

Concerning the revolutionary potential of Black Power, however, Rustin seems to me absolutely right. "From the revolutionist point of view," he says, "the question is not whether steps could be taken to strengthen organization among the *lumpenproletariat* but whether that group could be a central agent of social transformation. Generally, the answer has been no." But these observations, again, do not necessarily lead to the conclusion that Black Power has no validity. Rather they suggest the need to divorce Black Power as a program of collective self-advancement from the revolutionary rhetoric of the New Left, while at the same time they remind us that other ethnic minorities, faced with somewhat similar conditions, created new institutions that had important (though not revolutionary) social consequences. Black people cannot be considered a "nation" and a revolutionary *class* at the same time.

Robert Blauner

INTERNAL COLONIALISM AND GHETTO REVOLT

Robert Blauner, a sociologist, who has done considerable work on black culture and ghetto revolt, takes issue with white intellectuals who deny the validity of the colonial analogy. Blauner in his writings on black culture supports the view that there exists within the ghetto a dynamic and separate culture. Black culture, according to Blauner, is an ethnic rather than a lower-class culture. For whites to deny the existence of a distinctive ethos and value system in the black community, Blauner charges, is another means by which internal colonialism is practiced in the United States. He sees a connection between cultural nationalism and other forms of ghetto revolt, such as urban riots and ghetto control politics. Cultural nationalism as well as other manifestations of black power represent a black collective response to colonialism. In the following essay Blauner argues that internal colonialism is a realistic description of the relationship of the black ghettos to white America. It provides a "framework that can integrate the insight of caste and racism, ethnicity, culture, and economic exploitation into an overall conceptual scheme."

It is becoming almost fashionable to analyze American racial conflict today in terms of the colonial analogy. I shall argue in this paper that the utility of this perspective depends upon a distinction between colonization as a process and colonialism as a social, economic, and political system. It is the experience of colonization that Afro-Americans share with many of the non-white people of the world. But this subjugation has taken place in a societal context that differs in important respects from the situation of "classical colonialism." In the body of this essay I shall look at some major developments in Black protest—the urban riots, cultural nationalism, and the movement for ghetto control—as collective responses to colonized status. Viewing our domestic situation as a special form of colonization outside a context of a colonial system will help explain some of the dilemmas and ambiguities within these movements.

The present crisis in American life has brought about changes in social perspectives and the questioning of long accepted frame-

From Robert Blauner, "Internal Colonialism and Ghetto Revolt," *Social Problems* XVI, No. 4 (Spring 1969), pp. 393–406. Reprinted with the permission of The Society for the Study of Social Problems.

works. Intellectuals and social scientists have been forced by the pressure of events to look at old definitions of the character of our society, the role of racism, and the workings of basic institutions. The depth and volatility of contemporary racial conflict challenge sociologists in particular to question the adequacy of theoretical models by which we have explained American race relations in the past.

For a long time the distinctiveness of the Negro situation among the ethnic minorities was placed in terms of color, and the systematic discrimination that follows from our deep-seated racial prejudices. This was sometimes called the caste theory, and while provocative, it missed essential and dynamic features of American race relations. In the past ten years there has been a tendency to view Afro-Americans as another ethnic group not basically different in experience from previous ethnics and whose "immigration" condition in the North would in time follow their upward course. The inadequacy of this model is now clear—even the Kerner Report devotes a chapter to criticizing this analogy. A more recent (though hardly new) approach views the essence of racial subordination in economic class terms: Black people as an underclass are to a degree specially exploited and to a degree economically dispensable in an automating society. Important as are economic factors, the power of race and racism in America cannot be sufficiently explained through class analysis. Into this theory vacuum steps the model of internal colonialism. Problematic and imprecise as it is, it gives hope of becoming a framework that can integrate the insights of caste and racism, ethnicity, culture, and economic exploitation into an overall conceptual scheme. At the same time, the danger of the colonial model is the imposition of an artificial analogy which might keep us from facing up to the fact (to quote Harold Cruse) that "the American black and white social phenomenon is a uniquely new world thing."

During the late 1950s, identification with African nations and other colonial or formerly colonized peoples grew in importance among Black militants. As a result the United States was increasingly seen as a colonial power and the concept of domestic colonialism was introduced into the political analysis and rhetoric of militant nationalists. During the same period Black social theorists began developing this frame of reference for explaining American realities. As early as 1962, Cruse characterized race relations in this country as "domestic colonialism." Three years later in *Dark Ghetto*, Kenneth Clark demonstrated how the political, economic, and social structure of Harlem was essentially that of a colony. Finally in 1967, a full-blown elaboration of "internal colonialism" provided the theoretical framework for Carmichael and Hamilton's widely read *Black Power*. The following year the colonial analogy gained currency and new "respectability" when Senator McCarthy habitually referred to Black Americans as a colonized people during his campaign. While the rhetoric of internal colonialism was catching on, other social scientists began to raise questions about its appropriateness as a scheme of analysis.

The colonial analysis has been rejected as obscurantist and misleading by scholars who point to the significant differences in history and social-political conditions between our domestic patterns and what took place in Africa and India. Colonialism traditionally refers to the establishment of domination over a geographically external political unit, most often inhabited by people of a different race and culture, where this domination is political and economic, and the colony exists subordinated to and dependent upon the mother country. Typically the colonizers exploit the land, the raw materials, the labor, and other resources of the colonized nation; in addition a formal recognition is given to the difference in power, autonomy, and political status, and various agencies are set up to maintain this subordination. Seemingly the analogy must be stretched beyond usefulness if the American version is to be forced into this model. For here we are talking about group relations within a society; the mother country—colony separation in geography is absent. Though whites certainly colonized the territory of the original Americans, internal colonization of Afro-Americans did not involve the settlement of whites in any land that was unequivocally Black. And unlike the colonial situation, there has been no formal recognition of differing power since slavery was abolished outside the South. Classic colonialism involved the control and exploitation of the majority of a nation by a minority of outsiders. Whereas in America the people who are oppressed were themselves originally outsiders and are a numerical minority.

This conventional critique of "internal colonialism" is useful in pointing to the differences between our domestic patterns and the overseas situation. But in its bold attack it tends to lose sight of common experiences that have been historically shared by the most subjugated racial minorities in America and non-white peoples in some other parts of the world. For understanding the most dramatic recent developments on the race scene, this common core element —which I shall call colonization—may be more important than the undeniable divergences between the two contexts.

The common features ultimately relate to the fact that the classical colonialism of the imperialist era and American racism developed out of the same historical situation and reflected a common world economic and power stratification. The slave trade for the most part preceded the imperialist partition and economic exploitation of Africa, and in fact may have been a necessary prerequisite for colonial conquest—since it helped deplete and pacify Africa, undermining the resistance to direct occupation. Slavery contributed one of the basic raw materials for the textile industry which provided much of the capital for the West's industrial development and need for economic expansionism. The essential condition for both American slavery and European colonialism was the power domination and the technological superiority of the Western world in its relation to peoples of non-Western and non-white origins. This objective supremacy in technology and military power buttressed the West's sense of cultural superiority, laying the basis for racist ideologies that were elaborated to justify control and exploitation of non-white people. Thus because classical colonialism and America's internal version developed out of a similar balance of technological, cultural, and power relations, a common *process* of social oppression characterized the racial patterns in the two contexts—despite the variation in political and social structure.

There appear to be four basic components of the colonization complex. The first refers to how the racial group enters into the dominant society (whether colonial power or not). Colonization begins with a forced, involuntary entry. Second, there is an impact on the culture and social organization of the colonized people which is more than just a result of such "natural" processes as contact and acculturation. The colonizing power carries out a policy which constrains, transforms, or destroys indigenous values, orientations, and ways of life. Third, colonization involves a relationship by which members of the colonized group tend to be administered by representatives of the dominant power. There is an experience of being managed and manipulated by outsiders in terms of ethnic status.

A final fundament of colonization is racism. Racism is a principle of social domination by which a group seen as inferior or different in terms of alleged biological characteristics is exploited, controlled, and oppressed socially and psychically by a superordinate group. Except for the marginal case of Japanese imperialism, the major examples of colonialism have involved the subjugation of non-white Asian, African, and Latin American peoples by white European powers. Thus racism has generally accompanied colonialism. Race prejudice can exist without colonization—the experience of Asian-American minorities is a case in point—but racism as a system of domination is part of the complex of colonization.

The concept of colonization stresses the enormous fatefulness of the historical factor, namely the manner in which a minority group becomes a part of the dominant society. The crucial difference between the colonized Americans and the ethnic immigrant minorities is that the latter have always been able to operate fairly competitively within that relatively open section of the social and economic order because these groups came voluntarily in search of a better life, because their movements in society were not administratively controlled, and because they transformed their culture at their own pace—giving up ethnic values and institutions when it was seen as a desirable exchange for improvements in social position.

In present-day America, a major device of Black colonization is the powerless ghetto. . . .

Of course many ethnic groups in America have lived in ghettoes. What make the Black ghettoes an expression of colonized status are three special features. First, the ethnic ghettoes arose more from voluntary choice, both in the sense of the choice to immigrate to America and the decision to live among one's fellow ethnics. Second, the immigrant ghettoes tended to be a one and two generation phenomenon; they were actually way-stations in the process of acculturation and assimilation. When they continue to persist as in the case of San Francisco's Chinatown, it is because they are big business for the ethnics themselves and there is a new stream of immigrants. The Black ghetto on the other hand has been a more permanent phenomenon, although some individuals do escape it. But most relevant is the third point. European ethnic groups like the Poles, Italians, and Jews generally only experienced a brief period, often less than a generation, during which their residential buildings, commercial stores, and other enterprises were owned by outsiders. The Chinese and Japanese faced handicaps of color prejudice that were almost as strong as the Blacks faced, but very soon gained control of their internal communities, because their traditional ethnic culture and social organization had not been destroyed by slavery and internal colonization. But Afro-Americans are distinct in the extent to which their segregated communities have remained controlled economically, politically, and administratively from the outside. . . .

Colonization outside of a traditional colonial structure has its own special conditions. The group culture and social structure of the colonized in America is less developed; it is also less autonomous. In addition, the colonized are a numerical minority, and furthermore they are ghettoized more totally and are more dispersed than people under classic colonialism. Though these realities affect the magnitude and direction of response, it is my basic thesis that the most important expressions of protest in the Black community during the recent years reflect the colonized status of Afro-America. Riots, programs of separation, politics of community control, the Black revolutionary movements, and cultural nationalism each represent a different strategy of attack on domestic colonialism in America. Let us now examine some of these movements.

Riot or Revolt?

The so-called riots are being increasingly recognized as a preliminary if primitive form of mass rebellion against a colonial status. There is still a tendency to absorb their meaning within the conventional scope of assimilation-integration politics: some commentators stress the material motives involved in looting as a sign that the rioters want to join America's middle-class affluence just like everyone else. That motives are mixed and often unconscious, that Black people want good furniture and television sets like whites is beside the point. The guiding impulse in most major outbreaks has not been integration with American society, but an attempt to stake out a sphere of control by moving against that society and destroying the symbols of its oppression. . . .

Despite the appeal of Frantz Fanon to young Black revolutionaries, America is not Algeria. It is difficult to foresee how riots in our cities can play a role equivalent to rioting in the colonial situation as an integral phase in a movement for national liberation. In 1968 some militant groups (for example, the Black Panther Party in Oakland) had concluded that ghetto riots were self-defeating of the lives and interests of Black people in the present balance of organization and gunpower, though they had served a role to stimulate both Black consciousness and white awareness of the depths of racial crisis. Such militants have been influential in "cooling" their communities during periods of high riot potential. Theoretically oriented Black radicals see riots as spontaneous mass behavior which must be replaced by a revolutionary organization and consciousness. But despite the differences in objective conditions, the violence of the 1960s seems to serve the same psychic function, assertions of dignity and manhood for young Blacks in urban ghettoes, as it did for the colonized of North Africa described by Fanon and Memmi.

Cultural Nationalism

Cultural conflict is generic to the colonial relation because colonization involves the domination of Western technological values over the more communal cultures of non-Western peoples. Colonialism played havoc with the national integrity of the peoples it brought under its sway. . . .

The most total destruction of culture in the colonization process took place not in traditional colonialism but in America. As Frazier stressed, the integral cultures of the diverse African peoples who furnished the slave trade were destroyed because slaves from different tribes, kingdoms, and linguistic groups were purposely separated to maximize domination and control. Thus language, religion, and national loyalties were lost in North America much more completely than in the Caribbean and Brazil where slavery developed somewhat differently. Thus on this key point America's internal colonization has been more total and extreme than situations of classic colonialism. . . .

Yet a similar cultural process unfolds in both contexts of colonialism. To the extent that they are involved in the larger society and economy, the colonized are caught up in a conflict between two cultures. Fanon has described how the assimilation-oriented schools of Martinique taught him to reject his own culture and Blackness in favor of Westernized, French, and white values. Both the colonized elites under traditional colonialism and perhaps the majority of Afro-Americans today experience a parallel split in identity, cultural loyalty, and political orientation.

The colonizers use their culture to socialize the colonized elites (intellectuals, politicians, and middle class) into an identification with the colonial system. Because Western culture has the prestige, the power, and the key to open the limited opportunity that a minority of the colonized may achieve, the first reaction seems to be an acceptance of the dominant values.

Cultural revitalization movements play a key role in anti-colonial movements. They follow an inner necessity and logic of their own that comes from the consequences of colonialism on groups and personal identities; they are also essential to provide the solidarity which the political or military phase of the anti-colonial revolution requires. In the United States an Afro-American culture has been developing since slavery out of the ingredients of African worldviews, the experience of bondage, Southern values and customs, migration and the Northern lower-class ghettoes, and most importantly, the political history of the Black population in its struggle against racism. That Afro-Americans are moving toward cultural nationalism in a period when ethnic loyalties tend to be weak (and perhaps on the decline) in this country is another confirmation of the unique colonized position of the Black group. (A similar nationalism seems to be growing among American Indians and Mexican-Americans.)

The Movement for Ghetto Control

The call for Black Power unites a number of varied movements and tendencies. Though no clear-cut program has yet emerged, the most important emphasis seems to be the movement for control of the ghetto. Black leaders and organizations are increasingly concerned with owning and controlling those institutions that exist within or impinge upon their community. The colonial model provides a key to the understanding of this movement, and indeed ghetto control advocates have increasingly invoked the language of colonialism in pressing for local home rule. The framework of anti-colonialism explains why the struggle for poor people's or community control of poverty programs has been more central in many cities than the content of these programs and why it has been crucial to exclude whites from leadership positions in Black organizations.

The key institutions that anti-colonialists want to take over or control are business, social services, schools, and the police. Though many spokesmen have advocated the exclusion of white landlords and small businessmen from the ghetto, this program has evidently not struck fire with the Black population and little concrete movement toward economic expropriation has yet developed. Welfare recipients have organized in many cities to protect their rights and gain a greater voice in the decisions that affect them, but whole communities have not yet been able to mount direct action against welfare colonialism. Thus schools and the police seem now to be the burning issues of ghetto control politics.

During the past few years there has been a dramatic shift from educational integration as the primary goal to that of community control of the schools. Afro-Americans are demanding their own school boards, with the power to hire and fire principals and teachers and to construct a curriculum which would be relevant to the special needs and culture style of ghetto youth. Especially active in high schools and colleges have been Black students, whose protests have centered on the incorporation of Black Power and Black culture into the educational system.

This movement reflects some of the problems and ambiguities that stem from the situation of colonization outside an immediate colonial context. The Afro-American community is not parallel in structure to the communities of colonized nations under traditional colonialism. The significant difference here is the lack of fully developed indigenous institutions besides the church. Outside of some areas of the South there is really no Black economy, and most Afro-

Americans are inevitably caught up in the larger society's structure of occupations, education, and mass communication. Thus the ethnic nationalist orientation which reflects the reality of colonization exists alongside an integrationist orientation which corresponds to the reality that the institutions of the larger society are much more developed than those of the incipient nation. . . .

There is a growing recognition that the police are the most crucial institution maintaining the colonized status of Black Americans. And of all establishment institutions, police departments probably include the highest proportion of individual racists. This is no accident since central to the workings of racism (an essential component of colonization) are attacks on the humanity and dignity of the subject group. Through their normal routines the police constrict Afro-Americans to Black neighborhoods by harassing and questioning them when found outside the ghetto; they break up groups of youth congregating on corners or in cars without any provocation; and they continue to use offensive and racist language no matter how many inter-group understanding seminars have been built into the police academy. They also shoot to kill ghetto residents for alleged crimes such as car thefts and running from police officers.

The various "Black Power" programs that are aimed at gaining control of individual ghettoes—buying up property and businesses, running the schools through community boards, taking over antipoverty programs and other social agencies, diminishing the arbitrary power of the police—can serve to revitalize the institutions of the ghetto and build up an economic, professional, and political power base. These programs seem limited; we do not know at present if they are enough in themselves to end colonized status. But they are certainly a necessary first step.

Harold Cruse

POSTSCRIPT ON BLACK POWER—
THE DIALOGUE BETWEEN
SHADOW AND SUBSTANCE

A major critic of both the integrationists of the early sixties and the black nationalists of the late sixties is Harold Cruse, author of The Crisis of the Negro Intellectual *and* Rebellion or Revolution. *Cruse, a black intellectual, who refuses to take up the rhetoric of black nationalism, attempts instead to examine the reasons why the black movement of the sixties suffered from an "identity vacuum."* The Crisis of the Negro Intellectual, *from which this selection is taken, is a study of the black intelligentsia in the twentieth century. Cruse argues that black intellectuals must play a central role in the movement for racial change, if race progress is going to be a reality. They must formulate a political philosophy before they can decide on what means to use to reach the goals established. Cruse is critical of black intellectuals who attempt to resolve the black dilemma in America with imported ideologies, such as Marxism or Pan-Africanism. Blacks must develop an intellectual response that is appropriate to black America. Integration is no solution for black America; all it creates is cultural negation. This is true, Cruse argues, whether one discusses the writers of the Harlem Renaissance, the Marxists of the thirties, or the liberals of the postwar period. Also Cruse suggests that black militants should cease talking about guerrilla activity and concentrate on building a viable political philosophy. In the following essay, Cruse gives the Black Power movement an historical perspective and provides the reader with an excellent summary of the black dilemma in twentieth century America.*

The old proverb, "Necessity is the mother of invention," was given a unique civil rights configuration when the slogan of Black Power was popularized during the summer of 1966. The necessity lay in the fact that the SNCC–CORE united front, in its direct-action-protest phase, had bogged down. Like an army that had outdistanced its supply units, it had finally been stopped by the enemy counterattack—the backlash.

The slogan Black Power was conjured up and used in the manner of a rallying victory cry. In effect it covers up a defeat without

199

having to explain either the basic reasons for it or the flaws in the original strategy; it suggests the dimensions of a future victory in the attainment of goals while, at the same time, dispelling the fears of more defeats in the pursuit of such goals. Yet, each and every goal was already implicit in the direct-action movements even before the slogan was projected. Black Power, then, was raised when social reality forced so-called revolutionaries to put action aside and start thinking. A movement that up to then had placed its highest premiums on practical activism now turned over a new leaf and began to get theoretical about the real *substance* of its civil rights objectives. The old slogans about "justice," "liberation," "Freedom Now," etc., were now mere shadow terms. If direct action-protest had been defeated by certain structural barriers of society, the new slogan became a commitment to deal with the real substance of those barriers that block the attainment of civil rights. Thus fears, opposition, and startled cries of alarm were immediately raised. A new threat fell across the land like an ominous shadow, even though the exact concept of Black Power has not yet been clearly defined. At this writing, as a concept it remains as vague as the former abstractions—Justice and Liberation. Although the Black Power concept is a more specific and provocative abstraction than Freedom, it is open to just as many diverse and conflicting interpretations. While it tries to give more clarity to what forms Freedom will assume in America as the end-product of a new program, the Black Power dialogue does not close the conceptual gap between shadow and substance, any more than it plots a course for the program dynamic. Whatever Black Power is supposed to mean to its adherents and its foes, its implications cannot be clearly understood unless one examines the slogan's aims and origin. Who originated the slogan? Are its aims revolutionary or reformist?

It was originated by a leading member of the radical wing of the black bourgeoisie, Adam Clayton Powell: He first mentioned it at a Chicago rally in May, 1965, and elaborated upon it in his Howard University Commencement speech of May 29, 1966. It was picked up and popularized by a leading member of the radical wing of the civil rights movement, Stokely Carmichael, from the lower-middle-class students' front. Carmichael was then joined by certain nationalist elements from integration-minded CORE, the radical wing of the civil rights movement in the North. Thus, the slogan of Black Power appeared to signal a concerted shift from SNCC–CORE radical-protest integrationism—not to nationalist separatism—but to some intermediate position between separatism and racial integration.

Since all of these diverse protest elements, separatists, nationalists, and direct actionists, had made up the sum total of what was called the Black Revolution, formal logic would conclude that this tumultuous shift to Black Power denoted a turn to a more revolutionary posture than formerly held by SNCC and CORE when their direct-action battering rams were at full strength North and South. But a closer examination of every analysis by each Black Power exponent from SNCC and CORE reveals that while the slogan cast a revolutionary *sounding* theme and a threat of more intense revolt across the land, the *substance* was, in fact, a methodological retreat to black social reforms. In pragmatic America the slogans catch the imagination while the implicit substances are glossed over and ignored. The Negro thinks and acts like the American he is; thus the leaders of the Black Revolution who seized so readily upon Black Power had never made the distinction between social revolution and social evolution, or social reform.

As this entire critique has tried to show, there can be no such thing in America as a *purely* economic, or political or civil rights revolution. There *can* be economic or political or civil rights reforms, but these are all *evolutionary* social changes that are part and parcel of the very gradualism of the NAACP. Never mind the fact that Roy Wilkins and his "class-brothers" are frightened by Black Power—that proves nothing. What a Wilkins is really saying is—"Please don't start throwing around power you don't really have, or power which you *might* have but which you obviously don't know how to use. All you are doing is scaring people (like me) and provoking other people to mobilize white power for a showdown which you are not ready for." What these gentlemen want most avidly are a number of civil rights, legal, economic, social, and educational reforms in America. But the radical direct-action civil righters (plus the nationalists) vociferously claim that this is inadequate. They say: "Those bourgeois NAACP Uncle Toms can't reform this white man's society. Man, you got to resort to revolutionary tactics if you want to shake up these white folks!" But what were these so-called revolutionary tactics? The Black Revolution included everything in the pot: sit-ins, freedom rides, demonstrations and marches of all kinds, ghetto uprisings, stall-ins, voter registration, self-defense, boycotts, black (third) party attempts, etc. These were the elements of the revolution, particularly in the South. But today when the main bulk of the direct actionists of SNCC and others have quit the South, what have they left behind? Scattered groups devoted to voter registration and economic programs for self-help. CORE has left a "cooperative marketing program for farm produce" in Louisiana. There were a few local election victories here and there, but the political reform movement of the Mississippi Freedom Democrat Party has closed its doors in LeFlore County. This is not to say that the achievements of the direct actionists are not valuable bases upon which other things can be structured, but they are still *reformist and gradualistic ideas with which not a single NAACP-er nor King passive resister could argue.* The question arises: Why was it necessary for all those idealistic and intrepid direct actionists to submit themselves to such a terrible physical and psychological battering in the South to establish a few struggling groups for local reforms in politics and economics, attempting in vain to breach the jimcrow barriers, which are, in effect, "separate" movements? It was because these young radicals did not understand, at the outset, the divergent natures of reforms and revolutionary movements for social change. They confused the methods without understanding them, thus imputing revolutionary interpretations to merely reformist methods. Hence, when direct-action methods failed against hardening barriers, they had to fall back on what few political and economic reform gains they had won. From this point on, the direct actionists advanced to the slogan of Black Power, as if to convince themselves that they were taking a revolutionary step forward, to wit: instead of radical integrationism the theme became *economic and political control by blacks in the black ghettoes and in geographical areas of black majority in the South.* But is this a step forward or backward . . . or perhaps a one-step-backward-two-steps-forward sort of gambit? Whatever it is, it is essentially another variation of the old Communist leftwing doctrine of "self-determination in the black belt areas of Negro majority"—but with certain innovations. The old Communist Party doctrine did not include the Northern ghettoes in this scheme as the Black Power exponents do. Moreover, the Communists did not envision any separatist black party movements as part of "self-determination," nor include any separatist economic reforms for self-help (such as cooperative consumers and producers movements). For the Communists then, and forever more, trade unionism was of paramount importance. The Northern CORE found itself in the 1960s, for instance, still forced to battle for integration in certain unions such as the building and construction trades. But when the subterranean nationalists inside the organization came to the fore in 1966 in answer to Carmichael's Black Power call, they demanded that Negroes reject integration as their major aim. Negroes were called on to band themselves into a racially oriented mass movement, using political power and economic boycotts to win complete economic and political control of Northern ghettoes and Southern counties in which they are in the majority. Except for time, place, circumstances, plus a few innovative, ideological twists, there is very little that is new in all of this.

In essence Black Power represents nothing more than a strategic retreat for a purpose. It proposes to change, not the white world outside, but the black world inside, by reforming it into something else politically and economically. In its own way and for other purposes the Nation of Islam has already achieved this in a limited way, substituting religion for politics.

Malcolm X quitted the Nation of Islam because this type of Black Power lacked a dynamic, was static and aloof to the broad struggle. He proposed to create another movement (the Organization for Afro-American Unity, OAAU) and link up with all the direct actionists and even passive resisters, believing that one must be involved in all forms of struggle wherever they are on all fronts. But after Malcolm's passing, the most dynamic of all the direct actionists gave up their dynamism and took a position almost in the lap of the Nation of Islam. They merely substituted politics for a parochial religion to go along with economics, but they added a more secular religion of Black Power invented by a Baptist minister-politician. As the fates would have it, all of this took place at a time when

Powell, in whom more black political power was invested than in anyone else at the moment, was under fire from a Congressional white backlash in Washington, D.C.

On the face of it, Black Power adds up to some profound questions: Does this strategic retreat from integrationism mean that the civil righters are settling for gradual evolutionary reforms within the black communities? Can these economic and political reforms be achieved without effect on, and interaction with, the white world? Will the achievement of certain levels of Black Power enable the exponents to deal more effectively with the white world than the dynamics of direct-action integrationism? What manner of social dynamic is to be added to Black Power to make up for the dynamic that was discarded along with direct action? The real answer at this stage is that the Black Power slogan has no other dynamic than what is implied in its emotional necessity. Taken by themselves, all purely economic and political reorganizations of any type in America can be only reformist movements, whether in black ghettoes or the white world. In order to be revolutionary in method to effect social change, such as transforming ghettoes, other dynamic elements must be added to the economic and political combination. The Black Power exponents have not understood these elements. . . .

There is too much romanticizing about Africa going on in certain nationalist circles; too much rhetoric and too much Garveyite Back-to-Africa lip service by certain black redemptionists in America who haven't the least intention of going to Africa unless there is the guarantee of a good job or a money-making scheme in the offing, or the possibility of a "top echelon" marriage into the African diplomatic corps.

Africans such as Chief Adebo are just as much in the dark about the inner dynamic demands of the American Black Revolution as the Black Power exponents are about the dynamic substances of their new slogan. As a result, the readiness of most Black Nationalist trends, to lean heavily on the African past and the African image, is nothing but a convenient cover-up for an inability to come to terms with the complex demands of the American reality. . . . The trouble with the Black Nationalist Africanists is that most of their intellectual capacities are used up glorifying the most attractive aspects of Africa's pre-slavery past, while most of the African elite today have ceased being revolutionaries (if they ever were). In fact, most American Negroes who have been to Africa and back have almost as low an opinion of the African elite in Africa as some of the Africans have of the American Negroes' lack of cohesion. Hence, it would serve a very good purpose here in America for Negroes to cease romanticizing Africa and pre-feudal tribalism.

The radical wing of the Negro movement in America sorely needs a social theory based on the living ingredients of Afro-American history. Without such a theory all talk of Black Power is meaningless. One of the keys to the confusion over the meaning of the slogan, is the ambivalence in CORE's publication over the choice of historical leadership symbols and the interpretation given to the implications of these leadership trends. For example, the strong tendency of the Black Power theorists to associate only the names of Denmark Vesey, Harriet Tubman, Nat Turner, Marcus Garvey, Elijah Muhammed and Malcolm X with the social, political and ideological implications of Black Power is being absolutely false to history. Even the addition of Frederick Douglass to this historical leadership gallery is insufficient. For one thing, Douglass was no nationalist, and no pre-Civil War data is complete without the name of Martin R. Delany, the real prototype of Afro-American Nationalism.

But of more relevance to the present-day Negro movement as a whole are the twentieth-century leaders and their trends—Washington, DuBois, and Garvey. *These are the big three for our century.* Anyone who does not understand this cannot talk seriously about Black Power or any other slogan. But the Black Power theorists are romantics who do not understand this. Of course, spokesmen like Roy Inniss, Ben-Jochannan, etc., will find it difficult to accept this. In their conceptual scheme of things they would accept Marcus Garvey and reject Washington and DuBois. But this is predicated not on any profound theoretical or scientific examination of historical facts but on passion, emotionalism, and prejudice. They accept Garvey without Washington because they have not examined the reasons Washington was Garvey's only American hero. Similarly, they accept Douglass without DuBois, although it was DuBois who upheld Douglass and carried his abolitionist-protest-civil rights trend into the twentieth century. Although in terms of economics, Elijah Muhammed carried out Booker T. Washington's philosophy of economic self-sufficiency and self-help more thoroughly than any other movement, the Black Power theorists accept the Nation of Islam, yet reject Booker T-ism. They fail to see the fallacy of such reasoning because they have no understanding of economics as a science or the different schools of economic theory and how to apply them to the Negro movement. With such an innocence about economics, politics becomes child's play once the direct-action dynamic is taken away. Unschooled in the deep politics of the Negro movement since World War One, the leaders of CORE and SNCC are unaware that even the few economic cooperatives they initiated in the South are forty years too late. How can people like this expect to cope with the economic policies of Anti-Poverty today?

In terms of economics, the Negro's heritage today is New Deal capitalism and Anti-Poverty, broadly speaking. His only "race" economics of any importance are those of Elijah Muhammed. Garvey's economic ideology which was tied to the African scene is useless today, since there is no Back-to-Africa momentum. The only leader of the big three who left behind, in writing, an economic program for the United States was W. E. B. DuBois, yet nationalist prejudice against him prevents Negro leaders from acknowledging this. Moreover, it was DuBois' brand of Pan-Africanism that won out in Africa, not Garvey's, *because Garvey was not a socialist but a thoroughgoing capitalist.* In terms of economics, neither Africa nor the West Indies has achieved the kind of independence and autonomy Garvey wanted. However, the unreality of Garvey's program in the 1920s meant he would have had even less chance of expunging neo-colonialism from Africa than the leaders of the African Revolution have had today. The result has been that Garveyism has failed to muster up any aid or political and economic assistance from Negroes in the Western hemisphere. The real foreign aid must come from both capitalist and socialist governments. The politics of certain African leaders are sufficiently ambivalent that they avidly seek this capitalistic and socialistic aid with one hand (for their version of Black Power), while with the other they either point the finger of criticism at the American Negro or else mouth vague platitudes about black cooperation. They simply do not understand the Afro-American's complex problem and its imperatives.

The Black Power enthusiasts practice the same dubious verbal skin-game in another way. They cannot cope with the realities of the economics of their own foreign aid, i.e., Anti-Poverty, yet they talk boldly about economic independence as the basis of real power. How can such people talk seriously of cooperating with Africa when they cannot help themselves with a definitive economic program for Black Power in America? The "reluctant African" in the United States has adequate reasons for his stand-offishness. He has deep personal problems of identity to cope with, in the midst of a situation that has trapped the American Negro both physically and intellectually. The worst effect of his American conditioning is not his color-complex about blackness, but that it renders him unable to look at his own history and influence in America objectively and understand it scientifically. He is so bedazzled by the personalities of his chosen leadership symbols that he cannot peer behind the façade and examine what were the political, economic, class, and cultural trends that influenced the actions of those chosen leaders.

Another important issue the Black Power theorists evade is the class problem among Negroes. When one talks bravely about developing political and economic black power one had best start clarifying which class is going to wield this power. Better yet—which class among Negroes has the most power now? And which class will benefit from Black Power when it arrives? Here is another clue to the essential reformism inherent in the Black Power slogan: The theorists, although they snipe at the black bourgeoisie, are themselves prey to bourgeois aspirations—major or minor. This is by no means a bad thing in itself. To better one's material (if not spiritual) condition in America necessarily means adopting either the petty or the garish trappings of middle-class existence. However, the Black Power theorists are thrown into a reformist muddle involving class aspirations and economic power for the simple reason that they have no recognizable basis for economic power. To be brutally frank, some do not even know what economic theory is, while others do not want to be bothered with it. Despite their vaunted anti-Americanism, they are more American than they think. Congenitally pragmatic to the core, they are anti-theoretical. Thus, the white power structure does their economic theory and practice for them. New Deal economics, in force for thirty-four years, **de-**cides how Anti-Poverty funds are allotted to black ghettoes, but people in ghettoes have no say in how much funds or how often they are to be allotted. Is *this* economic Black Power? If not, ask any Black Power theorist what kind of politics can change this arrangement. Or better—ask any Black Power theorist whether economics determine politics, or vice versa? Ask any Black Power theorist why Anti-Poverty funds pay out so much money in middle-class salaries? Is this good or bad—for Black Power economics? You will get no clear answers. . . .

The last outstanding leader was Malcolm X, but did his followers really understand the man's positive side, or his limitations, or why he acted as he did? Did they see any Afro-American historical trends repeating themselves in Malcolm X's career? Unfortunately, they did not. The editors of CORE's magazine leaned heavily on quotations from Frederick Douglass' speeches and writings. But, historically, Douglass' Abolitionism and Reconstructionism are nineteenth-century achievements that became overshadowed by American twentieth-century developments. Besides, Frederick Douglass is also the chief hero of the NAACP integrationists, hence, the Black Power fellows are in strange company, sharing "heroes." Yet Malcolm X was no hero to the NAACP worshippers at Douglass' shrine, so how then, do divergent integrationist and nationalist trends wind up honoring the same hero? Because neither integrationists nor nationalists truly understand the crucial impact of the integrationist vs. nationalist conflict within the contours of American Negro history.

The Black Power exponents who uphold Malcolm X, yet cannot come to terms with either Washington or DuBois as historical leaders, understand neither the break between DuBois and Washington, nor the break between Malcolm X and Elijah Muhammed. These two breaches are historically related and stem from the same root in Afro-American history, albeit under different circumstances. Malcolm X broke with the Nation of Islam because of Muhammed's refusal to participate in the broad struggle for human rights, as

Malcolm X explained it. But W. E. B. DuBois, the turn-of-the-century radical, broke with Booker T. Washington's leadership school for the same reasons (as a reading of *The Souls of Black Folk* will show). DuBois said that Washington shied away from participating in the struggle for the Negro's manhood rights. Malcolm X's break was that of a radical nationalist with the conservative nationalism of Elijah Muhammed, the latter inherited from Booker T. Washington, by way of Garvey who had "radicalized" Washington's economic philosophy.

The only way to understand this process is not to be led astray by mere slogans, but to see the fundamentals at work: the underlying conflict between integrationist and nationalist tendencies historically projected in the contrasted outlooks of Douglass and Delany. No matter how nationalistic Malcolm X remained after his break, he was forced by circumstances to swing closer to the civil rights-integrationist forces in order to participate more fully in the broad struggle. That was why certain of Malcolm X's former followers could charge him with "selling out" by seeking an alliance with the direct-action-integrationist forces.

American Negro history is basically a history of the conflict between integrationist and nationalist forces in politics, economics, and culture, no matter what leaders are involved and what slogans are used. After Malcolm X's death, the Black Power slogan was actually a swing back to the conservative nationalism from which Malcolm X had just departed. The pendulum swings back and forth, but the men who swing with it always fail to synthesize composite trends. W. E. B. DuBois came the closest of all the big three to understanding this problem, when he wrote in *Dusk of Dawn:* "There faces the American Negro therefore an intricate and subtle problem of combining into one object two difficult sets of facts."

The "two difficult sets of facts" DuBois refers to are integrationism (civil rights, racial equality, freedom) versus nationalism (separatism, accommodationist self-segregation, economic nationalism, group solidarity and self-help). This was truly the first theoretical formulation of the historic conflict between tendencies, but DuBois never developed his basic theoretical premise. He failed to go beyond this first principle into a greater synthesis of all the historical ingredients of Afro-Americana, which he knew better than all the

Washingtons and the Garveys combined. Like Karl Marx, W. E. B. DuBois was one of history's great researchers—a sifter, interpreter and recorder of historical and contemporary knowledge; but unlike Marx, he could not reinterpret his data into new conceptions of social reality. Still, he came close, albeit late in life.

It was historically unfortunate that the American Negro created no social theorists to back up his long line of activist leaders, charismatic deliverers, black redemptionists, and moral suasionists. With a few perceptive and original thinkers, the Negro movement conceivably could long ago have aided in reversing the backsliding of the United States toward the moral negation of its great promise as a new nation of nations. Instead the American Negro has, unwittingly, been forced to share in many of the corrupted values of the society—not enough, to be sure, to cancel out completely his inherent potential for social change. However, the intellectual horizons of the black intelligentsia have been so narrowed in scope and banalized by the American corrosion that Negro creativity has been diminishing since the 1920s. An examination of the pronouncements of the Black Power theorists reveal that they have not advanced one whit in their thinking, beyond the 1919 writers of A. Phillip Randolph's *Messenger* magazine. They have, in fact, retrogressed. There is not a single Negro publication in existence today that matches the depth of the old *Messenger*. CORE's new Black Power publication talks of developing "political and economic power" as if speaking for the first time. But back in the 1920s, when Randolph's writers were chastising DuBois and boasting of how they were "correctly" giving precedence to economics and politics over culture and art, they knew what they were talking about and said it with infinitely more expertise than today's Black Power exponents. In fact, the Black Power theorists do not even know how to deal with culture and art, as the CORE publication reveals. This is shocking to contemplate.

Black Power slogans reveal the depth of unpreparedness and the lack of knowledge that go along with the eagerness of the new black generation of spokesmen. The farther the Negro gets from his historical antecedents in time, the more tenuous become his conceptual ties, the emptier his social conceptions, the more superficial his visions. His one great and present hope is to know and understand his Afro-American history in the United States more profoundly. Failing that, and failing to create a new synthesis and a social theory of action, he will suffer the historical fate described by the philosopher who warned that "Those who cannot remember the past are condemned to repeat it."

Suggestions for Additional Reading

In writing a bibliographic essay on the black man in the city, one must be selective. The relationship of the black American to the city manifests itself in almost every aspect of the black experience in America. Mary L. Fisher and Elizabeth W. Miller have compiled the definitive bibliography, *The Negro in America** (2nd edition, Cambridge, Massachusetts, 1971). The major historical survey of the black experience is John Hope Franklin, *From Slavery to Freedom: A History of American Negroes** (3rd edition, New York, 1967). A more interpretive history is *From Plantation to Ghetto** (New York, 1966) by August Meier and Elliott M. Rudwick. Meier and Rudwick have also edited a collection of secondary sources, *The Making of Black America** (New York, 1969; 2 vols.). Two major sociological works are Gunnar Myrdal, *An American Dilemma* (New York, 1944; 2 vols.) and E. Franklin Frazier, *The Negro in the United States* (revised edition, New York, 1957). Two general works that deal with the ante-bellum urban experience are Richard C. Wade, *Slavery in the Cities: The South, 1820–1860** (New York, 1964) and Leon F. Litwack, *North of Slavery: The Negro in the Free States, 1790–1860** (Chicago, 1961). W. E. B. DuBois has made a number of important contributions to the study of the black man and the city. He edited *Social and Physical Condition of Negroes in Cities* (Atlanta, 1897) and *Some Notes on Negroes in New York City* (Atlanta, 1903). He wrote a major sociological study, *The Philadelphia Negro* (Philadelphia, 1899), as well as the series of articles for the *New York Times*, "The Black North: A Social Study," (November 17, 1901–December 15, 1901).

There are a number of studies of blacks in particular cities. These include Robert A. Warner, *New Haven Negroes: A Social History* (New Haven, 1940), Wendell P. Dabney, *Cincinnati's Colored Citizens* (Cincinnati, 1926), J. S. Himes, "Forty Years of Negro Life in Columbus, Ohio, 1900–1940," *Journal of Negro History* XXVII (April, 1942), August Meier and David Lewis, "History of the Negro Upper Class in Atlanta, Georgia, 1890–1958," *Journal of Negro Education* (Spring, 1959).

The literature dealing with the lure of the city is voluminous. The

---

* Available in paperback.

selections included in this anthology are taken from W. E. B. Du-Bois, "The Black North," *New York Times* (November–December, 1901), which is reprinted in book form by the Arno Press (New York, 1969), Paul Laurence Dunbar, *The Sport of the Gods* (New York, 1902), Allan H. Spear, *Black Chicago: The Making of a Negro Ghetto, 1890–1920** (Chicago, 1967), and Gilbert Osofsky, *Harlem: The Making of a Ghetto, Negro New York, 1890–1930** (New York, 1966). Seth M. Scheiner has also written a monograph on New York, *Negro Mecca: A History of the Negro in New York City, 1865–1920** (New York, 1965).

Two major reference works on the Great Migration are Frank A. Rose and Louise V. Kennedy, *Bibliography of Negro Migrations* (New York, 1934) and the U.S. Bureau of the Census, *Negroes in the United States, 1920–1932* (Washington, 1935). For an impressionistic survey of the lure of the city see Arna Bontemps and Jack Conroy, *Anyplace But Here** (revised edition, New York, 1966). Earlier studies on the black migration are Emmett J. Scott, *Negro Migration During the War* (New York, 1920), Thomas J. Woofter, *Negro Migration* (New York, 1920), Carter G. Woodson, *A Century of Negro Migration* (Washington, 1918), Louise V. Kennedy, *The Negro Peasant Turns Cityward: Effects of Recent Migrations to Northern Centers* (New York, 1930), Clyde V. Kiser, *Sea Island to City** (New York, 1932), and Abraham Epstein, *The Negro Migrant in Pittsburgh* (reprint, New York, 1969). Two of the better contemporary articles on the migration are Charles S. Johnson, "How Much Is the Migration a Flight from Persecution?," *Opportunity*, I (September, 1923) and Donald Henderson, "The Negro Migration, 1916–1918," *Journal of Negro History*, VI (October, 1921). Two recent scholarly articles are Dewey H. Palmer, "Moving North: Negro Migration During World War I," *Phylon* XXVIII (Spring, 1967) and T. Lyman Smith, "Redistribution of the Negro Population of the United States, 1910–1960," *Journal of Negro History*, LI (July, 1966).

The view that the city is the "promised land" is seen in the selections taken from The Chicago Commission on Race Relations, *The Negro in Chicago: A Study of Race Relations and a Race Riot* (Chicago, 1922), St. Clair Drake and Horace R. Cayton, *Black Metropolis: A Study of Negro Life in a Northern City** (revised edition, New York, 1970; 2 vols.), Robert Bone, *The Negro Novel in America**

(revised edition, New Haven, 1965), and Alain Locke, ed., *The New Negro: An Interpretation** (New York, 1925).

The North was pictured as the "promised land" in black newspapers, especially the Chicago *Defender* and in letters of black migrants. For a sympathetic biography of the editor of the Chicago *Defender* one should consult Roi Ottley, *The Lonely Warrior: Life of Robert S. Abbott* (Chicago, 1955). Many letters of black migrants were collected by Emmett J. Scott. See his "Letters of Negro Migrants of 1916–1918," *Journal of Negro History*, IV (July and October, 1919).

A number of essays dealing with the Harlem Renaissance appear in Seymour L. Gross and John Edward Hardy, eds., *Images of the Negro in American Literature** (Chicago, 1966). One should also see Hugh M. Gloster, *Negro Voices in American Fiction* (Chapel Hill, 1948) and two of the many anthologies that have recently appeared, Addison Gayle, Jr., ed., *Black Expression: Essays by and about Black America in the Creative Arts** (New York, 1969) and James A. Emanuel and Theodore L. Gross, eds., *Dark Symphony: Negro Literature in America** (New York, 1968). James Weldon Johnson's *Black Manhattan** (New York, 1930), Claude McKay's *Harlem: Negro Metropolis* (New York, 1940), and Langston Hughes' autobiography, *The Big Sea** (New York, 1940), all provide insight into Harlem as the "promised land" during the twenties. E. David Cronon has provided a starting point for the study of the Garveyite movement in *Black Moses: The Story of Marcus Garvey and the Universal Negro Improvement Association** (Madison, Wisconsin, 1955). A brief, but interesting, contemporary view is E. Franklin Frazier, "The Garvey Movement," *Opportunity*, IV (November, 1926).

Events of the twenties and thirties brought an end to the dream of the "promised land." This is seen in the selections taken from Constance McLaughlin Green, *The Secret City: A History of Race Relations in the Nation's Capital** (Princeton, 1967), Elliott M. Rudwick, *A Race Riot at East St. Louis, July 2, 1917** (Carbondale, Illinois, 1964), E. Franklin Frazier, "Some Effects of the Depression on the Negro in Northern Cities," *Science and Society*, II (Fall, 1938), and Ralph Ellison, *Invisible Man** (New York, 1952). Further studies of race riots include the already mentioned *The Negro in Chicago*, Arthur I. Waskow, *From Race Riot to Sit-in: 1919 and the 1960s**

(New York, 1966), and Robert Shogan and Tom Craig, *The Detroit Race Riot* (Philadelphia, 1964). For a discussion of the 1943 riots see Kenneth B. Clark, "Group Violence . . . : A Study of the 1943 Harlem Riot," *Journal of Social Psychology*, XX (July, 1944) and Havard Sitkoff, "The Detroit Race Riot of 1943," *Michigan History*, LIII (Fall, 1969).

Black problems in the twenties were studied by contemporaries. An example of these views is found in Thomas J. Woofter *et al., Negro Problems in Cities* (New York, 1928). A valuable study on the impact of the Depression on the black American is Raymond Wolters, *Negroes and the Great Depression* * (New York, 1970). This work updates and expands on the scholarship of E. Franklin Frazier. Examples of Frazier's work in addition to the one included here are "Occupational Classes Among Negroes in Cities," *The American Journal of Sociology*, XXXV (March, 1930), "Negro Harlem: An Ecological Study," *Ibid.,* XLIII (July, 1937), and "The Impact of Urban Civilization Upon Negro Family Life," *American Sociological Review,* II (August, 1937). A number of important essays dealing with the thirties appear in Bernard Sternsher, ed., *The Negro in Depression and War: Prelude to Revolution* * (Chicago, 1969). For a journalistic account of Harlem in the thirties see Roi Ottley, *New World A-Coming* * (Boston, 1943). Two novels dealing with the black experience in the thirties are Richard Wright's *Native Son* * (New York, 1940) and Ralph Ellison's *Invisible Man.*

Two excellent studies on the ghetto are Robert C. Weaver, *The Negro Ghetto* (New York, 1948) and Karl E. Taeuber and Alma F. Taeuber, *Negroes in Cities: Residential Segregation and Neighborhood Change* * (Chicago, 1965). Weaver supplemented his study with an article, "Non-White Population Movements in Urban Ghettos," *Phylon* XX (Fall, 1959). A more limited study is Otis D. and Beverly Duncan, *The Negro Population of Chicago: A Study of Residential Succession* (Chicago, 1957).

General studies on black institutions have appeared throughout the twentieth century. An early history of the black church is Carter G. Woodson, *The History of the Negro Church* (Washington, D.C., 1921). The urban experience brought, at times, major changes to black religion. Arthur Huff Fausett discusses the impact of the urban experience on religion in *Black Gods of the Metropolis: Negro Reli-*

gious Cults of the Urban North (Philadelphia, 1944). For a more limited study see Robert A. Parker, *The Incredible Messiah: The Deification of Father Divine* (Boston, 1937). For a recent, brief survey one should consult E. Franklin Frazier, *The Negro Church in America** (New York, 1963).

An early study of black political activity is Harold F. Gosnell's *Negro Politicians: The Rise of Negro Politics in Chicago* (Chicago, 1935). For a broader study see James Q. Wilson, *Negro Politics: The Search for Leadership** (Glencoe, Illinois, 1960).

Beginning with the Moynihan Report, *The Negro Family: The Case For National Action** (Washington, D.C., 1965) controversy has developed over the impact of the ghetto. The report itself and the controversy it raised have been collected by Lee Rainwater and William L. Yancey in *The Moynihan Report and the Politics of Controversy* (Cambridge, Mass., 1967). William H. Grier and Price M. Cobbs devote part of their book *Black Rage** (New York, 1968) to an analysis of the black family, challenging the conclusions in the Moynihan Report. Moynihan relied heavily on the scholarship of E. Franklin Frazier. Frazier, a black sociologist, devoted most of his career to the study of the black family. Among his works are *The Negro Family in Chicago* (Chicago, 1932), *The Negro Family in the United States** (revised edition, New York, 1966), and *Black Bourgeoisie** (revised edition, New York, 1962). G. Franklin Edwards has added to the study of the black middle class with *The Negro Professional Class* (New York, 1959). A recent study of the black family is Andrew Billingsley, *Black Families in White America** (Englewood Cliffs, N.J., 1968).

A number of other studies have appeared in the sixties which treat black families in their own right and not as deviants from white norms. Some of these are Jessie Bernard's *Marriage and Family among Negroes* (Englewood Cliffs, N.J., 1966), Lee Rainwater's "Crucible of Identity: The Negro Lower-Class Family," *Daedalus* (Winter, 1966), and Joan Gordon's *The Poor of Harlem: Social Functioning in the Underclass* (New York, 1965).

Frazier in his study of the black urban dweller denied that he had a culture. Likewise Gunnar Myrdal in *An American Dilemma* argued that the black culture in the United States is not an independent phenomenon but a distortion of mainstream culture. Nathan Glazer and Daniel P. Moynihan in *Beyond the Melting Pot** (revised edition, Cambridge, Mass., 1970) generally follow the Frazier-Myrdal view. But many recent sociological and anthropological studies break with this view. Scholars like Frazier, Myrdal, DuBois, Cayton and Drake tended to see the black man and his institutions as responding only in a negative way to the white dominated racist society. The studies of the sixties for the most part emphasize both the impact of the racism of white society and the development of an autonomous black culture. Some of the best research of the past ten years appears in two anthologies, Lee Rainwater, ed., *Soul* (Chicago, 1970), a collection of articles which appeared originally in *Trans-action,* and Norman E. Whitten, Jr. and John F. Szwed, *Afro-American Anthropology: Contemporary Perspectives** (New York, 1970). The latter anthology is the more scholarly of the two.

A number of studies have appeared dealing with the role of the black male in ghetto society. Elliot Liebow in *Tally's Corner: A Study of Negro Streetcorner Men** (Boston, 1967) argues that the characteristics of streetcorner men are formed not by cultural inheritance but by economic pressures. Liebow's conclusions support the findings of Hylan Lewis, who in *Blackways of Kent* (Chapel Hill, 1955), rejects a uniquely black culture. Charles Keil in *Urban Blues** (Chicago, 1966) and LeRoi Jones in *Black Music** (New York, 1968) disagree with Liebow. Keil, as well as Jones, argues in favor of a positive culture within the ghetto and this is partly manifested in the blues. Bennett Berger attacks Keil's thesis in "Black Culture or Lower-class Culture?" *Soul,* edited by Lee Rainwater. Ulf Hannerz in *Soulside: Inquiries into Ghetto Culture and Community* (New York, 1969) attempts to show that the findings of Liebow and Keil do not necessarily contradict one another. Oscar Lewis in his studies, including "The Culture of Poverty," *Scientific American,* CCXV (No. 4, 1966) saw a separate culture in the ghetto. It was not a black culture, but a lower class culture, similar to poverty cultures elsewhere in the world. Charles A. Valentine, *Culture and Poverty* (Chicago, 1968) challenges Lewis' "culture of poverty" thesis. Valentine's book provides an excellent critique of the scholarship of the sixties. He deals with the work of Frazier, Moynihan, Lewis, Clark, Keil, and Liebow.

Linguistics is another area recently opened by the interest in black studies. Most linguists argue that the language of black Americans is not just a lower class dialect, but represents a cultural transference from one generation to the next. An early study of the influence of Africanisms on black language is Lorenzo D. Turner, *Africanisms in the Gullah Dialect* (Chicago, 1949). An example of the recent scholarship which favors the cultural interpretation of black behavior and which attacks the pathological interpretation is Stephen S. and Joan C. Baratz, "Early Childhood Intervention: The Social Science Base of Institutional Racism," *Harvard Educational Review*, XL (Winter, 1970). Frederick Williams, ed., *Language and Poverty: Perspectives on a Theme* (Chicago, 1970), a collection of articles on black language stresses the relationship between language and social class.

Black Power and the colonial analogy are important manifestations of black revolt in the sixties and seventies. An excellent bibliographic essay appears in John H. Bracey, Jr., August Meier, and Elliott Rudwick, eds., *Black Nationalism in America** (Indianapolis, 1970). The impact of the African independence movement is described in Harold Isaacs, *The New World of Negro Americans* (New York, 1963). Frantz Fanon's *The Wretched of the Earth** (New York, 1968) has had a great influence on the Black Power movement. The same is true of Eldridge Cleaver's *Soul on Ice** (New York, 1968). Important surveys of Black Power include Harold Cruse, *The Crisis of the Negro Intellectual** (New York, 1967), his *Rebellion or Revolution?* (New York, 1968), and Stokely Carmichael and Charles V. Hamilton, *Black Power: The Politics of Liberation in America** (New York, 1967). For a further discussion of Black Power see the essays in Floyd Barbour, ed., *The Black Power Revolt** (Boston, 1968) and the articles in *Partisan Review* during the winter and spring of 1968.

The "colonial thesis" is discussed by Robert Blauner in "Internal Colonialism and Ghetto Revolt," *Social Problems*, XVI (Spring, 1969), Charles V. Hamilton in "Conflict, Race and System-Transformation in the United States," *Journal of International Affairs*, XXIII (1969), Theodore Draper in "The Fantasy of Black Nationalism," *Commentary*, XLVIII (September, 1969), and Christopher Lasch in "Black Power: Cultural Nationalism as Politics," *The Agony of the American Left** (New York, 1969). Life in the ghetto is described in Kenneth B. Clark, *Dark Ghetto: Dilemmas of Social Power** (New

York, 1965) and William McCord *et al., Life Styles in the Black Ghetto** (New York, 1969). Nathan Wright, Jr. also gives a popular view of Black Power in *Black Power and Urban Unrest** (New York, 1967).

For works that deal with black unrest in the early sixties see Charles E. Silberman, *Crisis in Black and White** (New York, 1964), Thomas F. Pettigrew, *A Profile of the Negro American** (New York, 1964), Talcott Parsons and Kenneth B. Clark, eds., *The Negro American** (Boston, 1965), and James Baldwin's many works, especially *The Fire Next Time** (New York, 1962).

Numerous works have appeared on the riots of the sixties. The reader should, of course, begin with the *Report of the National Advisory Commission on Civil Disorders** (Washington, D.C., 1968). Other studies include Spencer Crump, *Black Riot in Los Angeles* (Los Angeles, 1966), Robert Conot, *Rivers of Blood, Years of Darkness** (New York, 1967), John A. McCone, *Violence in the City—An End or a Beginning?** (Los Angeles, 1965), Paul Jacobs, *Prelude to Riot: A View of Urban America From the Bottom* (New York, 1968), Tom Hayden, *Rebellion in Newark: Official Violence and Ghetto Response* (New York, 1967), Louis H. Masotti and Don R. Bowen, eds., *Riots and Rebellion: Civil Violence in the Urban Community* (Beverly Hills, 1968), Joseph Boskin, ed., *Urban Racial Violence in the Twentieth Century** (Glencoe, Illinois, 1969), and Nathan S. Caplan and Jeffrey M. Paige, "A Study of Ghetto Rioters," *Scientific American* (August, 1968). The riots are also discussed at length in William McCord *et al., Life Styles in the Black Ghetto.*

Black Nationalism of the early sixties is discussed in C. Eric Lincoln, *The Black Muslims in America* (Boston, 1961), E. Essien-Udom, *Black Nationalism** (Chicago, 1962), and Malcolm X and Alex Haley, *The Autobiography of Malcolm X** (New York, 1965). Another excellent autobiography of the mid-sixties is Claude Brown's *Manchild in the Promised Land** (New York, 1965).

3 4 5 6 7 8 9 10

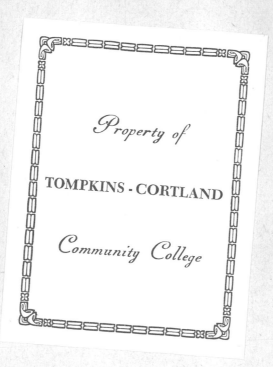